PACIFIC EXPLORATION

NIGEL RIGBY, PIETER VAN DER MERWE AND GLYN WILLIAMS

❋ PACIFIC ❋
EXPLORATION

Voyages of Discovery from
Captain Cook's Endeavour to the Beagle

ADLARD
COLES

LONDON · OXFORD · NEW YORK · NEW DELHI · SYDNEY

ADLARD COLES

Bloomsbury Publishing Plc
50 Bedford Square, London, WC1B 3DP

BLOOMSBURY, ADLARD COLES and the Adlard Coles logo are trademarks of Bloomsbury Publishing Plc

First published in Great Britain 2018

A catalogue record for this book is available from the British Library

Library of Congress Cataloguing-in-Publication data has been applied for

ISBN: PB: 978-1-4729-5773-3
ePDF: 978-1-4729-5774-0
ePub: 978-1-4729-5771-9

10 9 8 7 6 5 4 3 2 1

Designed and typeset in Baskerville by Austin Taylor
Printed and bound in China by Toppan Leefung Printing

To find out more about our authors and books visit www.bloomsbury.com and sign up for our newsletters

AUTHORS' NOTE

This book is a general introduction to European voyages in the Pacific from the 1760s to the 1830s. With some revisions, it combines chapters from two books previously published by the National Maritime Museum in 2002 and 2005. The original focus was on the principal British expeditions up to 1803, starting with those of Captain Cook, and the two European ones – French and Spanish – most immediately prompted by them. Here the coverage has been extended to include a new final chapter on the *Beagle* surveys of 1826–36 and additional sections on the artists who accompanied and illustrated the British voyages.

Nigel Rigby is former Head of Research at the National Maritime Museum, which he first joined in 1996. Pieter van der Merwe was on its full-time staff in various roles from 1974 to 2015, latterly as its General Editor for over 20 years. Glyn Williams is Emeritus Professor of History, Queen Mary University of London. His co-authors are especially grateful that, in his 86th year, he has been able and willing to assist with this combined new edition. He is the author of the Introduction and Chapter 6; Nigel Rigby of Chapters 4, 7, 8 and 9; and Pieter van der Merwe of Chapters 1, 2, 3 and 5 and the artist entries.

PREVIOUS PAGES THE WAR-BOATS OF THE ISLAND OF OTAHEITE [TAHITI], William Hodges's largest painting (nearly 2m x 3m) recollecting Cook's second Pacific voyage. It shows Tahitian preparations in an ongoing local war with the people of the neighbouring island of Moorea. It was completed and shown at the Royal Academy in 1777.

CONTENTS

FOREWORD

ANNIVERSARIES present opportunities for both museums and publishers. The former can seize the occasion to reinterpret historical events in special exhibitions and new galleries; the latter can do so more widely – including through museum bookshops – both to new generations of readers and to older ones enjoying aspects of a notable story again.

In 1768, after the ship's refitting for exploration at the Royal Dockyard, Deptford (a mere kilometre upriver from the site of the National Maritime Museum at Greenwich), Lieutenant James Cook set sail in the *Endeavour* on the first of his three great Pacific expeditions, which makes 2018 its 250th anniversary. This occasion also coincides with the opening of our new gallery about voyages to the Pacific in the late eighteenth century, which includes highlights from the Museum's large and rich collections on Cook and those who followed in his wake.

The story here covers even wider ground, from early European exploration of the great 'South Sea' in the 1500s to the 1830s voyage that led to Charles Darwin's theory of the origin of species. All three authors are masters in various aspects of this enormous subject, and are able to link and clarify its complex parts in an engaging as well as informative way. We are particularly grateful to Glyn Williams, for whom Pacific history has been a lifetime study. It is also a pleasure to thank Nigel Rigby and Pieter van der Merwe, not least since this is their last publication as staff members at Greenwich, after a combined service of over 60 years.

Dr Kevin Fewster, AM
DIRECTOR, ROYAL MUSEUMS GREENWICH

OPPOSITE CAPTAIN JAMES COOK;
oil painting by Nathaniel Dance.

INTRODUCTION

EL MAR DEL SUR

B Y THE EARLY sixteenth century the successors of Columbus were becoming aware that beyond the newly discovered Americas stretched an unknown ocean, possibly of great size. Its waters were first sighted by Europeans in 1513 when the Spanish conquistador Vasco Núñez de Balboa crossed the Isthmus of Panama from the Caribbean to the shores of el Mar del Sur, or the South Sea (so called to distinguish it from the Spaniards' Mar del Norte, or Atlantic). In a moment of high drama, Balboa, in full armour, strode in knee-deep to claim it for Spain, but the newcomers took many years to realise the vast extent of its waters and lands. The single most important advance in their knowledge came only a few years after Balboa's sighting.

In 1519 Ferdinand Magellan left Spain with five ships to search for a route from the South Atlantic into the new ocean and thence westward to the Moluccas (the Spice Islands), which were at this time being reached by Portuguese traders from the Indian Ocean. If the Spaniards were to find such a route it would demolish the hypothesis of Ptolemy, the Alexandrian scholar who in the second century AD

On their arrival off the west
coast of North America during
Cook's last voyage, his ships
were in a poor condition and
badly needed a refit. Webber's
informative panoramic
drawing shows *Discovery*'s
foremast being replaced.
The expedition's astronomical
observatory tents have been
set up on a rocky point at the
centre, and energetic contact
and trade with local people
are evident in the number
of canoes present.

had visualised the seas of the southern hemisphere as enclosed by a huge southern
continent that was joined to both Africa and Asia. The Portuguese navigators who
rounded the Cape of Good Hope had shown that there was open water between
the Atlantic and Indian Oceans, and Magellan in turn found a route near the tip
of South America in the form of the tortuous 350-mile strait that was soon to bear
his name. Battling against squalls, desertions and shipwreck, he took 37 days to
get through it and reach the ocean which he (or his chronicler, Pigafetta) named
the Pacific. As later storm-tossed mariners were to point out, it was not always
the most appropriate of names. Picking up the South-East Trades, Magellan's
two remaining vessels followed a diagonal route north-west across the ocean. For
15 weeks they sailed on, sighting only two small, uninhabited islands. Men died of
scurvy and starvation as the crews were reduced to eating the leather sheathing off
the rigging until, in March 1521, the ships reached the island of Guam in the North
Pacific, and from there sailed to the Philippines and the Moluccas. Magellan died
in the Philippines and only his ship, *Vittoria*, now commanded by Juan Sebastián
de Elcano, returned to Spain in 1522 to complete the first circumnavigation of the
globe. 'No other single voyage has ever added so much to the dimension of the
world', Oskar Spate has written, and dimension is the key word. For the tracks of
his ships had shown the daunting and apparently empty immensity of the Pacific,
where a voyage of almost four months' continuous sailing had encountered no
more than two specks of land.

An ocean traversed only across unprecedentedly unimpeded distances had been revealed; but to talk of its being 'unknown', then 'discovered' and 'explored' by Europeans – which this book necessarily does – hides the fact that long before Magellan it had already experienced a complex process of exploration, migration and settlement. The chart drawn for James Cook in 1769 by Tupaia, a priest, or *arii*, from the Society Islands, gives some indication of the range of geographical information held, almost solely in memory, by Pacific peoples before Europeans arrived. Centred on Tahiti, it marked 74 islands, scattered over an area of ocean 3,000 miles across and 1,000 miles from north to south. The type of craft used in Pacific voyaging ranged from the small single-hulled outriggers of Micronesia to giant double-hulled ones in Polynesia, some of which were longer than European discovery vessels and could make voyages of several thousand miles. Navigation was by observation of stars, currents, wave and wind patterns, and by the shape and loom of the land, rather than by instrument. Long-distance voyages were made that led to the occupation by Polynesians of lands as far distant from one another as the Hawaiian Islands and New Zealand. Europeans were slow to appreciate the navigational skills of the Pacific's inhabitants, and today there is still uncertainty about how many great voyages of the pre-European period were planned rather than fortuitously accidental, or a mix of the two.

Magellan's successors made slow progress in filling in the blanks on the map. Spanish attempts to follow his track and reach the Spice Islands from the east failed to find a commercial route, and in 1529 such ventures lost their point when the Treaty of Zaragoza assigned the Moluccas to Portugal, whose vessels came by way of the Cape of Good Hope. Shut out from the Spice Islands, the Spaniards turned northward to the Philippines, which they conquered in the mid-1560s. On the eastward return of the Spanish invasion fleet to Mexico, two vessels were pushed by wind and current far to the north. The curving track they followed soon became the regular route of the galleons sailing from the Philippines to Mexico with Chinese silks and porcelain, which were then taken overland to Vera Cruz before being shipped to Europe. At Acapulco the galleons loaded Peruvian silver for their return voyage, which followed a route well to the south of the eastbound track. West or east, it was the longest unbroken trading voyage in the world, and the galleons sailing from the Philippines took five to six months to make the run.

As Spanish settlement grew in Peru, efforts began to explore the South Pacific, spurred on by the long-standing belief in the existence of a southern continent, Terra Australis Incognita, a gigantic leftover from Ptolemaic concepts of the world. By the second half of the sixteenth century many world maps showed such a continent, including those constructed by the most celebrated geographers of the age, Mercator and Ortelius. In their depictions the continent covered most of the southern hemisphere, stretching towards the Equator as far as New Guinea, which

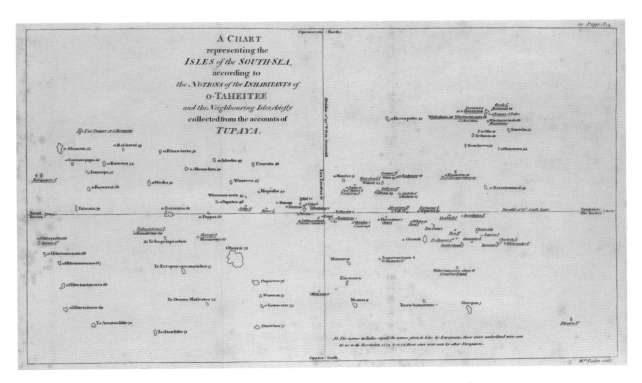

TUPAIA'S CHART.

The Tahitian priest/navigator Tupaia, who joined the *Endeavour* in Tahiti, knew of over 70 Pacific islands and sketched their positions from the ship's deck. His chart was reproduced on paper and later copied by J.R. and Georg Forster, the father-and-son team of naturalists who sailed on Cook's second voyage. The Forsters' chart attempts to accommodate the bearings, distances and identities of Tupaia's islands within the map of the Pacific being developed by Cook. It was later published in the Forsters' narrative of the voyage.

was often shown as a promontory. If an unknown continent was not incentive enough, there were also fabulous islands: those rumoured to have been found by the Incas sailing west from the coast of South America; Ophir, where King Solomon's ships were reported to have found gold; and Marco Polo's Locach. In 1567 ships commanded by Álvaro de Mendaña left Peru, and after sailing westward for two months reached islands which Mendaña named Yslas de Salomón. Despite the triumphant naming, no gold, silver or spices were found, and the expedition's estimate of the location of the islands was so erroneous that they were to be 'lost' for another two centuries.

Mendaña's voyage revealed the problems that faced navigators trying to establish their position in the vastness of the Pacific Ocean. European voyagers in the sixteenth century had no serious problems in finding latitude. Celestial observations of the Sun or stars could be made by astrolabe, simple quadrant or backstaff. Longitude was a very different matter, however, and no satisfactory solution was found until the

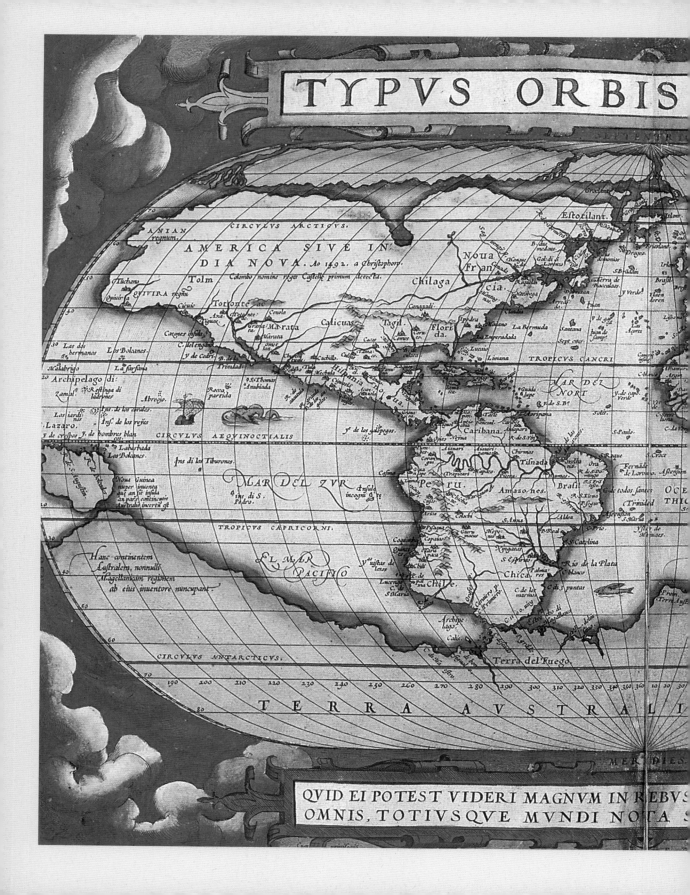

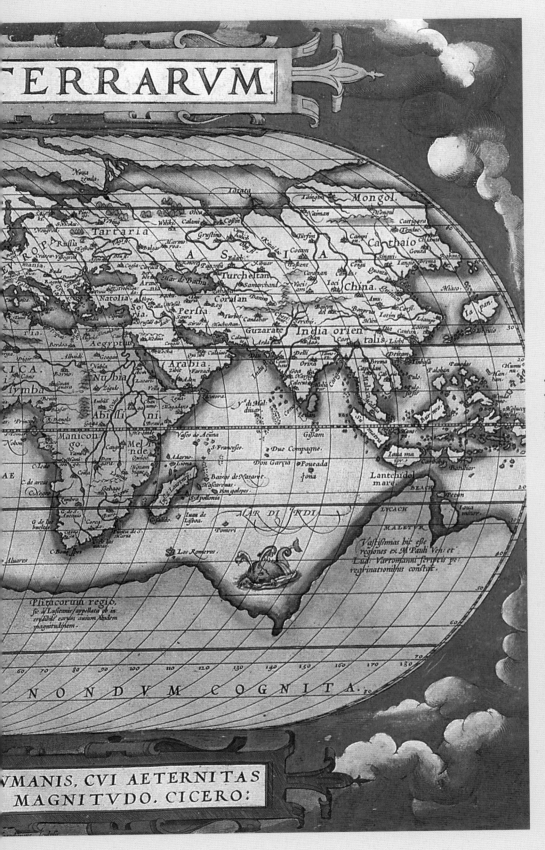

TYPUS ORBIS
TERRARUM; world
map by Abraham
Ortelius, 1573.
Ortelius's world
map is typical
of many of the
period in that it
shows an immense
southern continent,
though the legend,
Terra Australis, is
accompanied by
the cautionary words
Nondom Cognita ('not
yet known'). The
continent occupies
most of the southern
temperate zone,
crosses the Tropic of
Capricorn near New
Guinea and the East
Indies, and includes
Tierra del Fuego
off the tip of
South America.

development of the chronometer in the eighteenth century. Before then, navigators relied on keeping check of their longitude by dead reckoning. This involved a series of different estimates – compass course and magnetic variation, speed through the water, leeway and current. Many were not precise, leading to easy but significant errors that could accumulate on long Pacific crossings. Mendaña's sailing master underestimated the westward drift of the Pacific Ocean Current, and placed the Solomon Islands more than 2,000 nautical miles east of their true position.

A further handicap to comprehensive exploration was the system of prevailing winds. Ships entering the Pacific from the South Atlantic had to battle against gale-force westerlies – the notorious 'roaring forties' of sailors' narratives. Once in, they found themselves in the South-East Trades, carrying them on a diagonal line towards the Equator, which skirted the main island groups, while in the North Pacific they faced the even more persistent North-East Trades. Though the wind systems were helpful once known, they tempted sailing ships into relatively narrow sailing corridors, and venturing away from these could involve months of beating against head winds. It was not just a matter of extra time and heavy financial loss; the longer the voyage, the greater the chances of scurvy afflicting the crew. The only known cure for this terrible sea scourge was fresh food and rest on land, but in the Pacific ships were on unbroken passage for months while their crews, living on a diet of salt meat, stale biscuits and contaminated water, sickened and died.

Notwithstanding all the difficulties, by the second half of the sixteenth century the outlines of Spain's new Pacific empire were clearly visible. Its eastern rim along the American coastline had been explored from the Strait of Magellan to the Californian coast. From Peru silver was shipped to Panama on the first stage of its journey to Spain, while further north, New Spain (Mexico) tapped the resources of China by way of the Philippines. Through diplomacy, exploration and conquest, Spain claimed an ocean whose lands and waters covered one third of the surface of the globe. It was at this time that its position was challenged by the unexpected intrusion of another European power – the English. As relations with Spain worsened in Europe, so English mariners supported by the court and by merchants sailed for the South Sea in search of plunder. The first of these voyages was also the most famous: Francis Drake's circumnavigation in the *Golden Hind* (1577–80), which returned to England with a cargo of treasure that captured the public imagination and Queen Elizabeth's favour. None of its immediate successors enjoyed the same success, but it set the pattern for a tradition of further predatory raids. Drake's voyage and his landing somewhere on the coast of northern California or Oregon also left a tantalising English claim to the vast region of America north of New Spain, marked as New Albion on the maps. Almost 200 years later James Cook would be the next English navigator to sight that coast, and it was Drake's name of New Albion that he entered in his journal.

The engagement between George Anson's *Centurion* and the Spanish *Nuestra Señora de Covadonga* off Cape Espiritu Santo in the Philippines, 20 June 1743 (detail); oil painting by Samuel Scott.

The action was a one-sided affair between a specialist fighting ship and a poorly armed and smaller galleon, but it redeemed a venture that until then had been marked only by its losses of men and ships. The colossal treasure taken from the *Covadonga* seemed to epitomise the wealth of the South Sea and helped to pave the way for a renewal of British interest in it.

The English raids into the Pacific distracted Spanish energies from further significant exploration until 1595, when Mendaña once again sailed for the Solomon Islands, where he hoped to establish a new Spanish colony. He failed to find the islands of his earlier visit, although the ships touched at the Marquesas, where the slaughter of perhaps as many as 200 of the islanders made an ominous beginning to the relationship between Europeans and Polynesians. Mendaña died on the expedition but his chief pilot, Pedro de Quirós, returned to the South Pacific ten years later in an attempt to find and settle the great southern continent. In May 1606 he sighted and named Espiritu Santo, the main island in the group later known as the New Hebrides (today's Vanuatu), and decided that it was part of the continent. The attempt by Quirós to found a settlement there, New Jerusalem, ended in violence and abandonment of the venture. It was left to his second-in-command, Luis Váez de Torres, to make the more significant discovery that there was a passage between New Guinea and the coast stretching away to the south. Memory of this soon faded, until in 1770 Cook proved the existence of the Torres Strait by sailing through it. The discovery of Espiritu Santo was inflated by Quirós to epic and mystical proportions. It was, he claimed, 'the fifth part of the Terrestrial Globe', an earthly paradise, rich in spices, silver and gold, with numerous inhabitants, whom it would be the mission of the Roman Catholic Church to convert to Christianity. Despite all his hopes, Quirós never returned to the South Pacific, and it was appropriate that a different and more realistic view of the region should be taken by the Dutch, enemies to Spain both in Europe and overseas.

THE DUTCH IN THE EAST

As the Dutch East India Company began to establish itself in the Spice Islands at the expense of the Portuguese, it sent out expeditions to investigate the unknown seas and lands to the south. In 1605, a year before Quirós reached Espiritu Santo, the Dutch made their first landfall on the Australian coast, in the Gulf of Carpentaria. This was the first of a series of probings along the continent's northern and western coasts in the first half of the century, which culminated in the ambitious explorations of Abel Tasman. In 1642–43 he sailed south of New Holland (the original Dutch name for Australia), touched on the coast of Van Diemen's Land (Tasmania) and then sailed east to a land he named New Zealand before heading north to Tonga. In 1644 he surveyed much of Australia's northern shoreline but failed to find the Torres Strait. By circumnavigating the Australian land mass, albeit at a distance, Tasman had shown it could not be part of a greater unknown southern continent, which was pushed away south-east at least as far as the stretch of New Zealand coastline he had sighted. Maps of the region made that clear, but they could not convey the unenthusiastic Dutch reaction to New Holland, whose proud name flattered to deceive. Landing only briefly, and for the most part along the north and west coasts, the Dutch described a land that was arid and barren, devoid of exploitable resources, and inhabited by a few nomads who seemed as backward as any people in the world.

Tasman's brief encounter with the Maori of South Island, which left four of his men dead, strengthened the generally unfavourable view of the region. Amid the disappointments there were also some notable Dutch achievements, for it was in this period that the expedition of Jacob Le Maire and Willem Schouten (1615–16) found an alternative route into the Pacific from the east. Their ships sailed past the Atlantic entrance to the Strait of Magellan, round Cape Horn and into the South Sea; and in time the passage round the Horn, rather than through the narrow windings of the Strait of Magellan, became the normal route. A postscript to the seventeenth-century Dutch voyages was written in 1722, when ships under Jacob Roggeveen sailed far enough south as they rounded the Horn to encounter icebergs, touched at Samoa and the fringes of the Society Islands, and brought home the first reports of Easter Island and its mysterious statues.

BUCCANEERS AND WANDERING ISLANDS

Juxtaposed with the discoveries, mostly disheartening in terms of potential utility, was a continuing hope that somewhere in the unexplored stretches of the southern ocean lay rich and fertile countries. As the Americas and the Far East became known and exploited by Europeans, speculative attention focused on the Pacific. There the Quirós fantasy still shed its glow, and utopian visionaries set extraordinary lands and societies in the region that they vaguely identified as Terra Australis.

Accounts of voyages, real and imaginary, became bestsellers, especially in England, whose seamen were once more active in the South Sea as a multinational wave of buccaneering raids swept along the Pacific coasts of Spanish America in the later seventeenth century. Buccaneers from Henry Morgan onwards held a place in popular esteem that reflected admiration both for their perceived role as fighters against Spain and popery, and for the 'rags to riches' aspect of their depredations. An essential element in this heroising process came from their own writings, for some buccaneers went to sea with pen as well as sword in hand. Among them was William Dampier, who recounted his several South Sea voyages in books that became bestsellers. Dampier's visit to the western shores of Australia in 1688 produced a dismissal of the Aboriginal inhabitants as 'the miserablest People in the World', and it was this account that Cook turned to in 1770 when he viewed the east coast of Australia and its people for the first time.

Although on one of his voyages Dampier discovered and named the island (in fact three islands) of New Britain just east of New Guinea, his books and those of other buccaneers and privateers such as Bartholomew Sharp, Woodes Rogers and George Shelvocke provided literary entertainment more than they increased geographical knowledge. Certainly they influenced two of the best-known writers of early eighteenth-century England, Daniel Defoe and Jonathan Swift. The island adventures of Defoe's Robinson Crusoe were inspired by the marooning of the privateer Alexander Selkirk on Juan Fernández, while in *Gulliver's Travels* the first identifiable person named was 'My cousin Dampier', and many of its hero's experiences were set in Dampier's South Sea.

A map of the Pacific in the early eighteenth century makes it clear that the uncertainties still outnumbered the certainties. Although from Magellan onwards Europeans of several nations had ventured into and sometimes across the great ocean, their explorations were mostly inconclusive if not confusing. The immensity of the ocean, problems in establishing longitude, the twin threats of scurvy and mutiny on long voyages, and the constraints of wind and current presented formidable obstacles to methodical exploration. In the North Pacific stretched the one regular European trade route across the ocean – the galleon run between the Philippines and Mexico – but little was known outside the galleons' tracks. Japan's coasts had been charted by the Dutch, but the ocean to the north and east remained unexplored, and the Pacific coast of America was known only as far north as California. Russian expeditions sailing east from Kamchatka would be the first to explore the northern waters between Asia and America, but reliable information about their discoveries was slow to reach Europe. In the South Pacific there had been sightings of some of the island groups near the diagonal sailing course between the tip of South America and the East Indies, but their location seemed to shift from voyage to voyage. 'There are in the South-Sea many Islands, which may be called Wandering-Islands,' the English geographer John Green complained. The coasts of the western half of New Holland and of New Guinea and New Britain, together with short stretches of the shoreline of Van Diemen's Land and New Zealand, had been roughly charted, but their relationship with one another and with the hoped-for southern continent was unknown.

CULTURAL CROSS-PURPOSES

If the geography of the Pacific was blurred, so was knowledge of its inhabitants, for successive surges of migration across the ocean had produced a complex racial and cultural pattern. European explorers were entering a region where societies were organised in overlapping layers: there had been a mingling of peoples after migration, and a seeping of cultural influences from one island group to another. Once in the Pacific, Europeans found a bewildering and unpredictable variety of appearance and behaviour among the inhabitants. Their one undeviating characteristic, by European norms, was being incurably thievish, owing to differing concepts of property: as societies without metal, that was a principal lure, iron (being commonest) in particular. The constant conflicts arising from it, small and large, overshadowed attempts at understanding it and led to countless deaths. The observations of the discoverers were usually hasty and superficial, often the result of a visit of only a few days, even just a few hours. To Europeans, and only partly for language reasons, the beliefs and taboos on which Pacific island societies were based defied easy understanding but, being 'pagan' and 'uncivilised', they were axiomatically 'inferior'. To the islanders the strangers seemed apparitions, *atua*, or men from the sky, appearing and disappearing without warning. Encounters ranged from friendly to violent, but a concluding blast of gunfire on one side and a shower of stones and spears on the other was also often the outcome of confused mutual misunderstanding.

THE EIGHTEENTH-CENTURY REVIVAL

The intrusion by buccaneers, privateers and illicit traders into waters Spain regarded as its own was short-lived. The collapse in England and France in 1720 of a host of financial 'bubble' projects had a depressing effect on ventures to distant regions, and the Pacific became associated with the early South Sea Company, whose failure had ruined investors great and small. Revival of interest came with heightening international tensions in the middle decades of the century, and in particular after Commodore Anson's voyage across the Pacific and around the world (1740–44). This melodramatic episode of wartime achievement and disaster brought back memories of Drake and the feats of English arms against the Spain of Philip II. Anson's capture of the Acapulco treasure galleon off the Philippines brought back a colossal fortune to wartime Britain but at an appalling cost in lives. Out of over 1,900 men who left England with him almost 1,400 died – just four from enemy action, a few from accidents, and the rest from scurvy or other diseases. It was a grim reminder, if any were needed, of the perils of long oceanic voyages, and it prompted intensive research by Dr James Lind and other medical men into the causes of scurvy. The official narrative of the voyage became a bestseller, but it was more than a tale of adventure on the high seas. At one level it was intended to encourage 'navigation, commerce and the national interest'. At another it made an appeal to the imagination, for the life-saving months spent by Anson's scurvy-ridden crews at Juan Fernández and Tinian brought reminders of Crusoe's island, Rousseau's Nouvelle Héloïse and other tropical-island fantasies.

The publicity surrounding Anson's voyage led to new international speculation about the potential of the Pacific region. In France in 1756, Charles de Brosses published the first collection of voyages devoted exclusively to it, *Histoire des Navigations aux Terre Australes*, which was soon plagiarised by John Callander in an English edition. The narratives in these volumes confirmed that the earlier voyages had caused confusion as much as they had brought about enlightenment. Islands had been sighted and resighted, identified and then lost again; clouds on the horizon had been mistaken for continental ranges; straits had become bays, and bays straits. The map of the Pacific was marked by squiggles of coastline that hinted at lands of continental dimensions, and it was dotted with island groups whose names and locations changed with the whims of cartographical fashion. But for de Brosses, further exploration, especially the discovery of a southern continent, was a nobler objective of French ambitions than the endless European wars. Likewise, in Britain the geographer Alexander Dalrymple suggested that the southern continent might be 5,000 miles across and populated by 50 million inhabitants. The 'scraps' from its economy, he declared, 'would be sufficient to maintain the power, dominion and sovereignty of Britain, by employing all its manufactures and ships'.

After the ending of the Seven Years War in 1763 both Britain and France experienced a 'Pacific craze' in which a new type of naval hero emerged – namely, the explorer whose ships left for the unknown, to return years later laden with specimens from the South Seas, and with crews eager to publish accounts, maps and views of the exotic places they had visited. At home enthusiasts assumed that the unexplored lands of the Pacific held sufficient resources to tilt the commercial balance of power in Europe; for Britain, these would, they believed, confirm the overseas superiority brought by the wartime conquests of 1756–63, and for France, they would redress the humiliations that had led to an imposed peace. The first voyage in the new era of state-sponsored Pacific exploration was Commodore John Byron's in 1764. It was an unconvincing start, for Byron (the poet's grandfather) followed the normal north-westerly slanting sailing route from Cape Horn and made few discoveries of note. Perhaps sensibly, he ignored the part of his instructions that ordered him, after he had made discoveries in the South Pacific, to sail to its distant northern reaches in search of an entrance to the fabled North-West Passage. That formidable task would have to wait for Cook, on his final voyage. In 1766 the Admiralty sent out two more ships, commanded by Captain Samuel Wallis and Lieutenant Philip Carteret, with orders to sail into high southerly latitudes in search of the fabled southern continent. A few months later ships of the French navy also left for the Pacific under the command of one of the outstanding Frenchmen of the day, Louis-Antoine de Bougainville.

After becoming separated from Wallis's ship, the enterprising Carteret crossed the Pacific further south than any of his predecessors and in doing so removed part of the supposed southern continent from the maps. Wallis took a more cautious route, but his voyage was marked by a chance discovery whose emotional impact was out of all proportion to its geographical significance. In June 1767 he sighted Tahiti, an island of idyllic beauty, which for generations was to conjure up voluptuous images of the South Seas. To the crew of a discovery vessel after months on passage, the islands of Polynesia were an earthly paradise. To the breaking surf, the palm-fringed beaches and the towering volcanic peaks were added sensuous overtones – of women and girls, nubile, garlanded and welcoming. The opportunities, in the words of one of Wallis's officers, 'made all our men madly fond of the shore, even the sick who had been on the doctor's list for some weeks'. When Bougainville reached Tahiti the following year, reactions were even more effusive and extravagant. He called the island New Cythera after Aphrodite's fabled realm, while his naturalist, Commerson, preferred an even more resonant name – Utopia. From Tahiti, Bougainville sailed west through the Samoan group and on to the Espiritu Santo of Pedro de Quirós, which he found to be insular, not continental as the Spanish navigator had imagined. The expedition continued westward in search of the unknown east coast of New Holland before the outliers of the Great Barrier Reef forced it away north.

For all the activity that these voyages represented, the central issues of Pacific geography were no nearer to a solution. The fabled continent of Terra Australis had simply receded a little further south; New Holland was still the western outline of a land of unknown extent; islands discovered and undiscovered remained to be properly identified and located. In the North Pacific, Russian expeditions had found a few pinpricks of land that might or might not be part of the American continent, but a navigable North-West Passage remained as elusive as ever. Yet within a decade the outlines of both the North and the South Pacific took shape on the maps in much the same form as they stand today. The man responsible for this leap in knowledge was James Cook. As following chapters will outline, his three expeditions, begun in 1768 and ending in 1780 – a year after his own death on Hawaii – revealed the lands and peoples of the Pacific to Europe in a way none of those who had preceded him there had done.

AFTER COOK

The expedition of Lapérouse, which sailed from Brest in 1785, represented the first French response to Cook's voyages, though several other important ones were to follow. Cook was also an exemplar for the Spanish expedition that left Cádiz in 1789, commanded by Alejandro Malaspina, although his was also an ambitious attempt to survey Spain's existing overseas territories in the Pacific. In different ways both men were ill-fated. After sending home accounts of early success from the north-west Pacific to Australia (where he arrived at Botany Bay in 1788, within days of Arthur Phillip's British 'First Fleet'), Lapérouse simply disappeared, and a search expedition by d'Entrecasteaux found no trace of his lost ships. Malaspina completed a voyage of over five years, but on return to Spain his political activities led to his disgrace and to its elimination from contemporary record, although it has only fairly recently been retrieved by historical research. In the first years of the nineteenth century Nicolas Baudin commanded a French surveying and scientific expedition intended to complete the charting of the coastline of Australia. It did valuable work in surveying, ethnography and natural history, but its members were divided by political and personal differences. Baudin died at Île de France (Mauritius), and his voyage was widely regarded as a failure, although he has been more sensitively reappraised in modern scholarship. The contemporaneous British voyage by Matthew Flinders to the same region, in 1801–03, also had more than its fair share of ill luck, but his magnificent charts were to be used for many years, and his place names still mark the coastline of what he first consistently called 'Australia'. It would, it seemed, be left mainly to British seamen to complete and exploit Cook's work in the Pacific, as suggested by John Douglas, editor of the official account of his last voyage, when he wrote in its introduction that 'every nation that sends a ship to sea will partake of the benefit of such accounts; but Great Britain herself, whose commerce is boundless, must take the lead in reaping the full advantage of her own discoveries'.

It is the initial steps in this direction, rather than discovery itself, that the following chapters briefly outline in recounting the voyages of Arthur Phillip, William Bligh, Matthew Flinders, George Vancouver and Robert FitzRoy. While they all enlarged geographical knowledge, especially of specific areas on the Pacific rim, their main purposes – with the qualified exception of Vancouver – were to begin or at least enable the British practical 'advantage' from the prior discoveries to which Douglas alluded, and they did so in very different ways.

BOTANY BAY, BREADFRUIT AND SIR JOSEPH BANKS

Phillip's 'First Fleet' departure in May 1787 to establish a British penal colony at Botany Bay, Cook's first landing point in south-eastern Australia, was primarily motivated by a need to solve the domestic problem of where most usefully to exile convicted criminals who, after recognition of United States independence in 1783, could no longer be shipped as indentured labour to Britain's former North American colonies. Already claimed for Britain by Cook, New South Wales was to contemporary European opinion unowned *terra nullius*, with sparse and 'primitive' human inhabitants who could be accommodated or made compliant. As Evan Nepean, the official most concerned with the project, put it, the region 'appears to be a country peculiarly adapted for a settlement, the lands about it being plentifully supplied with wood and water, the soil rich and fertile, and the shores well stocked with shell and other fish'. Other factors almost certainly played a part: the need to forestall possible French initiatives; the advantages of having a base on the southern, or 'blind', side of the Dutch East Indies; and the hope that the region would provide much-needed naval stores such as timber and flax. In due course, after a hard but remarkably accident-free voyage, Phillip's 13 ships reached Botany Bay in January 1788, thereby launching British imperial possession of a new continent of which the full outline was still uncertain.

While most people have at least heard of the mid-Pacific mutiny on the *Bounty* in 1789, comparatively few also know that its commander, William Bligh, nevertheless completed the task set for him in that ship – the transplanting of Tahitian breadfruit to the West Indies. *Bounty*'s loss did not prevent the Admiralty from sending him on a second and better-prepared attempt (and may in part have prompted it to do so). However, his success on that occasion (like Malaspina's and Vancouver's) was largely overlooked both at the time (1793) and in later memory through his misfortune in reaching home during the early alarums and upheavals of the French Revolutionary War. The breadfruit project, unlike Phillip's, was primarily an economic one: to provide a cheap new foodstuff for the enslaved workforce on British plantations in the West Indies. Together with the East Indies trade, the West Indies were at that time the main overseas source of both British revenues and powerful political influence. While the breadfruit itself failed to meet expectations, Caribbean-generated wealth not only substantially funded Britain's early 'industrial revolution' which supported wartime survival, but – thanks to the trade-protecting role of the Navy – also grew inexorably, rather than diminished, during the long French wars to 1815. It was with West Indian 'plantation interest' in mind that Bligh's two voyages were planned, and the second also succeeded in the first's intention to transfer other Pacific and East Indian plants to various stopping points en route, the terminus (along with Caribbean additions) being the Royal Botanic Gardens at Kew.

Both expeditions had George III's keen support, and their presiding genius – who also steered Bligh into *Bounty*'s command – was Sir Joseph Banks. As a wealthy, botanically enthusiastic and knowledgeable Lincolnshire landowner, the young Mr Banks had become the prime authority on Pacific natural history from the three years in which, at his own request, he had been allowed to join Cook's first voyage in the *Endeavour* (1768–71). Thereafter, and as president of the Royal Society from 1778, he was the indispensable adviser on British scientific affairs at home and abroad, especially where botany and agricultural economy were concerned. In this he enjoyed the consistent support of George III – 'the farmer king' – in a period when geographical discovery made the extent of European botanical collections, especially royal ones, a focus of rivalrous prestige. Banks was also, for the same scientifically 'improving' reasons, an influential backer of the Botany Bay project, being literally the only man with direct and informed personal knowledge of the area, its flora, fauna, inhabitants and natural potentials for settlement. When it was eventually well established at what is now Sydney, it too became part of his network for ongoing international exchange of plants and related information.

Vancouver's voyage of 1791–95 also resulted from matters in which Banks had a hand, as one of those overseeing publication of Cook's last voyage in 1784. This had shown the potential for a trade in seal and sea-otter pelts on the Pacific north-west coast around Nootka Sound – or King George's Sound, as Cook named it – on the west coast of what is now Vancouver Island. This trade rapidly attracted Russian, Chinese and British mercantile interest, and Banks firmly supported home enterprise in the matter, especially the quickly formed King George's Sound Company. The company's projector brothers, Richard and John Etches, assiduously cultivated Banks and his royal influence, not least in the naming of their ships, of which the *King George* and the *Queen Charlotte* (the latter so christened by Banks) made their first successful fur-trading voyage to Nootka in 1788 under two former Cook third-voyage men, Nathaniel Portlock and George Dixon. Richard Etches's more ambitious vision led him to instruct James Colnett, a Cook second-voyage veteran who soon followed in the *Prince of Wales* and the *Princess Royal*, to establish at least one trading post on the nearby Queen Charlotte Islands. For, as he explained to Banks, 'Our purpose is to adopt a permanent system of Commerce direct from this Country to the N.W. coast and from thence to the Asiatic Coast and Islands' (China and the East Indies), with the further suggestion that such post or posts might in due course be manned by guarded convicts from Botany Bay, linking British enterprise in the North and South Pacific.

THE NOOTKA SOUND CRISIS

By the late 1780s the Pacific north-west was attracting the attention of geographers, merchants and governments, still in the hope (despite Cook's dismissal of it) that a navigable passage might yet be found that at least penetrated deep into

SEA OTTER; engraving after John Webber, 1784.

The dead young sea otter had been bought in Nootka Sound in 1778 and it was sketched by Webber and later included in the official narrative of the third voyage. It was, read the account, 'rather young, weighing only twenty-five pounds; of a shining or glossy black colour'. European ships were soon sailing to the north-west American coast to trade for sea-otter pelts, which were then resold in China, where they fetched considerable sums.

the North American interior, enabling a network of trade between there, China and Japan. Foremost among the advocates of renewed search was Alexander Dalrymple, hydrographer to the East India Company from 1779. He proposed a union between it and the Hudson's Bay Company that, with government support and using such a passage (if found), would link operations in the Americas and the Pacific, and dominate Europe's trade from northern Canada to Canton and Bombay. He pointed out that the Russians were already well established in Alaska, while the Spaniards were pressing north from Mexico and California. The urgency of the situation was confirmed by the Nootka Sound crisis, which began to unroll in the summer of 1789.

It centred on John Meares, a half-pay Royal Navy lieutenant who arrived on the coast as master of a small trader, *Nootka*, in 1786 and was the first European other than Russians to overwinter there, in Prince William Sound. He lost 24 of his men, mainly to scurvy, but returned to the coast in 1788 with two vessels, the *Felice Adventurer* and the *Iphigenia Nubiana*, both under nominal Portuguese command and colours to skirt the monopoly of the East India and South Sea Companies over British vessels trading in the seas east of China. By that May, in the *Felice*, he reached Cook's former harbour at Friendly Cove in Nootka Sound. There, in exchange for two pistols, he claimed that he bought an area of land from the leading local chief Maquinna (Ma-kwa-nee) on which he erected a trading hut and began building a small schooner with the help of Chinese carpenters and other workmen from his vessels. Looking for trade, he then sailed south as far as the Oregon coast, and on return to Nootka sent his longboat under the first mate, Robert Duffin, to explore a wide inlet found in 1787 by another voyager, William Barkley, who for historical reasons (explained in Chapter 7) named it the Strait of Juan de Fuca. (It is the wide sound looping round southern Vancouver Island, just north of modern Seattle.) Duffin was driven back by local attacks long before finding how far it went, but in his published voyage account of 1790, Meares speculated that it might even communicate with Hudson Bay.

In Meares's last two months at Friendly Cove, before he took the *Felice* to sell furs in China via Hawaii, he suppressed a mutiny and saw his little schooner completed and launched – under British colours on 20 September – as the *North-West America*. Even more significantly, he claimed that Maquinna (who had made deadly use of borrowed British muskets against local rivals) did 'obedience to us as his lords and sovereigns'. It is very doubtful that this submission by the chief bore the interpretation Meares and the British government later put on it; or that Meares's hut, on his purchased plot, was as substantial as he also claimed and illustrated in his voyage account. For after Maquinna and his people retreated to winter further inland, the crew of the *Iphigenia* pulled it to pieces before they also sailed for Hawaii, leaving only two American vessels temporarily in the cove.

Far to the north in the summer of 1788, a Spanish party from Mexico, under Esteban José Martínez, finally met one of the Russian groups by then fairly common in Alaska and heard of Russian intentions to advance further south. Spanish authority had long been apprehensive of Russian northern incursions into their claimed Pacific suzerainty, to which had now been added Cook's north-west coast survey, briefer French investigations by Lapérouse, and the steadily increasing British and American fur-trading expeditions. Although Martínez was mistaken in thinking Russian plans aimed as far as Nootka, he urged Spanish occupation of Friendly Cove against that possibility. In the spring of 1789 he was despatched from San Blas to effect it, commanding 200 men in two ships mounting 42 guns overall – a powerful force in regional terms. At the same time, British vessels were heading back for the trading season from Hawaii and China, and, given Martínez's impulsive temperament, confrontation was inevitable. In May the nominally Portuguese *Iphigenia* was only briefly detained, but in early June the tiny *North-West America* was seized and taken into Spanish service. Real crisis arrived with James Colnett in the Etches brothers' *Argonaut*, carrying Chinese workmen intended to build boats and a trading post (to be named Fort Pitt) at Nootka. The arrest of the *Argonaut* and its crew, followed by the seizure of the Etcheses' *Princess Royal*, was the prelude to scenes of high drama as Martínez and Colnett quarrelled, sometimes sword in hand. The Spaniard's fondness for alcohol did not help, and Colnett's unstable character resulted in at least one attempted suicide, while a Spaniard shot dead Maquinna's associate chief, Callicum, when he sought to intervene in a dispute. The Spanish authorities at San Blas, unaware of these developments, nonetheless eventually ordered the evacuation of Nootka. In October Martínez sailed south with his prisoners. Other American trade vessels had already left, and Maquinna's people had again gone inland for the winter, but this time the deserted silence at Friendly Cove was the lull before a brewing international storm.

First news of events at Nootka reached Britain in early 1790, by way of its diplomats in Spain. The government's immediate reaction was to secure an apology from Madrid, with recognition of British rights to trade and settle in areas Spain did not actually occupy. This was backed by preparations to send a naval expedition to the north-west by way of New South Wales, commanded by Henry Roberts, another veteran of Cook's last voyage. Draft orders specified his priority as finding out exactly what had occurred at Nootka in 1789; and then to explore the coast further (as Dalrymple was urging) and put about 30 Marines, overseers and convicts from Sydney ashore in the Queen Charlotte Islands, where they would establish a settlement (the scheme promoted by Banks and the Etcheses). In late April 1790 the expedition was cancelled when Meares's arrival in England put the matter on a different and more alarming footing. He claimed that in his dealings on the north-west coast he had acted as an officer of the Royal Navy, that he had bought the land at Nootka and taken possession of it in the King's name, and that he had secured recognition of British overlordship from Maquinna. If he was right, a British settlement was already established there, despite his trading post's demolition before the later Spanish arrival. An obscure scuffle with British traders and seizure of their property thereby became a Spanish insult to the British Crown, leading to a confrontation that raised the whole matter of trading and territorial rights on the north-west coast and beyond. As Henry Dundas, the British minister most involved, told the House of Commons: 'We are not contending for a few miles, but a large world,' for he had in mind a release from international restrictions that would massively benefit British traders. Or, as Richard Etches remarked to Banks, it was not a case simply of 'the immediate property seized' at Nootka, but of 'great and certain prospects' in trade and discovery.

Spurred on by bellicose public opinion, the British mobilised the fleet and prepared for war. Spain, however, faced with fighting yet another rearguard action in defence of its traditional claims in America, realised that France – its formal ally but now in revolutionary turmoil – was in no position to offer customary help. By the terms of the Nootka Sound Convention, signed in October 1790, Madrid conceded the main points at issue: the land and property seized in 1789 would be returned and free access and trade permitted along those parts of the north-west coast not occupied by Spain – in effect, all of it. British naval ships would go to the region under command of George Vancouver, also a Cook third-voyager and previously nominated first lieutenant to Roberts for his earlier, cancelled expedition. Vancouver's twin tasks were to receive the formal restitutions at Nootka and further explore the coast as far north as latitude 60°, to determine once and for all whether there was a navigable North-West Passage in temperate latitudes. This survey, all the more important because of Spain's abandonment of its exclusive claims, took him and his crews three seasons of wearisome work in open boats, often in poor weather, and with the threat of local attack always present. At the end, having found no north-westerly passage, he summed up his approach by justifiably asserting that his 'discovery that no such communication does exist has been zealously pursued, and with a degree of minuteness far exceeding the letter of my commission or instructions'.

On the diplomatic level, Vancouver met difficulties at Nootka, where the Spaniards had established a fort and other buildings more impressive than Meares's vanished hut. At a loss in his dealings with the affable but firm Spanish representative, Juan Francisco de la Bodega y Quadra, Vancouver broke off negotiations, which greatly irritated the British government. But by then, since he had received no further instructions or information from home, he could not know that Britain and Spain were now allies against revolutionary France. This soon led to an Anglo-Spanish accord whereby, after a symbolic restitution to new British commissioners, both nations would abandon Nootka. That took place in 1795, after which Maquinna's people began demolishing the Spanish fortifications in a search for nails and other ironwork. As there were fewer British ships on the coast after Vancouver's visit, and the sea-otter trade was in decline, the greatest beneficiary of the Spanish retreat was the United States, which played no part in the negotiations. It was American fur traders who thereafter dominated the coast, their numbers swelled in the new century by arrivals overland who spearheaded the westward American drive to the Pacific.

Perhaps even more disappointing to Vancouver than London's failure to keep in touch over the Nootka transactions was its failure to acknowledge his achievement – as he saw it – in negotiating cession of the Hawaiian Islands to Britain in February 1794. As Cook had first found, these islands provided the wintering base essential for ships working along the Pacific north-west coast. Oddly, however, while Vancouver left a letter in Hawaii explaining to the masters of all vessels calling there that Kamehameha and his chiefs had 'unanimously acknowledged themselves subject to the British crown', he seems never to have informed London of what he had done – or if he did, the letter has not survived: his last known one to the Admiralty from Hawaii is dated 8 February 1794, several weeks earlier. The affair was set out in detail in his voyage account, published in 1798, but this still prompted no official British reaction. Perhaps the government had doubts about the validity of Vancouver's act of cession or about the eventual value of possessing such remote Pacific islands, as Vancouver did himself. European affairs in 1798 were dominated by Napoleon's invasion of Egypt, Nelson's triumph at the Battle of the Nile, and the consequent formation of the anti-French Second Coalition: weighed against all this, Hawaii's status was of marginal importance.

WHALERS, TRADERS, MISSIONARIES AND THE *BEAGLE*

The Nootka Sound Convention also had implications for British enterprise in the South Pacific. By the 1750s the Greenland whale fishery could not meet the growing demand for oil. After Cook's broad charting of the Pacific both British and American whalers instead began to sail far south in pursuit of then-plentiful sperm whale there. One problem for British whalers (though not for the Americans) was that they were invading waters covered by the monopoly rights of the East India and South Sea Companies, but this was soon largely resolved. A different obstacle was the lack of bases in the southern oceans where whaling and sealing vessels could be repaired and crews refreshed. Again, the Britons suffered more than the Americans from Spanish intractability, and the problem became yearly more acute as increasing numbers of British whalers (more than 50 in 1791) entered the Pacific, many by way of Cape Horn. In the absence of a friendly port, some of them were at sea for up to a year, and their crews suffered heavy losses, mainly due to scurvy.

During negotiations over the Nootka crisis the British government was clear that its demands included freedom for British subjects to hunt whales in any part of the Pacific, and to land for repairs and relief in any unoccupied harbour. The first Nootka Sound Convention of 1790 formalised this, with its proviso that the coasts of Spanish America should be accessible to non-Spanish trade and settlement, except within 30 miles of an existing settlement. This not only gave practically unlimited range along the Pacific north-west but turned some of the uninhabited islands off South America's west coast into potential whaling bases. In 1792, given the lack of reliable surveys there, James Colnett (previously involved in the Nootka Sound crisis) commanded the *Rattler* on a joint government–private expedition to examine Pacific offshore islands from Chile to Mexico. However, by the time he returned in 1794 with an enthusiastic report on the Galápagos Islands, the problem had been solved a different way, since the whalers were by now using New Zealand, Hawaii and especially Sydney as supply bases.

VIEW OF SYDNEY FROM THE EAST SIDE OF THE COVE NO. 1; coloured aquatint by John Eyre, from D.D. Mann, *The Present Picture of New South Wales* (1811).

Government House, set in generous grounds, is on the far left; prison barracks crown the ridge behind.

After its difficult first years, the infant 'Botany Bay' penal colony at Port Jackson had made great strides in developing an agricultural and trading economy. It was becoming the bustling port city of Sydney, welcoming other types of immigrants, albeit still receiving convicts. By 1800 its huge natural harbour was a base not only for South Sea whalers but also for trading vessels, some heading for China and India and others to the islands of Polynesia for pork, sandalwood and later copra and coconut fibre. The islanders were willing traders for Western goods and tools, but adverse effects soon resulted from the as yet unpoliced sharp practice and violence of many of the Europeans involved – who also brought alcohol, firearms and disease. In 1796, too, the first missionary vessel, the *Duff*, sailed from England for Tahiti, and while missionaries generally supported Pacific peoples against European excesses, the concomitant Christianisation they pursued was no less damaging to local cultures and societal structures. In terms of volume and value, Pacific trade remained small compared with that of the North Atlantic and the Indian Ocean, but by now, almost 300 years after Magellan first crossed it, the great 'South Sea' was engaged, for better or worse, with the wider world.

Nevertheless, until the opening of the Panama Canal in 1914, the only eastern gateway to this sea remained round Cape Horn. For ships that had to enter westward that way, rather than by the longer but easier 'east-about' route across the southern Indian Ocean, there also remained the close-by Strait of Magellan. Winding, mountainous and with many hazard-ridden channels and strong currents, this had become little attempted in preference to the deep-water passage round the Horn, despite its difficulties, and by the 1820s the Strait was still not well surveyed. Filling that gap in detailed knowledge, and charting adjacent barren coasts and islands (including, thoroughly, the Galápagos further north) became HMS *Beagle*'s practical contribution to southern-ocean navigation, and its story forms the concluding chapter here.

For most but not all of the duration of its two voyages (1826–36), the *Beagle* was captained by Robert FitzRoy, a Royal Naval officer more emblematic of the early Victorian age than the late Georgian British commanders who largely populate this book. The latter were all meritocrats of modest origins who, from youth and often with only fairly basic schooling, learnt all their skills at sea, becoming wartime fighters of varied experience and distinction, as well as navigators. FitzRoy, by contrast, was a well-connected aristocrat, grandson on his father's side of the 3rd Duke of Grafton and on his mother's of the 1st Marquess of Londonderry. He was still a schoolboy when the Napoleonic War ended in 1815, never had fighting experience and went to sea only after public school education until he was 13 (the last year at Harrow, 1817–18), followed by shore-based naval training at the Royal Naval College, Portsmouth. He was an exemplary and distinguished student at Portsmouth, and later came top out of 27 in his lieutenant's examination of 1824.

OPPOSITE Like Cook before them, missionaries would have a powerful influence on the history of the Pacific islands. The first group was sent out in 1797 by the directors of the London Missionary Society, which commissioned Robert Smirke's huge oil painting, *The Cession of the District of Matavai in the Island of Otaheite [Tahiti] to Captain James Wilson* (1798–99). Wilson, captain of the *Duff*, can be seen to the right in the painting, holding his hat in his left hand. Tu, the future Pomare I, and his concubine, Tetua, are seated on their subjects' shoulders. The imposing ceremony was, however, not intended as a formal cession of land but was meant as a conditional offer of help and hospitality to the missionaries.

However, it is worth noting that many, if not most, sea officers of the Napoleonic Wars and earlier derided 'young gentlemen' who had had their first training at Portsmouth (where the college began as the Royal Naval Academy in 1733), rather than having, like them, simply gained practical experience at sea from late boyhood on.

While they had some justification for this view, both educational and disciplinary standards at Portsmouth had greatly improved by the time FitzRoy arrived, the Academy being reconstituted as the Royal Naval College in 1806 and being joined by the School of Naval Architecture in 1816. Even in the immediate wake of Nelson's victory at Trafalgar in 1805 (the year of FitzRoy's birth), the Navy recognised it was running into an age when its officer corps would require a better and more consistent underpinning of specialist theoretical literacy than could solely – and variably – be acquired by 'learning on the job'. What remained an invariable necessity was practical professional competence (without which everyone at sea was at risk), and despite also possessing a prickly aristocratic tendency to take offence, FitzRoy had that in abundance by the time he took command of *Beagle*, as well as considerable prior experience in South America. Thanks to ability and connection, he also had the concomitant luck, when the *Beagle* vacancy occurred, of being flag lieutenant to Admiral Sir Robert Waller Otway (1770–1846), the local British station Commander-in Chief and himself a distinguished practical and fighting seaman. It says as much for Otway's judgement as it does for FitzRoy's competence that the former gave his protégé the opportunity that enabled him to make his career as a leading scientific naval officer and later a pioneering meteorologist. FitzRoy's main *Beagle* survey (1831–36) is also inseparable from the work done on it by the gentlemanly recruit he enlisted to provide him with the conversation of an intellectually and socially equal companion. This appointment followed the suicide of FitzRoy's predecessor as commander of *Beagle*, Pringle Stokes, for with a degree of self-knowledge, FitzRoy rightly feared the potential solitude of an arduous command in a bleak and remote area he already knew.

Charles Darwin's later *Origin of Species* (1859) was rooted in his *Beagle* observations and closes the nearly 70-year separation between its second voyage and Cook's first in *Endeavour*. For in the same way that Banks made his name as the great gentlemanly

natural scientist of the late Georgian period by seeking to accompany Cook, so did Darwin in the early-to-mid-Victorian era by agreeing to go with FitzRoy. Unlike any of the other explorers treated here, FitzRoy also had the resources to repeat Banks's example of privately engaging landscape artists to accompany his second *Beagle* expedition, first Augustus Earle and then his replacement, Conrad Martens.

Regrettably, in the end, FitzRoy's fears of depression and tendency to suffer from it under stress proved well founded. Both he and Darwin were sincerely religious, but FitzRoy found the latter's theories of evolution alarming and hard to accept. Always a driven worker, he was a vice-admiral and only in his late fifties when he again became deeply affected by a conflict of views with his meteorological masters at the Board of Trade. On 30 April 1865, two months before his 60th birthday, he met the same end as Stokes, dying by suicide. Fortunately perhaps, given his beliefs, he did not live to see Darwin's *Descent of Man* (1871), the second of the two volumes that form a continental divide between the still-little-explored ocean of natural science in the age of Cook and Banks and the better-charted expanses of our own.

This 1970s cutaway model, based on the
Navy's original plans of the *Endeavour*, shows its
general internal arrangements after fitting-out
for Cook's first voyage of discovery, 1768–71.

COOK AND THE VOYAGE OF *ENDEAVOUR*

'A man, who has not the advantages of Education [...] who
has been constantly at sea from his youth, and who, with
the Assistance of a few good friends [has] gone through all
the Stations belonging to a Seaman, from a prentice boy
in the Coal Trade to a Commander in the Navy'

COOK'S DESCRIPTION OF HIMSELF, *c*.1775

IN JUNE 1766 the Council of the Royal Society of London resolved to send
observers to various parts of the world to record the six-hour transit of the planet
Venus across the face of the Sun, predicted for 9 June 1769. This rare event, first
recorded in 1639, was the subject of widespread but imperfect observation on its
next occurrence in 1761, and would not be repeated until 1874. The purpose of
the observations, which had to be made from widely separated latitudes on the
Earth's surface, and precisely timed, was to calculate the distance from the Earth to
the Sun. The result would give a unit for estimating the size of the universe.

The difficulties involved in ensuring observers were appropriately placed in
the northern hemisphere were manageable. Finding a suitable, cloudless, daytime
and safely accessible dry-land observation point south of the Equator was another
matter. In November 1767 the Society set up a Transit Committee, which shortlisted
a number of locations and potential observers. As far as the Pacific was concerned,
the Reverend Nevil Maskelyne, Astronomer Royal and leading Transit Committee
member, could only suggest a desirable general area, defined by latitude and longitude,
where as yet unknown islands might exist. Among individuals discussed, Alexander
Dalrymple was proposed as 'an able Navigator and well skilled in Observation' who
might be sent out in a ship which the government would be asked to provide.

Dalrymple (1737–1808) was a man of talent and ambition who was to become
the Navy's first official hydrographer in 1795. Having gone to India in 1752 as

an East India Company official, he there acquired a remarkable knowledge of early European exploration in the Indies and the Pacific. He rose to become the Company's deputy-secretary at Madras in 1758, and from 1760 to 1764 himself led several voyages through the Indonesian islands, with a professional sailing master. These opened new trading opportunities and Dalrymple returned to England to press for Company support to develop them. In putting himself forward to observe the transit in the Pacific, Dalrymple also intended to be the expedition commander, with a greater personal mission in view. This mission was to prove the existence of Terra Australis Incognita, the inhabitable but unknown 'southern continent' which geographers since Classical times had suggested must exist around the South Pole in order to balance the land masses in the northern hemisphere. His research had made him a leader in this still widely accepted belief, which was a central tenet in his important edition of early Pacific voyage accounts, *A Historical Collection of Voyages … in the South Pacific Ocean*, published in 1770–71.

The British authorities, less convinced, were at least alert to the potential benefits of such a continent and aware of rival French and Spanish interest. In 1764–66, they sent out Commodore John Byron to probe for it. He was instructed to examine and formally claim the Falkland Islands in the South Atlantic and to find a supposed 'Pepys Island' which, he rightly concluded, was a mis-sighting of the Falklands. Byron judged that his ships *Dolphin* and *Tamar* were unfit to pursue his further objective of seeking an equally fabled 'north-west passage' back to the Atlantic from the Pacific coast of Canada, and he encountered only Pacific islands, not continental land, as he took a circumnavigating route homeward via the East Indies. The *Dolphin* was then quickly sent out again in August 1766, under Captain Samuel Wallis, accompanied by the smaller *Swallow* under Philip Carteret, expressly to seek any land mass in the Pacific to the south of Byron's track.

Neither had returned when, in February 1768, the Royal Society petitioned George III for £4,000 to mount the proposed transit expedition. It was to be a voyage of scientific prestige, not a continental search, and cited the well-proved case that advances in astronomy brought benefits to practical navigation – the basis of British sea trade and power. Maskelyne's first publication of the *Nautical Almanac* in 1766, and the 'lunar distance' method of finding longitude which it facilitated, were important recent examples. The King agreed to grant the money and the Admiralty supplied a ship, bought for a further £2,800 in the form of a stout Whitby collier. The admirals, however, refused to have a civilian rather than a naval officer in overall command. Dalrymple was neither a naval officer nor a professional seaman: compromise was impossible and he withdrew from the project.

The Board of Admiralty could have chosen a commander from many commissioned sea officers but accepted its secretary's recommendation to appoint the master of the schooner *Grenville*, a well-regarded warrant officer and notable marine surveyor. He was a steady married man of 39 who had proven navigational and astronomical skills and had shown much expertise in charting difficult waters, most recently in his thorough surveys of the coast of Newfoundland. His name was James Cook.

COOK'S EARLY YEARS

James Cook was born on 27 October 1728 at Marton-in-Cleveland, a small country parish in the North Riding of Yorkshire, his father – also James – being an agricultural day-labourer of lowland Scots origin. His mother, Grace, was a young Yorkshire woman. Young James was the second child and second son in a family of eight, but only he and two sisters lived beyond 1750.

Cook's father was a poor man and James was fortunate in gaining a modest education in reading, writing and arithmetic, principally at the charitable Postgate School at Great Ayton where James senior became a farm foreman in 1736. In 1745, at the small Yorkshire fishing port of Staithes, 17-year-old James junior began a trial employment as shop boy to William Sanderson, a grocer and haberdasher, but after 18 months both realised that this was not his métier. Supported by Sanderson, Cook instead went over to nearby Whitby and entered a three-year apprenticeship to become a seaman in the coastal colliers of John Walker, a respected Quaker sea captain and ship owner. Walker was to become Cook's lifelong friend, and their association was also responsible indirectly for the start of another – that of Cook and the greatest British voyages of scientific exploration with the local 'cat-bark' colliers, the workhorses of the east coast and North Sea trade.

Cook, like most boys apprenticed to become seamen, entered as a 'servant' and his first voyage (with nine fellow apprentices in a crew of 19) was in the *Freelove*, a 341-ton Yarmouth-built ship, under John Jefferson. Two years later he helped Jefferson fit out a new ship of Walker's, the *Three Brothers*, and sailed in her from June 1748 to December 1749, initially carrying coal and then taking troops home from Flanders to Dublin and London under government contract. In April 1750 Cook completed his apprenticeship and continued as an able seaman in this and other ships until December 1752. He then rose to be mate of the *Friendship*, a new Walker vessel, in which he remained for another two and a half years under three successive masters, one from Whitby, one from Norway and one from the Netherlands. In the *Friendship*, there is no doubt that his skills expanded into mature competency in North Sea coastal navigation and pilotage, since Walker invited him to become the ship's next master.

Astonishingly, it was an offer Cook declined. He instead decided to enter the Royal Navy, volunteering as an able seaman at Wapping, London, on 17 June 1755.

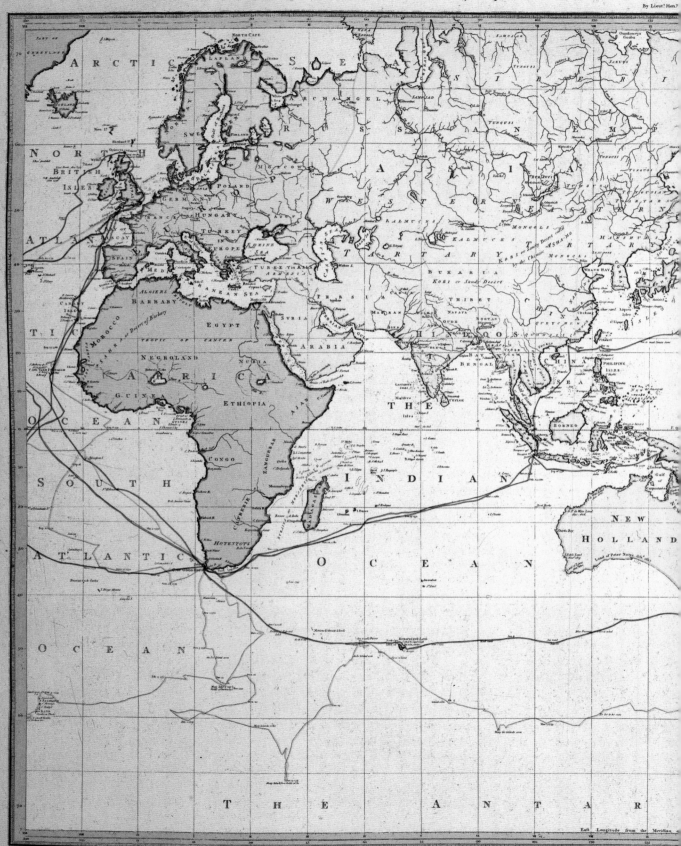

CHART

eceding VOYAGES; with the TRACKS of the SHIPS under his Command.

TY's Royal Navy.

ARCTIC SEA

NORTH

ARCTIC CIRCLE

BAFFIN'S BAY

GREENLAND

NORTH

HUDSONS BAY

LABRADOR OR NEW BRITAIN

SOUTH WALES

ESKIMAUX

NEW BRITAIN

NORTH

ATLANTIC

NEW MEXICO

NEW LOUISIANA

OCEAN

GULF OF MEXICO

CARIBBEAN SEA

TIERRA FIRMA OR NEW GRANADA

SOUTH

AMERICA

PARAGUAY

NORTH

PACIFIC

OCEAN

LINE

SOUTH

PACIFIC

TROPIC OF CAPRICORN

NEW HEBRIDES

NEW CALEDONIA

NEW ZEELAND

PACIFIC

OCEAN

SOUTH

ATLANTIC

OCEAN

ARCTIC CIRCLE

TIC OCEAN

EXPLANATION.

This shews the Endeavours Track in the Years 1768,1769,1770 & 1771.
Resolutions First Voyage in 1772,1773,1774 & 1775.
Resolution's Second Voyage in 1776,1777,1778,1779 & 1780.

In terms of pay and status it was a backward step; for, as Nelson later said of his own experience in the 1770s, merchant seamen then had 'a horror of the Royal Navy'. Cook himself gave no reason for this decision except for a later hint, after his second Pacific voyage, that his 'ambition' led him to range further than other men. Although in 1755 he could not know how far and in what remarkable capacity this would be, the Navy was already embroiled in the undeclared phase of the Seven Years War with France (1756–63). Fought substantially in North America and India, this was to take Cook further than he had yet been and give him opportunities beyond those open to a provincial short-trade shipmaster.

He was assigned to the 60-gun *Eagle* at Portsmouth, and within a month was advanced to master's mate. On 1 October, after she was driven back to repair weather damage from a cruise in the western approaches, a fellow Yorkshireman who would play an important part in Cook's career took over command – the competent, energetic and experienced Hugh Palliser (1723–96). A week later, the *Eagle* sailed out again on a stormy and active cruise, taking part in the capture of one French warship before the end of the October and in the sinking, on fire, of another in November. In January 1756 Cook became her boatswain in addition to his mate's duties and that spring, while patrolling off the southern Brittany coast, Palliser gave him temporary command of the cutter *Cruizer*. He subsequently brought home a merchant prize, taken in the Bay of Biscay, and in January 1757 took part in a severe fight when the *Eagle* and *Medway* captured a well-armed French Indiaman south-west of Ushant. That June, after Cook's friend John Walker solicited his local MP to approach Palliser, the captain recommended Cook's promotion to master – the senior warrant officer of a ship of war, charged with her routine navigation and maintenance of her sailing capacity. By then he had also learnt the techniques of celestial navigation necessary for ocean voyaging. On 29 June 1757 he was success-fully examined by Trinity House, Deptford, and the next day was appointed master of the *Solebay*, a 24-gun frigate patrolling Scottish waters.

In October 1757, at Portsmouth under Captain John Simcoe, Cook became master of the 64-gun *Pembroke*, which in February 1758 sailed as part of Admiral Boscawen's fleet for Halifax, Nova Scotia. This appointment was to make his name

in a major theatre of war, for the fleet and the troops it conveyed were being sent to help loosen the French hold on Canada, first by destruction of the fortress of Louisbourg on Cape Breton Island, guarding the Gulf of St Lawrence, and then by ascending the lower St Lawrence River and taking Quebec. The day after Louisbourg fell in July, Cook had a fortuitous meeting ashore with a military surveyor called Samuel Holland, whom he had watched busily taking angles with a surveyor's plane table. Holland was delighted to instruct him in its use. Cook's interest was actively supported and shared by his scientifically minded captain, Simcoe, and Cook himself conducted a small survey of the Bay of Gaspé in 1758. This became his first chart to be published, in London later that year, although Cook spent the long winter with the small squadron left at Halifax. There, under the joint guidance of Simcoe and Holland, he developed his skills as a cartographer and studied the higher reaches of navigational astronomy.

Simcoe unfortunately died in the spring of 1759, which saw the return of the main fleet from England under Admiral Sir Charles Saunders, bringing back

Major-General Wolfe for his second season's campaign. Then followed the difficult advance up the St Lawrence River to Quebec, in which Cook and the rest of the masters in the fleet were heavily involved, both as ship handlers and in surveying and recording the passage. Quebec fell to Wolfe's assault on 13 September, with himself and his opponent, Montcalm, heading the list of dead. Cook was shortly afterwards transferred to the *Northumberland* under Captain Lord Colville and again spent the winter at Halifax, although the great 'New Chart of the River St Lawrence' that Saunders published in England in 1760 included a large element of his work. A French counter-siege of Quebec was lifted that May, and when Montreal fell in September to British army assault from upper New York, Canada was secured. In January 1761, still at Halifax, Colville awarded Cook a bonus of £50 – over eight months' salary – for 'his indefatigable industry in making himself Master of the Pilotage of the River Saint Lawrence', and two years later in England he was even more warmly to recommend his 'Genius and Capacity' as a surveyor to the Admiralty. In the interim Cook gave further proof of this. He made detailed observations of the coast of Nova Scotia and took significant part as a surveyor and pilot in operations that repelled a French assault on St John's, Newfoundland, in the summer of 1762. He then returned to England with Colville.

The charting of Newfoundland, especially its southern and western coasts, was to occupy Cook from 1763 to 1767 – the first years of peace – and on a regular pattern: he would systematically survey ashore and afloat in the late spring and summer, and then return to London to work up and submit the results over the winter. He was to begin publishing them as charts in 1766. That year he also observed an eclipse of the Sun in Newfoundland – the subject of his first brief scientific communication to the Royal Society.

Set across the mouth of the St Lawrence, Newfoundland was sparsely populated but strategically placed and was the seasonal base for working the Grand Banks fishery – itself economically important to Britain. Many nations fished the Banks, but on and around Newfoundland the Royal Navy maintained jurisdiction through a naval governor sent out each spring. Charts of the island, and adjacent lesser ones, were poor and Cook was keenly sought to remedy this by the new governor, Captain Samuel Graves, who had recognised his expertise in the anti-French operations there of 1762. Palliser had also been involved and added his recommendations to those of Graves (whom he succeeded as governor, holding the position from 1764 to 1766). The Admiralty agreed and on 15 May 1763 Cook sailed from Plymouth, in Graves's *Antelope*, to begin his work, for which the schooner *Grenville* was locally bought. He had been back in London just over six months, but only six weeks had passed before he was married on 21 December 1762 to 21-year-old Elizabeth Batts of Barking, Essex. How and when they met is a mystery and, like many seamen's wives, she was to see little of her husband. Their six children were born and largely raised (and three died) in his absence; all were dead long before she herself died, aged 93, in 1835 after a widowhood of 56 years.

ENDEAVOUR: THE VOYAGE OF 1768–71

On 29 March 1768, the Navy Board reported that it had bought, in the Thames, the Whitby-built collier *Earl of Pembroke*; 14 months old, of 368 tons burthen, and 106 feet long overall. The ship was seaworthy and strong, roomy for its small size, and capable of being beached upright on a flat bottom. The Admiralty directed that the name be changed to '*Endeavour*, bark' (there was already an *Endeavour* in the navy list) and that the vessel be armed and fitted at Deptford Dockyard to sail for the South Seas. Cook was appointed to command only in April, and as the proposed complement rose to 70 (deaths being expected) the Admiralty decided to commission him as a lieutenant, and gave him a second lieutenant in Zachary Hicks. It later added a third, John Gore, who was formerly a master's mate under both Byron and Wallis in the *Dolphin*. Others of note who had also sailed with Byron were seaman (later Lieutenant) Charles Clerke, and Richard Pickersgill, master's mate. The official naval and Marine complement was eventually 85, but additions made the total company 98 when they finally left England, although over 170 men – including five Tahitians – passed through *Endeavour*'s books during the expedition, most replacing fatalities to illness in 1770–71. One of these losses was the Royal Society's civilian astronomer Samuel Green, who, with Cook, observed the transit of Venus and who had arrived with his servant in July 1768. So did a further party of nine, or possibly ten, for the already crowded ship. Joseph Banks, FRS, aged 25 and 'a Gentleman of large fortune … well versed in natural history', had persuaded both the Society and the Admiralty that the botanical and natural sciences would be well served by his inclusion – at his own expense – and came aboard with a 'suite' of eight: the Swedish botanist Daniel Carl Solander, a pupil of Linnaeus; the artists Alexander Buchan and Sydney Parkinson, to perform the recording roles that would today be achieved by photography; also Banks's Swedish secretary, Dr Herman Diedrich Spöring, and four servants (two black), as well as two greyhounds. A boy called Nicholas Young, while first noted as being on board at Tahiti, seems to have been one of those who arrived with Banks and was later the first to sight New Zealand, where he is commemorated by 'Young Nick's Head'. A famous addition – among the usual livestock that all ships carried – was a milking goat, just home from its first round-the-world voyage in the hard-worked *Dolphin*, with Captain Wallis. Wallis returned to England in May 1768 as the first European discoverer of an earthly paradise that he called 'King George's Island', right in the centre of Maskelyne's prescribed area for the transit observation.

He also had an accurate latitude and longitude for it (17° 30 S, 150° W), the latter calculated by his mathematically inclined purser using 'Dr Masculine's method, which we did not understand' – that is, by lunar-distance observation. This island now became Cook's intended goal. Its local name was Tahiti.

Although only the Admiralty took note of it from the official voyage journals (all handed in as restricted documents, as were Cook's), some of Wallis's men also reported seeing extensive high land well south of the new island. Investigating this latest rumour of Terra Australis headed the supplementary 'Secret Instructions' Cook was to fulfil after completing the transit work. He was also to claim possession, in European legal terms, of useful places he discovered, although friendship with all Pacific peoples was to be cultivated. They were to be treated with respect, civility and caution, their ways observed and, where possible, fair trade conducted for fresh food and other items. Lord Morton, President of the Royal Society, also supplied an enlightened and perceptive memorandum on observations to be made and cultural

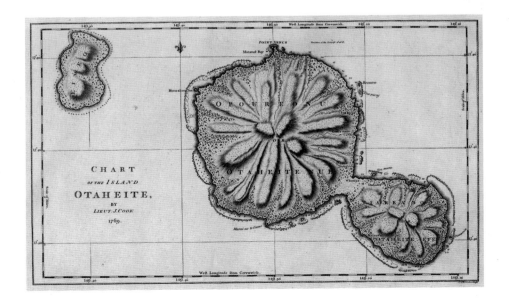

CHART OF THE ISLAND OTAHEITE, BY LIEUT. J. COOK 1769.

and moral issues likely to arise in encounters with 'primitive' populations. All this Cook absorbed, not as a romantic self-motivated adventurer, but as a professional seaman determined to achieve objectives laid down by others. Humanity in his general dealings and a conscientious pursuit of the aims set for him were to be the hallmarks of all his Pacific voyages, albeit with some lapses under stress. His genius lay in the exceptional judgement with which he interpreted his instructions, and in the professional skill with which he met and surpassed their expectations.

The crowded *Endeavour* left Plymouth on 26 August 1768 and reached Rio de Janeiro on 13 November. At Madeira, Cook obtained onions and distributed them among the crew, and flogged two men for refusing to eat fresh meat – the start of an insistence on fresh food and greens of any palatable sort to prevent scurvy (Vitamin C deficiency); he was equally strict in his demand for cleanliness of both ship and crew. *Endeavour*'s voyage was unprecedented in having few cases of scurvy and no deaths from shipboard-generated illness, and as such it became the model for both Cook voyages that followed. Leaving Rio on 7 December after problems with the authorities, they landed briefly on Tierra del Fuego, where an unwise foray resulted in Banks's two black servants, Thomas Richmond and George Dorlton, being frozen to death in a snowstorm (through falling asleep in it while drunk), and Solander only narrowly escaped. Cook then passed through the Strait of Le Maire and rounded Cape Horn on 27 January 1769. He reached his furthest point south in *Endeavour* three days later, in latitude 60° 4'S, before altering course north and then west for Tahiti. This was sighted on 11 April after *Endeavour* passed through, and Cook recorded, much of the Tuamotu Archipelago.

On 13 April they found the *Dolphin*'s anchorage in idyllic Matavai Bay, on the north-west coast near modern Papeete. Welcoming Tahitian canoes came out as soon as the ship was sighted and, despite the language barrier, trade and cordial relations rapidly began. The endemic South Seas problem, based on different values and common to nearly all the islands Cook visited, was the inhabitants' persistent thievery and expertise at it. Iron of any portable sort vanished, especially nails (the common currency of trade); also stolen were clothes, a gun, a valuable quadrant and many other items. Those of any significance were mostly recovered as the expectations and firepower of the visitors became clear, though one Tahitian was shot dead in a rare lapse of control, which Cook greatly regretted. He also began to develop his practice of 'detaining' local property, and sometimes people, against restitution of purloined items and flogged his own men when they could be identified for theft, or for abetting it. The usual reason the latter stole was to trade for the sexual liberality of the Tahitian women. Cook was well aware of the dangers of this and of his duty to his hosts: the Tahitians (though not all Pacific islanders) suffered from yaws, which gave immunity to syphilis, but not to gonorrhoea. Anyone suspected of infection was confined to the ship until pronounced clear although, as soon became apparent, it had already reached the island through Hitaa on the east coast. Cook suspected a Spanish source but it was in fact the French, from when Bougainville's *Boudeuse* and *Etoile* had stopped off there, shortly after Wallis, whose own crew was another possible source of the disease.

Banks and Solander were in heaven, collecting and recording plants – although their ethnographic and landscape artist Alexander Buchan had died of an epileptic fit just after arrival – and in the fort and observatory that Cook built on 'Point Venus', Green set up equipment to observe the transit. This was successfully done on 3 June in a daytime temperature of 119°F (48.3°C), with two parties under Hicks and Gore also recording it from other positions as back-up.

Endeavour sailed from Tahiti on 13 July to explore islands to the north-west, which Cook named the 'Society Islands' from their close grouping. He surveyed Huahine and made a particular friend in Ori, the chief there. Pressed by Banks, he had agreed to take on board a young Tahitian chief and priest Tupaia, who wished to see England, and his servant boy, Taiata. Neither survived the voyage but Tupaia quickly proved an asset as an interpreter and pilot, naming well over 100 central Pacific islands, of which Cook managed to sketch a chart of 74. Among drawings from the voyage originally held by Banks (and now in the British Library) are a few naively stylised but striking watercolours, whose painter was a mystery for over 200 years. Eventually, in the 1980s, he was called the 'Artist of the Chief Mourner', from one that showed a Tahitian in the ritual dress of that role. Finally, in 1997, a note by Banks was found clearly identifying them as by Tupaia, probably using Parkinson's colours and with a little guidance from him or Spöring.

On 9 August, complying with his 'secret instructions', Cook sailed south. He had already scotched earlier reports of continental land further east in his southern sweep from Cape Horn. By 2 September he had crossed well beyond latitude 40° south but there was no sign of the land reported by *Dolphin*, nor did the long ocean swell from that direction suggest the presence of any. As also instructed, he then cast westward to seek the eastern side of New Zealand, whose western coast was first discovered by the Dutch navigator Abel Tasman in 1642.

On 6 October they sighted land, but on reaching it two days later, they found the Maori inhabitants unfriendly and unwilling to trade, although Tupaia was understood by them. Three approaches were violently repulsed and, to Cook's grief, several Maori were killed as he and his men defended themselves. Empty-handed, the *Endeavour* left Poverty Bay, as Cook named it, heading south and finding only further hostility ashore. Having reached beyond latitude 40° south once more, with the coast still running south and west, Cook named the point they had reached 'Cape Turnagain' and reversed his course there. The ship then made a sweep northward to replenish water among more friendly people below East Cape, before heading north-west across the Bay of Plenty. They stayed for 11 days at

Mercury Bay, so named because Cook and Green observed the transit of Mercury there, which gave them an accurate longitude. Despite one more fatal incident they established friendly relations with the people, visited an impressive Maori fortified village, or *pa*, and found strong evidence suggesting that the Maori were cannibals, though this was later questioned in England. Over 80 years later a local chief, Te Horeta, who had visited *Endeavour* as a child and met Cook, could recount a vivid memory of the occasion. The ship headed north after a further edgy landing in the Bay of Islands, but Cook's running survey of the heavily fragmented coast was interrupted by a sustained gale on 13 December. This blew him out of sight of land, but on 15 December its resighting, and an increase in the south-western swell, showed that they had passed Cape Maria van Diemen, the northern point of New Zealand.

Cook managed to plot this from a distance and with great accuracy before continuing his running survey down the dangerous west coast. On 14 January 1770 a huge bay opened to the eastward, on the south side of which Cook found what was to become a favourite harbour, Ship Cove, in the narrow Queen Charlotte Sound. Surrounded by plentiful wood, water, greenstuff, exotic birds and a friendly, if possibly cannibalistic people, the *Endeavour* was here thoroughly overhauled. By climbing a hill Cook also confirmed what Tasman had suspected: the bay he had entered was in fact the wide strait that now bears his own name, dividing the two islands of New Zealand. On 6 February he sailed into it, narrowly avoiding being carried ashore by its treacherous tidal current. He then completed his survey of North Island by stretching north to resight Cape Turnagain before reversing course once more and heading down the east coast of South Island in tempestuous weather. By 13 March he had rounded the southern end and was again sailing up the western side, completing (in Banks's words) 'the total demolition of our aëriel fabrick' that it might be part of a southern continent. His survey was to result in the first chart of New Zealand, compiled on a single pass to an extraordinary level of thoroughness and accuracy.

By the end of March 1770, *Endeavour* had again resupplied at Admiralty Bay in the Cook Strait as her captain used the discretion granted by his orders to consider

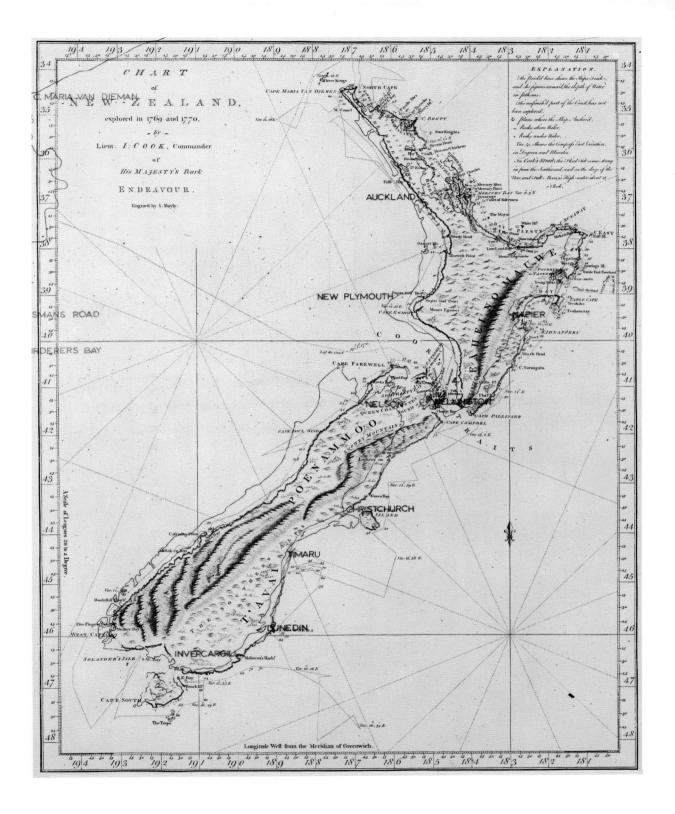

BELOW A 4-pounder gun from the *Endeavour*.
After striking the Great Barrier Reef the crew had to lighten the ship, throwing overboard the six carriage guns, and eventually managing to refloat it. Two hundred years later they were retrieved by divers, and this one was presented to the National Maritime Museum by the Australian government in 1969.

OPPOSITE A view of the Endeavour River on the coast of New Holland (detail), where the ship was laid on shore, in order to repair the damage which she received on the rock; engraving by William Byrne, probably after a lost drawing by Parkinson.
Endeavour was beached for seven weeks in June 1770 for repairs.

his route home. Although he was tempted, the state of the ship argued against further hunting for a 'southern continent' on a high-latitude Pacific passage to Cape Horn. The same applied to a route directly to the Cape of Good Hope by passing south of Van Diemen's Land (Tasmania). Cook listened to the views of his officers and Banks and decided to sail via the East Indies – where *Endeavour* could refit properly – but with the variation of heading west and falling in with the totally unknown east coast of New Holland. He hoped to confirm whether Van Diemen's Land was joined to it and then to follow it north – with luck, directly to the Indies.

They sailed at daylight on 31 March, and on 19 April, driven too far north to see Van Diemen's Land, they sighted the main south-east Australian coast. Cook decided to turn north along it, but the weather prevented a landing for another ten days. On 29 April, *Endeavour* finally entered a sheltered bay inhabited by a few shy, unfriendly people, apparently primitive even by comparison with the Pacific islanders, and with whom Tupaia could not communicate: they were the first Aboriginal people encountered. 'Isaac, you shall land first,' said Cook to his wife's young cousin, Isaac Smith, as their boat rowed ashore in what was first called Stingray Harbour. Later, after Banks and Solander had begun studying the harvest of new plants brought aboard, it became Botany Bay. Cook left on 6 May, naming but not entering the great inlet of Port Jackson, just to the north, where modern Sydney now stands. On 23 May he entered another good haven north of modern Brisbane, which he called Bustard Bay after the birds shot there, and then began his closest and worst brushes with disaster.

Cook's method of taking a running survey of land bearings required an inshore course, but doing this up the Australian coast funnelled him, almost unaware, into the open southern jaws of the Great Barrier

PACIFIC EXPLORATION

Reef. *Endeavour* avoided the clearly growing dangers until about 11 o'clock on the night of 10 June, when she suddenly struck a coral outcrop nearly 20 miles off the land. In an attempt to release her, about 50 tons of weight – ballast, stores and the carriage guns – were thrown overboard, but it was high tide and the ship was stuck fast, holed and flooding badly. With great difficulty she was hauled off a day later, a broken spur of coral fortunately jamming in the hole it had made, since the pumps could not otherwise have saved her. A sail was quickly fothered over the bottom and Cook laid the ship ashore a little to the north, in what has since been called the Endeavour River. Here, far-from-perfect repairs were made; sick and exhausted men recuperated on fresh turtle, shellfish and wild vegetables; and more plant collecting was carried out. It was also here that Cook's party were the first Europeans to see kangaroos, which Bank's surviving dog fruitlessly chased, although some were shot and eaten. The local people, however, proved as hard to engage as they had been at Botany Bay and caused panic by starting a bush fire, which destroyed the remains of the shore camp. On 6 August Cook sailed again, picking his way through the reef for a week until he found a passage to open sea. He had sailed over a thousand miles since mid-May, sounding the depth continuously.

Two days later, with an onshore wind falling to calm, their boats had to tow the *Endeavour* against an inexorable swell that was carrying her back into the breakers. At one point they were within 80 yards of destruction but were saved by a catspaw of breeze, before more towing and a turn of wind and tide took them safely back through a gap – the 'Providential Channel' – in the unending reef. From then on, with a boat sounding ahead, they pursued an intricately slow course northward within the reef and on 21 August reached the tip of the vast hinterland: this Cook named Cape York. That evening, from a hill on offshore 'Possession Island', he saw that only sea lay to the westward and that the 2,000-mile coast up which he had passed and now claimed as 'New South Wales' was not joined to New Guinea. He had confirmed the existence of the strait through which Torres had unwittingly sailed from the east in 1607 and that Tasman had sighted from the west in 1644.

On 29 August *Endeavour* raised the New Guinea coast and on 11 October anchored at Batavia (Jakarta), capital of the Dutch East Indies, on Java. From there Cook sent home the first news of *Endeavour* since she had left Rio nearly two years before, while the battered ship was taken into the Dutch dockyard and repaired. Her uncoppered hull was in a desperate condition with major damage to the keel, shipworm, and planking cut to barely an eighth of an inch thick in places. The Dutch did a good job, but the weeks at Batavia – a sink of malarial fever and dysentery – proved far more lethal to the crew than their past voyage had done. Banks and Solander went down but recovered; eight others died, including the Tahitians Tupaia and Tataia. After Cook sailed on 26 December, 23 more also died from illness contracted there on the way to the Cape of Good Hope. They included Herman Spöring, Banks's secretary; Sydney Parkinson, the hard-working botanical artist; and Charles Green, the astronomer. Heading north from Cape Town, Lieutenant Hicks was the final casualty, dying from long-standing tuber-culosis, which allowed Clerke to be promoted to his position. The goat finished its second circumnavigation but Banks's last greyhound died before *Endeavour* anchored in the Downs, off Deal, on 13 July 1771.

There Cook stepped ashore with his journals and 'charts, plans and drawings' for the Admiralty Board, with a covering letter to its secretary. This modestly expressed hopes that these items would 'be 'found sufficient to convey a Tolerable knowledge of the places they are intended to illustrate, & that the discoveries we have made, tho' not great, will Apologize for the length of the Voyage'. Given his unprecedented if not complete success – the question of the southern continent remained in the air – the apology must have appeared curiously unnecessary.

THE *ENDEAVOUR* ARTISTS

Cook's *Endeavour* expedition was the first scientific voyage to carry artists, though only unofficial ones, to draw what they found. They were in the private party of the wealthy Joseph Banks, who was allowed to sail with Cook to pursue his primarily botanical interests.

Alexander Buchan, a Scot of whom nothing else is known, was employed to record landscapes and other subjects, and made a few studies on the outward voyage, mainly in Tierra de Fuego, but died of epilepsy on 15 April 1769, two days after they reached Tahiti. Banks's Swedish–Finnish secretary, Dr Joseph Spöring (*c*.1733–1771), also later did technical drawings of Pacific canoes and some landscapes and coastal profiles; this left the botanical draughtsman, Sydney Parkinson (*c*.1745–1771), as the principal voyage artist.

Parkinson, a Quaker brewer's son from Edinburgh, was largely self-taught but was influenced by contemporary landscape watercolourists, especially Paul Sandby, of whom he became a neighbour after moving to London in the early 1760s. He exhibited flower paintings in London and Banks first employed him in 1767 before taking him on the *Endeavour* voyage at £80 a year. During the voyage

he produced just over 1,200 drawings of plants and animals for Banks, 280 being finished botanical studies for the latter's proposed *Florilegium*. This was not published at the time and appeared only in the 1980s, using the original engraved plates and drawings by Parkinson and others (all now in the Natural History Museum). With Buchan gone, Parkinson also extended his range into studies of Pacific peoples and landscape views. These

---

right The artist Sydney Parkinson (detail); self-portrait from his posthumously published *A Journal of a Voyage to the South Seas in His Majesty's Ship the Endeavour* (1773), edited by his brother.

opposite IPOMOEA INDICA; from the Banks *Florilegium*, after Parkinson. The plant is a form of morning glory; its pounded root was used in Hawaii and Tonga to treat bowel ailments.

show his artistic limitations, all being rather stiff in drawing terms, though with lively and distinctive character in the figures and notable atmosphere in some of the views. Many were not for Banks, however, but for his own interest and use, which led to later problems. A likeable, intelligent and observant young man, and a natural peacemaker, Parkinson further showed his good relations with Pacific peoples in his compilation – the first ever made – of words and phrases in the Tahitian, Maori and Australian Aboriginal vocabularies, and he also kept an illustrated fair-copy journal of the voyage. Unfortunately, he did not survive it, being among the 31 members of the crew who died from fevers contracted at Batavia while the *Endeavour* was refitting there on the way home. When he died at sea on 26 January 1771, two days after Spöring, his much-admired pictorial journal disappeared (and has never been found), but enough of his notes survived for his account of the voyage to be published by his elder brother, Stanfield Parkinson, after some difficulty in retrieving many of Sydney's figure and landscape studies from Banks. Reproduced in John Hawkesworth's official account of the expedition, with others appearing in Parkinson's, and then copied by others, they were the earliest views of the South Pacific and its inhabitants widely seen by a general public.

---

below A View in the Island of Huaheine; with the Ewharra no Etua, or House of God ... and a Tree Called Owharra with Which Houses Are Thatched (detail); engraved for the *Endeavour* voyage account (1773) after Parkinson, from an image made from two of his drawings.

opposite Head of a New Zealander, with a Comb in His Hair; engraved in 1773 after a drawing Parkinson probably made at Queen Charlotte Sound in January 1770. He wrote, 'Their faces were tataowed, or marked either all over, or on one side, in a very curious manner, some of them in fine spiral directions…'

PACIFIC EXPLORATION

A View of Maitavie Bay [in the
Island of] Otaheite [Tahiti] (detail);
oil painting by William Hodges, 1776.
    Resolution and *Adventure* are shown during
Cook's second voyage, airing sails off Point
Venus (left), where Cook first observed the
transit of Venus in 1769. He returned there
on subsequent voyages. This large canvas is
one of four Hodges did later for the Admiralty,
with two of New Zealand (see p. 62) and
one of New Caledonia (Vanuatu).

2
SHIPS IN COMPANY

The Second and Third Voyages

'*The ablest and most renowned Navigator this or any country hath produced.*'

COOK'S EPITAPH BY ADMIRAL JOHN FORBES

RESOLUTION AND *ADVENTURE*, 1772–75

BANKS was a well-known figure in society before he left England, but his triumphant return, with an epic story to tell in the highest circles and a scientific haul of lasting value, made him even more fêted than Cook. The more sober Admiralty was, however, well pleased with its man: its new First Lord, the highly intelligent John Montagu, fourth Earl of Sandwich, was henceforth Cook's most influential naval friend and quickly saw him promoted to commander. Unusually, he also received his new commission personally from the King, to whom Sandwich took him with his charts and plans, and with whom he had an hour's conversation.

With Alexander Dalrymple's influential *History* now in print, belief in the 'southern continent' was still strong and Cook's return to the region tended to raise rather than weaken confidence that it might be discoverable. Cook himself was sure that, if there, it had to be further south than so far envisaged and had already sketched a plan to resolve the question by embarking on a new voyage. This would not head west via the Horn but would sail east round the Cape of Good Hope, to quarter the southern Indian Ocean in the summer season, sped on their way by the high-latitude prevailing westerlies. After recouping in New Zealand, he would repeat the process in the southern Pacific at the start of the next summer. If nothing was found, a loop back north and west on the south-easterly prevailing winds might enlarge knowledge of islands, known and still unknown, in its central and western basin.

A View of the Cape of Good Hope
Taken on the Spot, from on Board
the *Resolution*, Captain Cooke (detail);
oil painting by William Hodges.

This picture was painted in November 1772,
probably ashore in Cape Town, shipped directly
home and exhibited at the Free Society of Artists
in 1774. A related drawing by Hodges, possibly
used for it, also survives (now in Australia).

As the French and Spanish were
now hard on British heels to establish or
reinforce Pacific claims, this was essen-
tially the plan the Admiralty adopted.
This time Cook recommended a two-
vessel expedition. *Endeavour* had firmly
convinced him that only 'North Country
built ships, such as are built for the coal
trade' were suitable, and he chose the
Marquis of Rockingham and the *Marquis of
Granby*, both owned by Captain William
Hammond of Hull. After purchase by
the Navy Board, of which Cook's friend
Palliser was Comptroller from 1770,
they were respectively renamed the
Resolution and the *Adventure*. Both were
relatively new, and the former of 462
tons burthen; the latter, commanded by Lieutenant Tobias Furneaux (who had
sailed with Wallis), of 340 tons.

Banks enthusiastically prepared to accompany Cook with an even larger party
than before, including his botanist-librarian Daniel Solander; the astronomer-
physician Dr James Lind; two reputable artists, Johann Zoffany and John Cleveley
junior; and the draughtsmen brothers John and James Miller. However, the
necessary extra accommodation added to the *Resolution* made her so unseaworthy
that the Navy Board had it removed. Banks threatened to withdraw if his needs
were not met, and when the Admiralty called his bluff, he felt obliged to do so,
although his relations with Cook were only temporarily strained; he instead led
most of his suite on a private foray to Iceland. It was a regrettable loss to Cook's
company as much as to science, for Solander was replaced by the learned but
difficult German naturalist Johann Reinhold Forster, accompanied by his gifted
artist son, Georg. The latter generally proved an asset, but Forster senior strained

everyone's patience. Some of the crew of the *Endeavour* were back again among the *Resolution*'s crew of 112 (the *Adventure* had 81): Clerke (second lieutenant), Pickersgill (now third lieutenant) and Midshipman Isaac Smith were among them. George Vancouver, another midshipman, was later to win fame as an explorer himself, while the work of William Hodges, the sociable landscape painter who replaced Zoffany, was to define both this voyage and the dominant visual image we still have of the eighteenth-century Pacific.

The astronomers this time were William Wales (one of Banks's team) and William Bayly, the latter going with the *Adventure*. Both were appointed by the Board of Longitude, on which Maskelyne was the key figure as Astronomer Royal. Their prime task was to use lunar-distance observation, of which Maskelyne was a champion, to test the reliability of four new-fangled marine timepieces as a simpler alternative for calculating longitude at sea. One of these was Larcum Kendall's faithful 'K1' copy of John Harrison's great 'H4' prototype – 'our trusty friend the

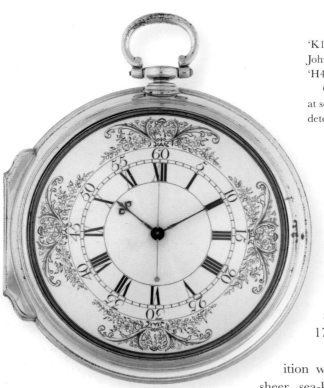

'K1', Larcum Kendall's first copy (1769) of John Harrison's prototype marine timekeeper, 'H4' of 1759.

Chronometers revolutionised navigation at sea by providing the easiest method of determining longitude.

Watch', as the admiring Cook was later to call it – which was making its maiden voyage. The others were different and unsuccessful models by John Arnold. Their modern name of 'chronometer' stuck only after it was proposed in 1794 by Alexander Dalrymple.

The *Resolution* and *Adventure* expedition was Cook's greatest in terms of its sheer sea-keeping endurance, as a feat of navigation, and in its accumulation of geographical and related knowledge of Pacific islands until then unknown to Europeans, or at least uncharted by them. However, although longer and no less dangerous than the *Endeavour* voyage, this expedition lacked its two big landmarks – the surveys of New Zealand and eastern Australia – and it is only the overall pattern rather than the detail that can be summarised here.

The ships sailed from Plymouth on 13 July 1772, exactly a year after the *Endeavour*'s return. As she had done, they replenished at Madeira and reached Cape Town on 30 October. Here Hodges painted the *Adventure* lying dwarfed below Table Mountain, on a big, breezy canvas which Cook left there for shipping home in an Indiaman. They sailed again on 22 November, heading south-east in search of 'Cape Circumcision' – a landfall reported in 1739 by the French voyager Bouvet de Lozier at latitude 54° south, longitude 10° 20' east. Instead they found a gale, cold and then ice, first in small quantities, and then vast fields of pack ice, and a new phenomenon – towering 'ice islands' (icebergs) up to 200 feet high. Early in January 1773 they made the important discovery that ice taken from round a berg melted down into fine drinking water. Rigging and sails froze, however; livestock brought from the Cape died and signs of scurvy began to appear. On 17 January they became the first men in history to cross the Antarctic Circle (66° 33' south). The following day, at latitude 67° 15' south, longitude 40° east, they turned back

VIEW IN PICKERSGILL HARBOUR, DUSKY BAY, NEW ZEALAND, APRIL 1773, by William Hodges, 1773–76.

Cook wrote that he moored the *Resolution* 'so near the shore as to reach it with a Brow or stage that nature had in a manner prepared for us by a large tree, which growed in a horizontal direction over the water [and] reached our gunwale'. Wales's observatory tent can be seen through the trees. Hodges painted this over an earlier view of Antarctic icebergs seen shortly before, though exactly when is not certain.

on a long dog-leg north and then on a sweep south-east again across the southern
Indian Ocean, to New Zealand.

On 8 February the ships were separated in a gale and Cook arrived in beautiful
Dusky Bay at the tip of South Island on his own, staying for seven weeks before
moving to Queen Charlotte Sound on the Cook Strait, where he found Furneaux.
The latter had touched on Van Diemen's Land and, although he had not resolved
the question of whether it was joined to Australia, he discovered a small group of
islands (now named after him) to the north-east. The southern winter was now
beginning but Cook did not intend to sit this out. He halted Furneaux's preparations to do so and they both sailed again early in June 1773, in a great loop west and
north to revisit Tahiti and the Society Islands, where they were warmly welcomed
in August. Supplies at Tahiti proved short but were made up at Huahine, where the
only major incident was the stripping to his trousers of Dr Anders Sparrman – the
assistant the Forsters had recruited at the Cape – when he made a lone botanising
foray, probably on to sacred ground. When they left on 17 September, Cook took
with them a young man known as Odiddy (O-Hedidee) from Raiatea, dropping
him back there in 1774. At Huahine, another islander called Mai begged Furneaux
to let him join the *Adventure* so persistently that he took him on board: thus 'Omai',
the first South Sea islander seen in England, steps into history and artistic celebrity
– at least in portraits by Sir Joshua Reynolds and others.

From the Society Islands, effectively Cook's central Pacific base, the expedition
sailed west to locate islands that Tasman had called Amsterdam and Middelburg
(Tongatapu and Eua) some 130 years earlier. These were sighted on 1 October.
The people were perceived as being as light-fingered as the Tahitians and equally
welcoming – though initially unwilling to trade – and Cook called the group the
'Friendly Islands' (otherwise known as Tonga). Red feathers obtained there were
soon found to have so high a value elsewhere that Cook had to exert on-board
'exchange control' to prevent inhabitants of other islands from refusing to supply
provisions in return for anything else. After a week both ships headed south for
New Zealand again, where they were finally separated in a storm off the east coast
at the end of October 1773 and did not see each other again during the voyage.

A View Taken in the Bay of Oaite Peha [Vaitepiha] Otaheite [Tahiti] (traditionally known as 'Tahiti Revisited'); oil painting by William Hodges, 1776.

Hodges painted this picture for the Admiralty after showing a previous version at the Royal Academy in 1776. Together with the romantic setting and the eroticism of the tattooed Tahitian bathers, the menacing presence of the *tii* (an ancestor carving) and the *tupapu* (a burial platform) behind in the distance to the right evokes a traditional European artistic idea of *et in Arcadia ego* (I [Death] also exist in Paradise).

Cook reached the Ship Cove rendezvous in Queen Charlotte Sound on 3 November 1773 and prepared for a rapid departure for his second Antarctic sweep, taking advantage of the southern summer. While there, he found explicit proof of Maori cannibalism, in a shipboard experiment that Clerke rather light-heartedly initiated with gruesome and thought-provoking results. Nonetheless, Cook's general opinion of the Maori remained high, not least because he found them honest among themselves and not rivals to other islanders in terms of thievery. On 25 November he sailed, unable to wait any longer for Furneaux, but leaving him a buried and marked message of his intended movements.

Furneaux's outlook and shipboard regime were more conventional than Cook's and his record of sickness and adverse incident less impressive. Delayed on the coast of North Island by the weather, he made Queen Charlotte Sound early in December, six days after the *Resolution* left. From Cook's message he realised there would be little chance of finding him and, after a brief respite, he was about to sail for home when he lost a boat and crew sent on a foraging trip: a search soon discovered that the men had been killed and eaten by accompanying Maori. The facts came out only later, but there had been a sudden quarrel over food, during which a seaman had first shot two Maori. Furneaux buried the remains and quickly sailed for Cape Horn, searching for land in intense cold as far south as latitude 61° and continuing directly east across the south Atlantic to make another grasp for Bouvet de Lozier's 'Cape Circumcision'. This remained elusive and he concluded that the Frenchman had mistaken ice for land. He then made for Cape Town in March 1774. It was a creditable performance and the *Adventure* reached England on 14 July, having lost 13 men in all, though only one from among her many cases of scurvy.

Meanwhile, the *Resolution* had again headed south through gale conditions for the Antarctic. On 7 December 1773 her crew drank toasts to home at the exact antipodes of England, north of the great Antarctic bight which James Clark Ross would discover in 1841, and now known as the Ross Sea. However, as their latitude rose from 62° to 66° south they were increasingly ensnared by loose summer sea ice, massive bergs, fog, snow, intense cold and high wind. From latitude 67° 31' south, again beyond the Antarctic Circle, Cook prudently hauled north again for over 1,200 nautical miles until 11 January 1774, before making a final plunge south in deep-freeze conditions to the furthest point yet reached by man. Here, on 30 January, at latitude 71° 10', longitude 106° 54' west, he was stopped by solid ice stretching as far as the lookouts could see; had it been further east he would have been ashore in the mountains of Palmer Land, at the base of the 800-mile Antarctic Peninsula. Despite the presence of petrels and penguins, Cook was now convinced that if land lay beyond, it was completely ice-bound, adding: 'I who had ambition not only to go farther than any one had been before, but as far as it was possible for man to go, was not sorry in meeting with this interruption.' '*Ne plus*

A View of the Monuments of
Easter Island (detail), painted (on panel)
by William Hodges, c.1776.

Cook's *Resolution* touched briefly at Easter
Island (Rapa Nui) in March 1774. Although
fascinated by the astonishing statues, Cook
reflected that no nation would ever contend
for the honour of discovering the island.

ultra! ('No further [has any man ever been]!') yelled young Vancouver – literally the furthest man south, out on the *Resolution*'s bowsprit – just as they turned north, leaving Antarctica itself for a future age to discover.

Having proved that no inhabitable southern continent existed, Cook would only have been using the discretion granted in his orders if he had headed home. Instead, with adequate stores, a healthy crew, a sound ship and vast areas of the central Pacific so little known to Europeans, he later wrote: 'I was of the opinion that my remaining in this sea some time longer would be productive of some improvements to navigation and geography as well other sciences.' Backed by his officers and the goodwill of his men, he launched north on a huge parabola, which by November 1774 would take him north to just below the Equator, west towards New Guinea, and then back south again to his favourite New Zealand base in Queen Charlotte Sound. The passage began with a violent storm, followed in February by serious illness for Cook himself, apparently a gall bladder and bowel problem, which caused great alarm. Fortunately he was nursed back to recovery by the surgeon, James Patten, aided by the only fresh meat still on board, the last of the edible Tahitian dogs. In March, the *Resolution* briefly visited the remote and deforested

SHIP COVE, QUEEN CHARLOTTE SOUND, NEW ZEALAND (detail); drawing by John Webber, 1777.

Queen Charlotte Sound, found on the *Endeavour* voyage, became a regular base, despite the killing and cannibalising there of a boat's crew from *Adventure* in 1773. Maori on the move lived in temporary hut encampments and set one up at Ship Cove while Cook was there. He is shown greeting the group's chief, and he later wrote in his journal: 'Mr Webber has made a drawing of one of these Villages that will convey a better idea of them than any written description.'

Easter Island – first described in any detail in 1722 – of whose massive and mysterious stone figures Hodges later painted a remarkable picture. Circling north-east,
Cook then rediscovered and fixed the position of the Marquesas Islands, found and
named by Álvaro de Mendaña in 1595 but unseen since. This brought him back
once more, via other minor landfalls, to Matavai Bay, Tahiti. The welcome was as
enthusiastic as ever and the island seemed in a much more prosperous state than
the previous year. Theft was just as bad and eventually, after the usual detentions
of persons or property failed to be an effective remedy, Cook ceremonially flogged
a Tahitian (as he did thieving seamen) to show he was both in earnest but also
even-handed. He also witnessed a spectacular review of several hundred Tahitian
war canoes, which were working up to attack nearby Eimeo (Moorea) in a local
dispute. This too provided the subject of one of Hodges's most famous paintings –
his largest Pacific canvas – *The War-Boats of the Island of Otaheite*, shown at the Royal
Academy in 1777 (see pp.2–3).

From Tahiti they went on to the usual elaborate and generous welcome on
Huahine and Raitaea (where Odiddy left them) and then west to relocate the
islands of 'Austrialia de Espiritu Santo', first found by Pedro de Quirós in 1606,
although more recently relocated by Bougainville and called the 'Great Cyclades'.
Cook was to rename them the New Hebrides (now Vanuatu) and to chart them with
great accuracy after he fell in with them in mid-July at Malekula, following other
small discoveries and a stop for supplies at Nomuka, Tonga. The New Hebrideans,
however, were Melanesians, a different race with a different language from his usual
Polynesian friends: he thought them uglier, certainly cannibals and hostile – not
surprisingly, since they believed the visitors to be ghosts. All attempts at friendship
were met with propitiatory offerings which, when Cook misread their significance,
were followed by some form of attack. Eating poisonous fish was another dangerous
novelty here that often led to illness. On Erramanga the hostility repeated itself and
the Marines had to open fire, wounding several islanders and killing their chief.
It was not until Cook reached the bay he called Port Resolution, on the actively
volcanic southern island of Tanna, that he was able to restock with wood and
water in still edgy but not openly dangerous circumstances. On 25 August he finally
anchored at Quirós' Espiritu Santo proper, the largest northern island in the New
Hebrides, and completed his general survey of the chain by sailing round it.

At the end of the month, the *Resolution* sailed south for New Zealand, but on
4 September a large and unknown island was sighted, later found to be the fourth
largest in the Pacific, running some 300 miles north-west to south-east. It reminded
Cook of New South Wales and he eventually called it New Caledonia, spending
most of the month surveying the eastern side. The people were prosperous and
friendly, happy to supply water and to trade. More remarkably, they neither stole
nor, in the women's case, could be persuaded to bestow sexual favours on Cook's

men, which gained the admiration of Cook and the puritanical J.R. Forster, at least. One nasty surprise was another poisonous fish, a small amount of which made Cook and the Forsters painfully ill, and which killed a pig that ate part of it. At the south end of New Caledonia, on the small Isle of Pines, they first mistook the huge trees for pillars of basalt, and had a near escape from wrecking the ship at night in the surrounding reefs as Cook tried to make the western coast. After that he reluctantly gave up any attempt to survey that side, resuming his course for New Zealand on 3 October. On the way he discovered and briefly landed on uninhabited Norfolk Island, and in mid-October the white volcanic cone of Mount Egmont, the north-western sentinel of the Cook Strait, again rose above the horizon.

On 18 October the *Resolution* once more anchored off Ship Cove again. Cook's message to Furneaux was missing and there were clear signs that the *Adventure* had come and gone. There were also unverifiable reports of Furneaux's casualties, although the local people assured Cook that the *Adventure* had left safely. Here, although very short of proper materials, Cook recaulked the ship and prepared for the last stages of the voyage. Wales, the astronomer, double-checked the longitude against an earlier result of Bayly's, and Cook, the perfectionist, was mortified to find that on the *Endeavour* voyage he had plotted South Island about 40 nautical miles too far east. More happily, he found that the accumulated error in the rate of Kendall's chronometer, after nearly a year at sea in all conditions, was a mere 19 minutes 30 seconds.

On 10 November 1774, in the high southern summer, the *Resolution* sailed east over the Pacific, crossing the tracks of her earlier passages in about latitude 55° south, just in case any land between had been missed. Cape Deseado, the western end of the Strait of Magellan, was sighted on 17 December. There were few provisions to be found on Tierra de Fuego, but after a cheerful Yuletide in Christmas Sound, the ship passed south towards Cape Horn, with Cook still making such coastal observations as conditions allowed. In the first week of January 1775 they were in the South Atlantic searching to just south of latitude 60° for a coastline predicted by Dalrymple, much of whose theorising had now been disproved by the voyage. When this also vanished into air Cook turned north, stumbling instead on what he first took for an ice island before it solidified into towering peaks of rock. Cook landed briefly on the desolate shore of Possession Bay and claimed the island as South Georgia, the future way station on Antarctic voyages undertaken by Shackleton and others. Conscientiously reasoning that where one island existed, Bouvet de Lozier's mysterious cape might also be nearby, he then briefly turned back to follow the 60th parallel eastward. This brought him one last discovery in the form of the small, remote and deserted South Sandwich Isles but took him south of the tiny speck of Bouvet Island, the hare which both he and Furneaux had so fruitlessly pursued. With the sight of a glacier calving on South Georgia and more bergs and broken pack ice floating north from

REVIEW OF THE WAR GALLEYS AT
TAHITI (detail); oil painting by William
Hodges, 1776.

On the *Resolution*'s return from its second
island sweep, which had taken in Easter Island
and the Marquesas, the officers and crew were
able to observe with professional interest
a fleet of over 150 Tahitian canoes gathered
for an attack on the neighbouring island of
Moorea. This small painting of it was later
engraved for the official voyage account.

the undiscovered Weddell Sea, Cook ended the voyage certain 'that there is a tract
of land near the Pole, which is the Source of most of the ice which is spread over
this vast Southern Ocean'. He was, however, correctly convinced that it lay largely
within the Antarctic Circle 'for ever […] buried under everlasting snow and ice' and
also, quite wrongly, that it never could or would be explored.

On 21 March 1775, after a stormy northerly passage and exchanging news
and messages with passing ships, the *Resolution* again anchored in hospitable Table
Bay, and spent five weeks there as her rigging was refitted. She sailed on 27 April
via St Helena, Ascension Island and Fernando de Noronha off the Brazilian Coast,
and anchored at Spithead, Portsmouth, on 30 July 1775. The ship itself and Mr
Kendall's timepiece had proved their worth through a voyage of over three years
and 70,000 miles – well over twice round the world. Only four men on the *Resolution*
had died: three by accident, one of disease, and none from scurvy.

THE *RESOLUTION* AND THE *DISCOVERY*, 1776–80

The *Resolution*'s return saw her ever-modest captain and his achievements at the centre of public admiration. This time his glory was undimmed by the presence of Banks, who made a late return from a yachting trip to find renewed friendship and respect, with past differences forgotten. Banks was now on the Council of the Royal Society, which unanimously elected Cook a Fellow and awarded him its prestigious Copley Medal. Royal and naval approbation came with a further visit to the King and promotion to post-captain on the establishment of Greenwich Hospital – an honourable paid retirement – although with Cook's own proviso that, if he wished, he could again request suitable active service. In the meantime there was much to do, including sitting (in his new captain's full dress) for Nathaniel Dance, for a portrait that Banks had commissioned.

At Cape Town, Cook had been 'mortified' to read the published account of his *Endeavour* work. This he had left to be edited by Dr John Hawkesworth as part of a more general publication of recent Pacific voyages, including those of Byron, Wallis and Carteret, who reached home in 1769. He found 'his' contribution to be an erroneous conflation of his own journals with those of Banks and others, prefaced by a misleading claim that he had checked it before sailing in the *Resolution*. This time, supported by Sandwich and others, he collaborated with a more meticulous editor: Dr John Douglas took over and polished his account of his second voyage (and later edited the third), although Cook never saw the fine, illustrated two-volume result, published in May 1777, for a third voyage was being planned and Cook began to realise that, its 'fine retreat and [...] pretty income' aside, 'the limits of Greenwich Hospital [...] are far too small for an active mind like mine'.

With growing knowledge of the Pacific, and old rivalries soon to re-erupt as France and Spain sided with the American rebellion against British rule (1776–83), a new variant on an old theme was being considered in terms of a resumption of the quest for a North-West Passage between the Atlantic and the Pacific, and possibly also a search for a north-eastern one above Arctic Russia. Two north-western straits were rumoured to debouch in Drake' s 'New Albion' (the Pacific north-west of Canada) – that of Juan de Fuca at about latitude 48°, and one attributed to a fictional 'Admiral de Fonte' at about latitude 53°. Finding these had been the discarded object of Byron's 1764 voyage. If they existed, it had been known since 1771 that they could connect with the Arctic Ocean only somewhere north of Hudson Bay, since this had been shown to have no westerly outlets. Much clarification was also needed about the Pacific coasts south-west and south-east of the Bering Strait. Both had been substantially investigated only by the Russians, who were conducting a fur trade there. On the way, a new expedition could also return Mai to Tahiti, after his engaging but rather vacuous career as resident 'noble savage' in London. With Banks as his protector and patron, he became a celebrity. Opinions of his intelligence varied, but by mixing in the best society, he added genteel manners and improving English to his natural grace and good humour: 'How do, King Tosh!' was reportedly his cheerful greeting when Banks presented him to George III and Queen Charlotte, just days after his arrival. Of several portraits painted during his stay, the most famous is the full-length (now in the Tate collection) by Sir Joshua Reynolds, first president of the Royal Academy.

The *Resolution* was judged fit for another voyage, which Clerke (now a commander) was initially due to lead. Cook advised on the purchase of her new consort, the *Discovery*. At 298 tons and with a total complement of 69, she would be the smallest of his ships, for shortly after her purchase, around the end of January 1776, the Admiralty had been gratified to hear that Cook wished to command once more, with Clerke now taking the *Discovery*. John Gore would be Cook's first lieutenant; the second, James King, and Cook himself would comprise the *Resolution*'s astronomical observers, with Bayly going again in the *Discovery*. The *Resolution*'s previous surgeon's mate, now her surgeon, William Anderson, was also the naturalist, with the *Discovery*'s surgeon's mate, William Ellis, doubling as a natural-history draughtsman. David Nelson, a gardener from Kew, also joined the *Discovery* as a plant collector. Dr Solander then found John Webber, another excellent and sociable draughtsman, landscape painter and portraitist, of Anglo-Swiss parentage, who agreed to join the *Resolution* at short notice.

Cook had another fine navigator, William Bligh, as master of the *Resolution*. His place in the European romantic myth of the South Seas was destined to be secured later as commander of the ill-fated *Bounty* and of a more successful later Pacific voyage with Nathaniel Portlock. The latter at this point was also a *Discovery* 'mid' as, again, was young Vancouver, as well as Edward Riou, later to die commanding Nelson's frigates at Copenhagen. James Burney, their first lieutenant (and brother of Fanny, the novelist), was himself to become a notable historian of Pacific voyages. Once again, on this one, they were all accompanied by 'Mr Kendall's watch', flawlessly ticking away the longitude in Cook's cabin.

The *Resolution*, with her complement of 112, sailed on 12 July 1776 from Plymouth, a voyage anniversary which all considered lucky. Clerke was detained by family business until 1 August, but the ships met at Cape Town in mid-October, where they reprovisioned for a two-year voyage. This included so much livestock for themselves and as gifts for the islands (including horses) that they seemed a floating zoo. The *Resolution* had already proved wet and leaky thanks to poor dockyard work, and the continuing voyage south-east in cold weather and gales was as unpleasant as ever. Crossing the southern Indian Ocean, Cook confirmed the position of minor recent French island discoveries, the largest being the bleak Island of Desolation, later renamed Kerguelen after its original finder.

After the *Resolution*'s fore-topmast and main topgallant were carried away in a gale, a brief stop in Adventure Bay on Van Diemen's Land provided a necessary staging post towards the usual anchorage at Ship Cove, in New Zealand's Queen Charlotte Sound. Cook spent nearly a fortnight here, finding the Maori fearful of his possible vengeance for the death of Furneaux's men. He had no such intention, however, and did his best to resume friendly relations, while taking sensible care against surprises. Everyone benefited from the wild celery, scurvy grass and other produce of the place which they left for the last time on 25 February 1777, heading slowly north and east against contrary winds. This delay, based on ignorance of local seasonal variations, was to affect the whole progress of the voyage. By the time they touched on Mangaia in the Cook Islands, Cook was short of fresh supplies and decided that he would have to visit Tonga first, delaying his planned arrival at Tahiti. Arriving at the end of April, he was to stay 11 weeks in the 'Friendly Isles', surveying and observing, and pestered as ever by local theft. Clerke eventually found that shaving or half-shaving culprits' heads and throwing them overboard as objects of ridicule was the most effective deterrent. Thirty years later it transpired that, during this visit, Tongan chiefs plotted to kill the entire party and seize the ships, one of the leaders calling it off at the last moment for personal reasons. Cook, unaware of the danger, considered the visit a success, and eventually sailed for Tahiti on 17 July.

Since his last visit there, Spaniards from Peru had been to and gone from Tahiti in a feeble attempt to reassert their Pacific sovereignty and 'convert the heathen'. Their leader had died there, and despite their pious warnings to the islanders about the British, Cook was made as welcome as before. After his landing at Vaitepiha on 12 August, the old camp at Matavai Bay was recommissioned, fireworks were let off and Cook and Clerke were pleased to land the last of their livestock, with their own appearance on horseback, and Mai's less expert attempts at horsemanship, causing general astonishment. Cook declined to become involved in the continuing local war against Moorea, but he did attend a human sacrifice connected with its poor progress (the victim had, in fact, been killed earlier). He also had to refuse the Tahitian chief Tu's gift of a canoe for King George as too large to take, but had Webber paint his own portrait as a present for Tu. The portrait was much treasured by Tu, and Bligh was asked to repair it in 1788 when he arrived in the *Bounty*. It was last seen four years later. At the end of September, Cook moved on to Moorea, so far unvisited, and where the noticeable shortening of his patience for theft burst out in full fury, as houses and canoes were burned in order to gain restitution of a stolen goat. This was followed just before they reached Huahine by a new escalation: 'in a Passion', he ordered not only that a Moorean pilferer's head be shaved but also that his ears be cut off. The man lost his hair and one earlobe to the barber before Cook relented and made him swim ashore. Another 'hardened Scounderal' who stole a sextant on Huahine lost both hair and ears, and was put in irons when he threatened murderous revenge. It was nonetheless on Huahine that Mai was finally settled, in a house and garden Cook had built for him, along with two Maori who had joined him from New Zealand and who could not be returned. The final parting when they sailed on 2 November was, as Bayly wrote, 'a very Afecting Scean'.

Cook next made his final visit to Raiatea, an island of delight where several men were tempted to desert and settle, a thought entertained even by Anderson and possibly Clerke, both of whom were prone to consumption and feared the rigours of the Arctic. A simple-minded Marine called Harrison actually did desert there, but was recovered. More serious were the cases of a seaman called Shaw and a lovelorn midshipman and son of a naval captain, Alexander Mouat, both of whom fled to nearby Bora Bora. In response, Cook and Clerke rapidly and hospitably detained the son of the chief Orio, and also his son-in-law and famously beautiful daughter, Poetua, on *Discovery* against his men's return. As with the previous ear-croppings, it was further evidence suggesting that Cook's long patience was finally being more affected by the stresses of his three Pacific commands. Orio sent a message to Bora Bora, but also unsuccessfully planned to counter-seize Cook and Clerke when they were ashore, before finally ordering the return of the fugitives. A positive outcome of this anxiety-provoking drama, which only temporarily disturbed the general friendship, was the opening it gave Webber to make studies of Poetua in preparation for the fine portrait of her which he exhibited in London in 1785. After an emotional farewell, the ships briefly visited Bora Bora, obtaining there part of one of Bougainville's anchors to convert into hatchets for trade, and Cook then left the Society Islands for ever.

From Raiatea they sailed north and on 24 December discovered uninhabited Christmas Island, where Cook remained until 2 January 1778. Here an eclipse of the Sun was observed, English seeds were planted (Cook's invariable practice, for later use) and local supplies such as yams and turtles were gathered in large quantities. On 18 January, about 1,300 nautical miles north of the Equator, they became the first Europeans to sight the western elements of Cook's 'Sandwich Islands' (Hawaii). Canoes quickly came out to trade, and the people who came aboard spoke Polynesian and had the same infuriating talent as their southern cousins for spiriting away items that seized their fancy. When a scouting party eventually landed on Kauai there was an incident in which one islander was shot dead. However, by the time Cook himself landed, the crowds not only seemed friendly but prostrated themselves before him (as they would to one of their own half-divine kings) before he visited a nearby village and sacred site, or *heiau*. Cook rapidly saw that he had encountered a very sophisticated society, stretched over a large island group, but he was almost immediately driven from his anchorage by weather and found it difficult to regain a safe one in the offshore currents.

OPPOSITE POEDUA, THE DAUGHTER OF ORIO (born *c*.1758; died before 1788), by John Webber, *c*.1784.

Poetua (the usual modern spelling) was about 19 and in early pregnancy when Webber made the study of her on board *Discovery* in 1777 that he would use for this portrait, which was painted later in London and shown at the Royal Academy in 1785; he also painted two other versions. Its dreamy romanticism has come to embody the sexual fascination that Polynesia held in the European imagination.

After spending only three days ashore during his fortnight there, he sailed again on 2 February and sighted the coast of 'New Albion' – modern Oregon – on 7 March, at latitude 44° 33' north. This was his most southerly point on a coastline which he was to follow both north and far to the west for over 2,000 miles, until it tailed off in the shoals, tidal races and islands of the Aleutian chain. Although relatively low at first meeting, it was clearly backed by high ground, which further north piled up into the towering, snow-topped ranges of the Canadian Rocky Mountains. The coast below, from which the ships mostly stood well offshore in cold weeks of fog and storm from the west, also soon became as fragmented and complex as north-eastern New Zealand, but on a vastly grander scale. Urgently needing to reprovision and replace some of his spars, Cook tacked north and west in offshore gales looking for a suitable harbour. In doing so he missed the opening south of Vancouver Island which is now called the Juan de Fuca Strait, one of the mythical entrances to a 'north-west passage'; the so-called Admiral de Fonte Strait was to be equally elusive.

On the western side of the island, which he did not recognise as such, he put into what became known as King George's Sound, and later Nootka Sound, where the ships moored safely until 26 April, and where they were refitted. Here they cut new upper masts from the immemorial forest, set up an observatory and accurately determined their longitude, and conducted trade for fish and furs with the friendly local 'indians'. Shortly after leaving, the *Resolution* sprang a leak, which the pumps kept in check as they slowly tacked their way well to seaward across the Gulf of Alaska and put into Prince William Sound, south-west of modern Anchorage. The *Resolution* was recaulked there, but there was a risky incident when armed local people, now resembling 'Esquimaux' (Inuit), stormed the *Discovery* in the hope of easy pickings; they were driven off with cutlasses, resulting in no serious injury. Two weeks of May were subsequently spent in inconclusive probing of the nearby Cook Inlet (which leads up to Anchorage) and which Vancouver, 16 years later, was to confirm as no more than a huge, long bay into the continental hinterland.

They were now in regions known from the earlier eighteenth-century voyages of Bering and the Russians, and there were growing signs of Russian fur-trading contact amid local people as they sailed outside Kodiak Island and west by south down the Alaska Peninsula. Cook passed through the Aleutian Islands east of Unalaska early in July and landed on the Russian side of the Bering Strait, 800 miles to the north, on 10 August 1778. A week previously, on 3 August, he had lost his excellent naturalist and surgeon when William Anderson died, aged 30, and was buried at sea.

A week after passing through the Strait and heading north-east, the ships began to encounter the familiar dangers of floating Arctic ice, although the presence of large numbers of walruses – or 'sea-horses' as they were called – provided a copious supply of fresh meat. On 18 August, they were stopped by a solid wall of pack ice at their furthest point north, latitude 70° 44', and although Cook then altered his course westward to reach longitude 179° west, well above northern Siberia, ice also stopped them there. He thus resolved to try again at an earlier stage the following summer, and sailed south to Unalaska Island where there was a hospitable welcome from the local Inuit, the Russian fur-trading community and their resident factor, Gerasim Izmailov. Despite language difficulties, Izmailov was able to give Cook more information about the Russian coast, undertook to pass on a letter to the Admiralty via St Petersburg and provided other letters of introduction to the governor of Kamchatka, where Cook could have wintered. By the time he sailed on 26 October, however, Cook had instead already determined to winter in the Sandwich Islands, to enlarge his knowledge of the group and benefit everyone's health from fresh supplies and the warmer climate.

The passage began with a fearful storm in which a seaman on the *Discovery* was killed when rigging gave way, but a month later they sighted Maui and, on 31 November, Hawaii itself for the first time. Cook did not land, however, until the middle of January, preferring to avoid island entanglements and to trade with canoes that came off to do so as he recorded the group. Another storm at the end of December separated him from the *Discovery*, and by the time they rejoined on 6 January 1779, they urgently needed to find a harbour for repairs to ships with leaking decks, split sails and shattered rigging. On 17 January they anchored off Hawaii, in Kealakekua Bay.

Their landing brought large numbers of people and ecstatic demonstrations of honour. The unfathomable earlier prostrations resumed. Koa, a chief and a priest whom Cook had already met, led elaborate rituals of welcome at a nearby *heiau*, where Cook was draped in red cloth and had a hog offered to him. Cook also learnt that he had had the title of 'Orono' bestowed on him. Although the matter is still much debated, what he failed to understand – fatally, as the early stages in a tragedy of cultural cross-purposes unrolled – was that the islanders may have believed his 'second coming' to be that predicted for Lono, a Hawaiian year god.

Throughout the rest of the month he was consequently honoured like a returning deity, with visits from the Hawaiian king, Kalini'ōpu'u, and other chiefs, as well as ceremonies and such a quantity of 'offerings' and supplies that his hosts naturally began anxiously to hope for his early departure.

On 4 February Cook therefore set sail to survey the coast and find a new anchorage, sped on his way with further gifts and a fleet of canoes as a final escort. Two gale-filled nights, however, split his sails and the *Resolution*'s foremast; no other harbour could be found, and on 11 February he regretfully re-anchored at Kealakekua Bay. It proved strangely deserted, and while mast repairs ashore were permitted and the king again paid a formal visit, there were soon signs of increasing local hostility. For the Hawaiians, a disorientating and unwelcome third return for Lono was not in the script as they understood it. A spate of thefts, at which Cook protested, raised the temperature and led him to double his guards. Then, on the night of 13 February, the *Discovery*'s cutter was stolen (and in fact broken up for its iron).

BELOW A PARTY FROM HIS MAJESTY'S SHIPS *RESOLUTION* AND *DISCOVERY* SHOOTING SEA-HORSES, LATITUDE 71 NORTH, 1778; oil painting by John Webber. Exhibited at the Royal Academy in 1784, Webber's painting shows a walrus hunt from the ships, north of the Bering Strait. The third voyage, in particular, generated great commercial interest in the exploitable natural resources of the Pacific.

THE DEATH OF CAPTAIN COOK
AT KEALAKEKUA BAY, HAWAII,
14 FEBRUARY 1779.

Francesco Bartolozzi's print of 1784, after Webber, is probably the best representation since the latter was a distant witness of it by telescope from the *Resolution*'s deck and spoke to those more closely involved. Sudden violence broke out amid general misunderstandings triggered by a separate fatal incident on the other side of the bay. In addition to Cook, four Marines and 17 Hawaiians died.

The next day Cook led an armed party to 'invite' King Kalini'ōpu'u aboard against the cutter's return, following his Tahitian practice. The chief came willingly enough as far as the beach but was backed by an armed crowd, who prevented him going further. Seeking to avoid bloodshed, Cook abandoned his attempt to negotiate for the boat's return and was about to re-embark. At that moment news broke that another important chief had been shot and killed in an incident on the far side of the bay, and the infuriated crowd began hurling stones. Cook was violently threatened by one man, replying first with a charge of buckshot that caused no serious harm and then shooting dead another assailant. As the mob charged, his Marine party opened fire, but four of them were killed before they could reload or reach the boats. Cook was struck down and knifed from behind, then hacked and clubbed to death into the shallows.

Clerke, a sick man but no less clear-headed or humane than Cook, now took command of both the stunned expedition and the immediate situation. When a watering party was also attacked it immediately set fire to a village, but he would allow no further premeditated acts of vengeance. A truce was quickly established in which repairs to the *Resolution*'s foremast were finished and the ship was re-embarked, Clerke's firm requirement being the return of Cook's body. His bones (though not the Marines') were ceremoniously restored six days later by Kalini'ōpu'u. The Hawaiians had sustained considerable losses themselves (17, including four chiefs) and regretted the incident equally, and they had treated Cook according to their custom for great men. His body had been largely burnt and the flesh stripped from the bones, of which the longer ones, together with the skull and the preserved hands and feet, were handed back. Many small bones were beyond retrieval, having already been distributed as honoured relics. On 21 February Clerke consigned his captain's last remains to the waters of the bay, with full naval honours. The following day, with Clerke in command of the *Resolution* and John Gore, her first lieutenant, taking *Discovery*, they weighed anchor and departed from the beautiful but tragic scene.

Clerke, too, never returned home. He made a gallant attempt to complete Cook's Arctic mission, sailing north once more and making port on the Kamchatka Peninsula, where the Russians helped him both with supplies and with repairs to his increasingly weather-worn ships. On 22 August 1779, while returning to Kamchatka from a fruitless second foray beyond the Bering Strait, he died, aged 38, of the tuberculosis he had carried from England. He was buried ashore at Petropavlovsk, where the Russians again gave notable assistance and sent home the ships' reports: their grim news broke in London seven months later. Gore succeeded to the command of the *Resolution*. Lieutenant James King, the most adept manager of encounters with indigenous populations apart from Cook, took over the *Discovery*, and after a stormy passage down the coast of Japan both ships reached Macao, in China, in the first week of December. From there they trod the well-worn paths of the East India trade homeward, through the Sunda Strait to Cape Town, arriving there in good health on 9 May 1780.

Three months later, an Atlantic gale blew them so far north that their British landfall was at Stromness, in the Orkneys. Sailing 'north-about' and down the English east-coast route to the Thames, on which Cook first learnt his trade, they anchored off Sheerness on 4 October, after a voyage of nearly four years and three months. The news of the deaths of Cook and Clerke was already old and, whatever the private welcomes, the return of the ships was both less noticed and more sombre than those of 1771 and 1775. In an idiom of that age rather than of our own, a homecoming crowned with the cypress of mourning rather than with laurels of triumph closed Cook's unique chapter of success in the history of European discovery of the Pacific.

WILLIAM HODGES
AND THE *RESOLUTION*

Sydney Parkinson's illustrations of Cook's first Pacific voyage demonstrated the value of taking artists, even before the rather sensationally edited official account of it was published in 1773.

When Cook sailed again in 1772 he carried with him William Hodges (1744–97), 'a Landskip Painter', whom the Admiralty this time engaged 'to make Drawings and Paintings of such places in the Countries you may touch on … as may be proper to give a more perfect idea thereof than can be formed from written descriptions only'. Hodges was thus the first official British expedition artist. The learned but difficult Johann Reinhold Forster went as the first official natural historian with his gifted son, Georg, as botanical draughtsman (from whom Banks later bought 568 drawings). Like Parkinson, Hodges was of modest origins: his father was a respectable London blacksmith off Piccadilly, who encouraged William's drawing talents under good tuition. In 1758 this gained him apprenticeship to Richard Wilson, a portraitist and pioneering landscape painter greatly influenced by French seventeenth-century classical masters such as Claude Lorrain. Hodges in turn acquired classical painterly ambitions, but his drawing training also made him an accurate recorder of coastal profiles, landscape views and incidents of the voyage. While he painted very few oil portraits (Cook's was among those he did), he nevertheless drew good ones of individual and often identified Pacific people, mainly in red and black chalk. He was probably recruited through Lord

Palmerston, an early patron, and was certainly the first oil painter to work in the Pacific, bringing back a number of atmospheric and mostly small pictures done on the spot. One of the earliest was a view of Antarctic icebergs made early in the voyage – the first-ever attempt at this subject – though now visible only as an X-ray image since he was clearly dissatisfied with it and painted it out, under his *View in Pickersgill Harbour, Dusky Bay* (p.63). Whether he did this in New Zealand or later is still uncertain, but Georg Forster also did a watercolour version of the same polar scene, probably under his guidance, and Midshipman John Elliott recorded that Hodges gave drawing instruction to others on board as well.

The influence of French classicism on Hodges is most clearly seen in *View of Cape Stephens in Cook's Straits, with Waterspout* – a real incident but compositionally modelled on Gaspard Dughet's *Seascape with Jonah and the Whale*, widely known from a print of 1748. Similar idealisation is seen in his other post-voyage works for the Admiralty, including small but complex figure subjects of Cook's landings in Melanesia. These were done for engraving in the official voyage account, which also included many of Hodges's more realistic drawings. The Pacific subjects that he exhibited in London from 1776 were only modestly successful, despite his use of classical formulas to make them seem less alien to his audience. However, as the first colour representations of the Pacific, they laid the foundations for European notions of the South Sea as a place of sultry romance, mystery and menace in ways still familiar today through melodramatic film and tourism representations. From 1779 to 1783 Hodges worked in India – most notably for Warren Hastings, the governor of Bengal. Since India was already more familiar to the British than the Pacific, this brought him greater public success and led to his election as a full Royal Academician in 1789. In 1794, early in the French Revolutionary War, his last project was to exhibit, and publish as engravings, two huge 'moral landscapes', *The Effects of Peace* and *The Consequences of War*. It proved disastrous, both commercially and then when the show was closed as subversive to the war effort by demand of HRH The Duke of York (who saw it as critical of his own poor record as an army field commander). Hodges sold up and retired to Devon, where he became partner in a small local bank. When this failed in a general crash early in 1797, he died and within six months his wife followed him, leaving six children 'in great want'.

right WILLIAM HODGES, after George Dance, 1810. This print is from a drawing of Hodges after he became a Royal Academician in 1789. It is one of a well-known series by Dance.

overleaf A VIEW OF CAPE STEPHENS IN COOK'S STRAITS, WITH WATERSPOUT, by William Hodges, 1776. This large oil painting is of an incident that occurred in 1773 and is one of a set of four for the Admiralty. Hodges also did a more naturalistic drawing of it for engraving. Both versions show just one waterspout (in the foreground here) and three stages of its development.

JOHN WEBBER (1751–93): A SWISS AT SEA

'Mr Webber excels equally in Oil, & in watercolours…'
— DOROTHY RICHARDSON, A VISITOR TO WEBBER'S STUDIO IN 1785

By training, John Webber was the best suited of the Cook voyage artists for an expedition-recording role. He was born in London in 1751 to a Swiss sculptor father from Bern and an English mother; financial hardships led to his being raised from the age of six by an aunt in Bern, where his family had long-standing merchant connections. She recognised his talent, and in 1767 he was apprenticed for three years to Johann Aberli, a leading Swiss topographical draughtsman, before going to study painting in 1770 at the Académie Royale in Paris, where he added rustic figure groups and portraiture to his skills. He returned to London in 1775, enrolled in the Royal Academy Schools and first exhibited

at the Academy in 1776. The three works he showed, two landscapes and a portrait, were spotted by Daniel Solander – Banks's botanical assistant on the *Endeavour* – and this led to his appointment as artist for Cook's third Pacific expedition at 100 guineas a year, sailing that July.

Webber was well liked on the *Resolution* and very methodical, working closely with Cook in recording landscape and coastal views, with publication in view. He proved adept at rapidly sketching ethnographic figure subjects and combining these into more finished scenes, and did portraits of Pacific people. Encouraged by the surgeon, William Anderson, he also expanded his range into natural-history drawings, often

with the assistant surgeon, William Ellis, who was amateur artist-recorder of the voyage. Webber worked mainly in pen, wash and delicate watercolour, with acute observation of detail, good atmospheric effects and a tendency to produce idiosyncratically elongated figures. When the expedition returned in 1780, after the deaths of Cook and Anderson, he brought back over 200 drawings and about 20 small portraits in oils, and showed a selection to George III. The Admiralty then re-engaged him at £250 a year to direct the engraving of illustrations for the voyage account, published in 1784, and to paint further Pacific oil subjects until 1785. They include his famous portrait of

Poetua – romantic icon of the eighteenth-century South Seas (see p.78) – painted from a now lost oil study. He exhibited these and others at the Academy from 1784 to 1791, successfully published a set of Pacific views as prints, and in 1785 helped his friend P.-J. de Loutherbourg with the scenery and costumes for the famous pantomime *Omai, or, A Trip Round the World* at the Theatre Royal, Covent Garden. Tours in Britain, France and the Alps provided the subjects for his later work and in 1791 – the year he was elected a full Royal Academician – he presented 101 ethnographic items he had collected under Cook to the library at his childhood home, Bern (where they are now in the museum). He died, still a bachelor, in London in 1793, leaving bequests to his servants, Swiss relatives and artistic friends, though his main heir was his younger brother Henry, a sculptor who did much work for the potter Josiah Wedgwood. Webber first painted a small oil portrait of Cook at Cape Town in 1776, which is now in the National Portrait Gallery, London. Three other later versions (and two of his portrait of Poetua) are still known; another of Cook, painted at Tahiti for Chief Tu, was last seen there in 1792.

above A VIEW IN ULIETEA [Raiatea] (detail); this Society Islands watercolour of 1787 is an example of Webber's Pacific subjects made after his voyage. He exhibited an oil version of 1786, at the Royal Academy in 1787. This followed, with two known copies, and prints made from one of them.

opposite A TONGAN DANCE; a rough water-colour study by Webber, probably made on 21 June 1777, of which no other version is known. The tall structures are 'yam posts' – square columns of yams supported in a framework of four tall poles about 30 feet high, which Cook described in his journal.

Arthur Phillip Esq.

Captain General & Commander in Chief in & over

the Territory of New South Wales.

3

'GENTLEMAN, SCHOLAR AND SEAMAN'

Arthur Phillip and Australia

C OOK'S exploration and charting of the eastern Australian coast in 1770 was a signal achievement but one without immediate practical consequence. For nearly 20 years there were no further European landings in the vast territory that he named New South Wales, whose scattered Aboriginal peoples were briefly left to its previously uncontested possession.

From 1775 British attention was instead diverted by the War of American Independence which, from 1778, became a European seaborne conflict as France, Spain and the Dutch in turn backed the American rebels. One consequence of their revolt was to stop the transportation of about 1,000 British convicts a year, most to Virginia and Maryland, as cheap plantation labour. But this suspension did not end the legal sentence of transportation – seven years, fourteen or life – and, while considering alternative destinations, the British government instituted a system of prison hulks, in which transportees were held and employed in heavy dockyard and river work. Run by the contractor Duncan Campbell, the hulks were effective but had limited capacity, and London was soon being assailed by local complaints about the costs of the overflow backing up in civic jails. Among new places of exile considered, three suggested in 1784 and 1785 combined both distance and utility.

For practical reasons, proposals for two convict colonies in southern Africa, envisaged as staging posts on the route to India, quickly gave way to the third, on which Cook and Banks had already reported. This was Botany Bay, Cook's first landing point in south-eastern Australia at the end of the long but straight-forward voyage running before the prevailing westerlies from the Cape of Good

OPPOSITE ARTHUR PHILLIP ESQ CAPTAIN GENERAL & COMMANDER IN CHIEF, IN & OVER THE TERRITORY OF NEW SOUTH WALES; engraved by William Sherwin after Francis Wheatley, 1789

Hope. It also seemed to offer other advantages more vaunted than real – as a base against the French in the Indian Ocean, the Dutch in the East Indies or the Spaniards in the Philippines and even on the western American coasts. Occupation of New South Wales would also deny this region to the French and possibly offer new natural resources: Cook had already indicated the naval potential of Norfolk Island pine and New Zealand flax.

The costs and outline of the scheme were approved in August 1786, but a voyage to establish a convict colony would require an exceptional leader and, thereafter, resident governor. Since political responsibility fell principally within the remit of the Home Secretary, Lord Sydney, it was he – advised by his under-secretary, Evan Nepean – who chose an obscure 47-year-old naval captain, Arthur Phillip. That this choice was against the preference of the formidable Lord Howe, First Lord of the Admiralty, itself suggests unusual qualifications in the nominee.

BEFORE AUSTRALIA

Few personal documents relating to Phillip survive; his low personal profile and the secret work in which he was sometimes involved help make him one of the least-known founders of any modern state – in his case, Australia. It was also characteristic of him that, like Cook, he succeeded by doing nothing more romantic than carrying out his instructions in a highly competent manner.

Arthur Phillip was born in the parish of St Olave's in the City of London on 11 October 1738. His father, Jacob, was a German from Frankfurt who taught languages. His mother, Elizabeth, had already been widowed from her first marriage to a seaman called John Herbert and had a useful connection in a cousin, Michael Everitt, a naval captain. Jacob and Elizabeth probably married in 1736, when a daughter, Rebecca, was born, but after a few years of modest prosperity Jacob seems to have been dead by 1751. In June that year Arthur was admitted to the Greenwich Hospital School for the sons of poor seamen. While his mother's connection with Everitt may have helped, the school's records give Jacob's occupation as both a 'steward' and an 'able seaman'. Whether his life at sea was before his marriage or in the 1740s is unknown, but the Marquess of Lavradio, the Portuguese Viceroy of Brazil, later reported that Arthur first went to sea in the Navy at the age of nine, and it might have been briefly with his father. Jacob's principal legacy to his son, who would have been around 12 when he died, was fluency in spoken and written German, 'an excellent grounding in Latin […] and some knowledge of French', which his later career enabled him to perfect. Lavradio said that he spoke six languages, of which he learnt Portuguese in Brazil, and circumstances suggest that he also had Spanish. The sixth, assuming Latin did not count, is uncertain.

In 1753, the Reverend Francis Swinden, headmaster of the Greenwich Hospital School, was able to write at the end of his pupil's brief education there: 'Arthur Phillip is noted for his diplomacy [and] mildness. [He is] nervously active, unassuming, reasonable, business-like to the smallest degree in everything he undertakes, always seeking perfection.' Similar characteristics – of reserve, honesty, educated principle and frank but respectful reasonableness, not least in contrast with other deplored English 'excesses of temper' – were to be echoed in the praise he received from the Viceroy. Swinden would also have been pleased to hear his old pupil described much later as a combination of 'the Gentleman, the scholar and the seaman'.

All Greenwich boys were educated for sea careers, and on 1 December 1753 Phillip was apprenticed to William Redhead, master of the Arctic whaler *Fortune* of London, which, like many others, also traded in other cargoes out of season. Between April and July 1754 he made his first whaling voyage, followed by one in August to the Mediterranean, before returning to London via Rotterdam in April 1755. Another Arctic voyage immediately ensued, returning in July, when Phillip's apprenticeship to Redhead was prematurely ended. Exactly why is unknown, but the initial skirmishes of the Seven Years War with France (1756–63) were then beginning and, at a rather earlier age than Cook before him, Phillip must have seen greater opportunities in a naval career. He embarked on this in the traditional role for officers of 'captain's servant' under his relative Captain Everitt in the 68-gun *Buckingham*, flagship of Vice-Admiral Temple West in the Channel Squadron. He joined at Plymouth six days after his seventeenth birthday, and by mid-November had taken part in the capture and burning of a French 74-gun ship. The following year in the Mediterranean the *Buckingham* shared in the incompetent fleet action with the French off Minorca that led to Britain's loss of that island. Phillip sent his sister an indignant account of it and the 'Cowardice of Admiral Byng' – who was subsequently court-martialled and shot.

On Everitt's recall, Phillip remained in other ships in the Mediterranean (including, briefly, as a captain's clerk) until rejoining him and West as a midshipman in the 98-gun *Neptune* at Portsmouth early in 1757. That July he was hit by one of the bouts of periodic ill health that dogged his life and went ashore, only definitely returning to sea in mid-1759 and rejoining Everitt in the *Stirling Castle* in February 1760. The ship sailed for the Leeward Islands in September and on 7 June 1761 he was appointed the ship's fourth lieutenant by the local commodore. As such he was involved in Admiral Rodney's capture of Martinique from the French early in 1762, and in the great amphibious expedition later that year that briefly took the Cuban capital Havana from the Spanish. Phillip seems to have shown his good qualities there and came to the notice of Captain Augustus Hervey, whose patronage proved important to him two years later. The Admiralty confirmed his commission when he returned to England in March 1763, but the onset of peace

that year saw him discharged on half-pay, albeit with £130 of Havana prize money to ease the transition.

In July 1763 Phillip married Mrs Charlotte Denison, 16 years older and the well-off widow of a London cloth merchant. Given his new wife's background and his own later interests, he may have been involved in some aspect of trade for the next two years, but at some point, probably by the end of 1765, they had bought a small farm near Lyndhurst in Hampshire. Gentlemanly management of it was to be valuable experience for Phillip, but unfortunately and for unknown reasons his marriage failed and he sought a legal separation. By mid-1769 he was on his own again and in debt to his wife, who had retained control of her own property. For the

GREENLAND
WHALERS IN THE
ARCTIC, by Charles
Brooking, 1723–59.

The *Fortune*, in which
Phillip first sailed, was
probably very similar
to the English whaler
shown here.

next four years he appears to have oscillated between two long periods of official leave 'for the benefit of his health' in France and the Low Countries, interspersed with eight months of home naval service, primarily in the *Egmont*, in 1770–71.

It seems fairly certain that Phillip earned enough money abroad to settle his debts to Charlotte, possibly by acting as an agent in the cloth trade on behalf of London friends. He may also have pursued engineering and military studies in Europe, for by the 1770s he had acquired an unusual theoretical knowledge. Sometime before 1778 he had assessed the French naval base at Toulon, so he may have volunteered, or been asked for, intelligence about a fleet fitting out there early in 1773. Phillip's portraits show his mild, unremarkable appearance: along with discretion, thoroughness and a command of languages, unobtrusiveness is a valuable asset to a spy.

Following his return to peacetime England in 1774, Phillip adopted a fairly common option for unemployed but ambitious officers: he enlisted abroad. Portugal and Spain were then in dispute over territory on the northern side of the River Plate estuary in what is now Uruguay and southern Brazil. Here the Portuguese had established a fortified outpost at Colonia del Sacramento, across the Plate from Buenos Aires. A Spanish assault on it in 1773 was repulsed by the Viceroy, Lavradio, who also sought reinforcements from home. Portugal requested naval help from Britain, her oldest ally, which was limited to allowing the recruitment of a few unemployed naval officers. The British had long sought to penetrate Spain's jealously guarded South American trade and Hervey, now at the Admiralty, knew that information on those coasts could prove valuable. The only volunteer he unreservedly recommended was Lieutenant Phillip, praising his experience, knowledge, judgement and good French (then the international language). That he would acquire information of possible use for London would have been tacitly understood.

Phillip obtained generous terms from the Portuguese, including the rank of a captain in their navy. He left for Lisbon in December 1774 and arrived at Rio on 5 April 1775. There he swiftly confirmed his good qualities with the viceroy, not least in contrast to Robert M'Douall, the blustering British officer who was already commodore of the local naval forces. Lavradio gave him independent command of the *Nossa Senhora do Pilar*, a merchantman under conversion to a 26-gun frigate. With this ship he put new fibre into the defence of Portuguese interests on the disputed coast and at Colonia, where Phillip was also put in command of a small squadron. When a large Spanish force arrived off Lavradio's southern naval base of Santa Catarina Island early in 1777, M'Douall's irresolution led to its unresisting surrender, with only one Portuguese captain and Phillip demurring. They probably both felt their honour redeemed by their sharp attack in April on the superior Spanish 70-gun *San Augustin*, which then surrendered to the squadron. Phillip's reward was to take command of her until peace was restored in April 1778, when Spain gained Colonia in exchange for the return of Santa Catarina and for recognising Portuguese sovereignty in southern Brazil.

Phillip gained much else from his Brazilian service. Through Lavradio's friendship he enjoyed a high level of social engagement, including gaining entry to local scientific circles, and within a year he was writing and speaking fluent Portuguese. He charted the coast or obtained charts of it as part of his official duties, and learnt about local settlements and defences, agriculture and produce. His experience at Colonia also taught him the hardships of sustaining an isolated outpost with an unwilling population, and he may have been the first Englishman to enter the forbidden interior zone of Minas Gerais to observe gold and diamond mining, which hardened a distaste for slavery that he probably first acquired in the West Indies. Lavradio saw him leave with regret, sending him back to Lisbon in mid-1778 with a report praising his judgement, integrity, tact and sometimes high-handed bravery. With the American War now in full swing, Phillip wanted to return to the Royal Navy: Lisbon, echoing Lavradio's praise of his 'zeal and honour', could only regretfully comply with his wishes.

On arriving home in September, Phillip lost his Portuguese rank of captain but was appointed first lieutenant of the 74-gun *Alexander* in the Channel Squadron and in September 1779 was raised to master and commander of a fireship. When this did not go into service he substituted for absent captains in two larger vessels, but his movements were otherwise shadowy until late 1781, when he was finally made post-captain in the frigate *Ariadne* and sent to collect Hanoverian troops from the Elbe. A reputation for dealing with unusual situations and his command of German probably recommended him, and both skills came into play when *Ariadne* was trapped by ice and had to be secured for the winter there, returning only in spring 1782.

More significant at this time was his likely role as an adviser on naval policy in South America. It brought him into direct contact with Lord Sandwich, First Lord of the Admiralty, and with others who were to be important to him, including Evan Nepean – later secretary in both the Home Office and the Admiralty – and Nepean's master in the former, Thomas Townshend, later Lord Sydney. Spanish and Dutch alliance with the American rebels in 1779–80 was then prompting a series of complex expeditionary proposals. They included revived plans for action against the Spanish in South America, seizure of the Cape of Good Hope from the Dutch and the ongoing need to safeguard British interests in India. Commodore George Johnstone's expedition to take the Cape sailed in 1781, with Plate operations from there a later possibility, but the plan collapsed when the French intercepted him in a drawn action off the Azores.

In all this it is fairly clear that Phillip supplied advice to Sandwich and the government, as well as copies of his South American charts. Early in 1781, he may also have commanded a merchant ship taking Portuguese army recruits (including convicts) to Rio. If so, his real purpose would have been to gather intelligence for anti-Spanish moves, and success in this mission might help explain his promotion to post-captain that autumn. In December 1782 he was appointed captain of the 64-gun *Europe* in a squadron sent to reinforce Admiral Sir Edward Hughes in India, but the *Europe* arrived at Madras alone, all the other ships having been forced back by bad weather. Phillip himself had had to put into Rio for repairs, where he had received 'every possible mark of respect and attention', but his stay in India was short. In October 1783 Hughes ordered him home in Commodore Sir Richard King's squadron, which reached Cape Town early in December, storm-damaged and heavily afflicted with scurvy. When Phillip was sent to ask permission to land the sick the Dutch at first refused, claiming they had no confirmation of a recent truce with England, and it was an indication of Phillip's standing that King sent him home in advance with official protests and Hughes's Indian despatches.

Arriving in April 1784 he again asked for a year's leave, from mid-October, to attend to private affairs in Grenoble, on this occasion certainly cover for a peacetime spying mission. In November, Nepean at the Home Office paid him £150 from secret funds to check reports of a French warship-building programme at Toulon. Phillip confirmed that this was underway and, tellingly, that the arsenal there was 'in very good Order and very superior to what it was when I saw it before the War'. He returned to England in October 1785 but left again in December for Hyères, just west of Toulon, for another year's official absence. Since Nepean authorised a second related payment to him of £160 there is no doubt that his undercover work continued there, whatever else he might have been doing for his London merchant friends.

'THE FIRST FLEET'

By 1786, Phillip was a man of wide experience in distant voyages, foreign service, diplomacy and languages, in financial matters of a commercial as well as an official nature, and in the observation of Portuguese, Spanish and Dutch colonial practice (the last at the Cape) in agriculture and defence. He had also advanced from modest origins by making the most of his steadiness, his proven courage and his talent for accomplishing unusual tasks. All these factors probably underlay his nomination for the Botany Bay project.

His response was to produce an imaginative and detailed paper on how the voyage and what followed should be conducted for the health and welfare of the convicts, and how reform, work and the success of the colony would open up opportunities for them. He considered the necessary supplies, equipment, plants, seeds and breeding animals; and the required laws, punishments and incentives, including making private grants of cultivable land both to transportees on expiration of their sentences and to the Marine force sent as their guards. He addressed the protection and segregation of women convicts but acknowledged the probable need to condone a degree of prostitution, while also wishing to encourage stable marriages, either among the transportees or with Polynesians (the last also applying to the Marines). He was also determined to encourage good relations with the Aboriginal people; to promote,

PACIFIC EXPLORATION

ABOVE ENTRANCE TO RIO DE JANEIRO
(BRASIL) FROM THE ANCHORAGE
WITHOUT THE SUGAR LOAF BEARING
NW. ½ N. OFF SHORE 2 MILES, by

George Raper, 1790.
The 'First Fleet' at anchor, with the *Sirius*
in the centre and the two-masted *Supply* third
to her right.

as Europeans saw it, their 'enlightened civilisation', and to protect them under the same English laws that governed the colony. He included the very specific tenet 'That there can be no Slavery in a Free Land – and consequently no Slaves', a provision which was rapidly abrogated by his military successors in New South Wales in their treatment of later transportees. Further complex legal arrangements were concluded to allow him to exercise law as civil governor under a number of technically separate jurisdictions.

Beyond such principles, Phillip immersed himself in all the practical details of fitting ships, such as appointing officers – including former shipmates like Philip Gidley King from the *Ariadne* and the *Europe*. He also exerted pressure to obtain 'Provisions and accommodations better than any Set of Transports' one harassed Navy Board colleague had ever seen, although much with which he was supplied proved inadequate. His one failure was to be formally appointed commodore by the Navy, although he was generally referred to as such, and was given a second captain in John Hunter for his 'flagship'. Overall, and with many delays, the process took nine months, with Phillip and Nepean ensuring that orders were issued by personally visiting all the heads of department concerned and waiting there until they were, as Cook had done.

For the voyage the Navy Board refitted the 540-ton naval transport *Berwick*, now renamed the *Sirius*, and the 175-ton brig *Supply*, and contracted nine civilian ships. The *Alexander*, the *Scarborough*, the *Charlotte*, the *Friendship*, the *Lady Penrhyn* and the *Prince of Wales* were convict transports. The first two took men only, the third and fourth took men and women, and the last two took women – except for one man, in the *Prince*. The last ship was added only late in the day, when the number of female transportees was increased, and to carry extra baggage and stores. The *Fishburn*, the *Golden Grove* and the *Borrowdale* were storeships, while the *Charlotte* and the *Lady Penrhyn* were chartered by the East India Company to reduce costs by collecting tea from China as a return cargo.

At 114 feet long and 452 tons, the *Alexander*, built in 1783, was the largest transport, carrying 195 male prisoners confined in an unlit and underventilated 'tween deck with a clearance of only 4 feet and 5 inches. (The 430-ton *Scarborough* carried even more, with a complement of 208.) The *Alexander* was also the dirtiest, delaying departure when typhus broke out on board. This was quickly contained, but the ship remained dirty and unhealthy until Phillip later insisted that the master have her regularly pumped and cleansed. The typhus outbreak at least gave Phillip late leverage to gain the level of fresh provisions that he wanted, although he still sailed short of clothes for female convicts and without adequate musket balls to contain a determined rebellion. Although it was suggested these might follow in the *Bounty* when she sailed for Tahiti, Phillip was able to make up this deficiency and others at Rio, and the 'First Fleet' of Australia's European history eventually sailed from Portsmouth on 13 May 1787. With Phillip in the *Sirius* went the Kendall chronometer ('K1') used by Cook on his last two voyages.

The fleet's convict cargo – 546 men and 190 women by one modern count, though the figures vary – comprised neither the greatest villains of Georgian society nor political prisoners, even though some of them were educated. Of the 262 whose ages are known, five were under 15, 234 were between 16 and 45, and 13 were older. Largely from London, they were a harvest of failure and destitution, most sentenced for crimes against property. This was sometimes serious – including theft from employers and burglary (93 cases), highway robbery (71), sheep and cattle stealing (44) and violent mugging (31). There were also a few dealers of stolen goods, swindlers and forgers, but the majority of known crimes (431 out of 733) were minor thefts, often through necessity: a hen or two, some cheese or bacon, a shilling's worth of butter in one case. A starving black West Indian called Thomas Chaddick took some cucumbers from a garden. John Hudson, a nine-year-old chimney sweep, stole some clothes and a pistol; Elizabeth Hayward, a clogmaker aged 13, took clothing to the value of seven shillings. These were the youngest. Dorothy Handland, a perjured rag dealer, was the oldest: aged 82, she would also be Australia's first recorded suicide. Most were ill-suited as colonial pioneers, with only a handful having carpentry or building skills; there was a brace each of tailors, weavers and butchers, five shoemakers and a single skilled fisherman. One man, other than Phillip and his old farm servant Henry Dodd, appears to have had significant experience of farming. Of two gardeners, one was a free man sent by Joseph Banks to collect plants who decided to stay at the Cape. Of the rest with any trade at all, most were labourers or menials. Many of the women, if not already de facto prostitutes, soon turned to trading their bodies for rum and other favours from male prisoners, guards and seamen alike. Ill-clothed, malnourished, lousy, some infirm and sickly, disorientated and banished from all they knew by a brutal law, these were the detritus of society sent wallowing south-west in Phillip's vomit-strewn convoy, in most cases for ever. The Marine guards also sailed anticipating an absence of years, some taking wives and children with them. Others had to leave them behind: 'Oh my God all my hopes are over of seeing my beloved wife and son,' wrote the recently married Ralph Clark, their second lieutenant, when the fleet did not put into Plymouth.

Fortunately the voyage was relatively uneventful, especially in the warmer first stages, apart from some rationing of food and water. A few convict plots were easily countered, with troublemakers, including several incorrigible women, put in irons or flogged (neither punishments unusual in the Navy). Later dissensions in Australia were heralded in the often harsher discipline for the Marines, one of whom got 200 lashes for passing forged coins at Rio de Janiero. Astonishingly, given the conditions, the forgeries had been made on board by convicts, who were less severely punished.

Fair weather also allowed a regime of regular deck exercise, while Phillip ensured the ships were kept as clean and ventilated as possible. All ports of call were foreseen in the sailing orders, Rio de Janeiro becoming necessary after adequate supplies, especially fruit, could not be found at Tenerife and because Phillip's experience anticipated hard bargaining at Cape Town. At Rio, from 5 August to 3 September, his local reputation helped him take on (in addition to musket balls) useful plants, seeds and other supplies, and a large stock of oranges for both convicts and crews. This suggests that his views on their efficacy against scurvy were more advanced than Cook's, whose success owed more to his advocacy of 'greens' and hygiene than to his mistaken trust in malt extract.

In fact, the health record of the voyage was unprecedented for its nature, and was a tribute to Phillip's regime. It covered a total of just over 15,000 miles in 252 days, of which 184 were at sea – making the average speed an unexceptional three knots. Between Portsmouth and Rio only 16 people died (ten in the mephitic *Alexander*), most being those already sick on departure. By Botany Bay the death toll had risen to 48: four female convicts, 36 male, five convicts' children, plus a Marine, a Marine's wife and a Marine's child. This was less than three per cent of a total company of about 1,350, while only about a third of the deaths were from scurvy. By contrast, when the Second Fleet arrived in 1790 it had already lost 267 out of 1,017 convicts and was riddled with other infirmities; in 1791 the Third Fleet lost 182 out of 1,864. Although both were run by appalling contractors who were mainly experienced in the slave trade, such numbers were more typical of long and crowded voyages.

On 13 October 1787 the First Fleet anchored in Table Bay. Phillip then increased the human crowding to embark an official stock, mostly for breeding, of 'one stallion, three mares, three colts, six cows, two bulls, 44 sheep, four goats and 28 hogs' plus poultry and all the feed for these creatures, as well as others bought privately by officers. He also obtained 'a vast number' of seeds and plants, including citrus and other fruit trees, the Cape having a well-stocked botanical and agricultural garden. This time the Dutch proved more courteous, but their merchants racked up prices, as expected. Phillip was nonetheless able to ensure that the convicts and his men were equally well fed on fresh provisions before the last leg of the voyage. In a phrase of Marine Lieutenant Tench, everyone was aware that their departure on 12 November cut them off indefinitely from 'every scene of civilization and humanized manners' as they understood these.

On 25 November, in the southern Indian Ocean, Phillip split the fleet and went ahead in the *Supply* with the three fastest sailers (the *Alexander*, the *Scarborough* and the *Friendship*) following as closely as possible. His aim was to find a settlement site and, aided by some 'convict artificers' moved into these ships, build a storehouse to speed the unloading and homeward passage of the transports. But in the stormy 'roaring forties' weather took a hand, blowing all ships on with hatches battened down, water rationed again, galley stoves often out and growing mortality among both personnel and livestock in cold, wet conditions. The small *Supply* struggled in the vast eastward-rolling seas, but the transports, including the slower ones under John Hunter in the *Sirius*, made better speed. On 3 January 1788 Phillip sighted southern Van Diemen's Land (Tasmania) and, after struggling with contrary winds, the *Supply* entered Botany Bay on 18 January. Her division came in a day behind and the rest on 20 January. Taken overall, it was a remarkable achievement that a fleet of 11 should finish the passage of 88 days from the Cape practically together and without major incident. However, the advance party had no time to do more than defuse a nervous armed welcome from the 'Indians', cut urgently needed grass for the livestock and catch fresh fish.

Phillip also quickly saw that the shallow bay was a poor harbour with inadequate soil for crops and little fresh water. Without disembarking the convicts, he ordered Major Ross, the Marine commandant and the colony's lieutenant-governor, to begin clearing the best available site as a precaution, but on 21 January he himself led a party ten miles north in three ship's boats. His destination was the

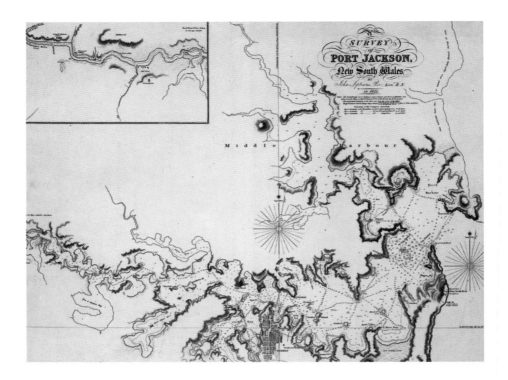

inlet called Port Jackson, in which David Collins, the new colony's Judge Advocate, recalled that 'Captain Cook, as he passed by, thought might be found shelter for a boat'. The entrance was through two prominent outer heads that concealed a vast, deep-water southern arm with many inlets and islands, the last one being of a 'Novel & Romantic appearance', according to the surgeon Arthur Smyth. Phillip explored it for two days, reporting almost prophetically to Lord Sydney that it was 'the finest harbour in the world, in which a thousand sail of the line may ride in the most perfect security'.

> [T]he different coves were examined with all possible expedition. I fixed on the one that had the best spring of water, and in which the ships can anchor so close to the shore that at very small expense quays may be made at which the largest ships may unload. This cove, which I honoured with the name of Sydney, is about a quarter of a mile across the entrance and half a mile in length.

Phillip returned to the bay – today surrounded by the southern districts of modern Sydney – on 24 January 1788, but not for long. In his absence two distant ships were seen heading in, and suspicions that they were the *Boussole* and *Astrolabe* of Lapérouse's Pacific expedition were soon confirmed. Governor Phillip – as he now was – would not risk being forestalled in Port Jackson and headed back immediately

in the *Supply*. Hunter was left to greet the French hurriedly on 26 January, with
an offer to send home despatches; the British convoy then weighed and struggled
out of the bay in contrary winds and a flurry of minor collision damage. Collins
reported that Lapérouse had used Cook's chart to guide him in and was a warm
admirer of their English forerunner. Surprised not to find a settlement already
established, Lapérouse stayed in the bay and in contact with Phillip's party for
six weeks, turning back several convict escapees who tried to join him before
disappearing northward to his grim fate.

Governor Phillip

Phillip took formal possession of Sydney Cove on the morning of 26 January; Hunter arriving that evening. The male convicts were disembarked the next day to clear ground and put up tents for the first night ashore. Phillip rapidly decided to establish his headquarters and the female convicts on the eastern side of the cove, with the male quarters on the western side with the Marine guards and the hospital. For himself he had brought a temporary framed canvas house from England and had picked up considerable private livestock, including a horse, dogs, two dozen sheep, poultry (and rabbits, later a bane). His own and other gardens were quickly planted on both sides of the cove, and on 1 February Farm Cove to the south began earning its name with a larger area being cleared for vegetables by Dodd. On 6 February the women were landed, with predictable results: a night of debauchery and drunken riot in the scrub by convicts, seamen and Marines indiscriminately, accompanied rather than discouraged by an apocalyptic storm and lashing rain.

Order was established at a parade the next morning, with the Marines marching in to stand over the circled, squatting convicts, while their band, colours, volleys of musketry and 'God Save the King' added pageantry to the formalities. Phillip heard Collins read out both his commission as governor and the letters-patent establishing the legal basis of the colony. He then gave a 'short speech, extremely well adapted to the people he had to govern' but also 'mild and humane' – at least in parts. He attempted to give hope to all who had so far behaved well and who realised that this was a new start in which only 'repetition of former demerits' would count against them. Those who did not work would not eat, since '*good* Men […] should not be slaves for the *Bad*'. Those who helped create a civil ordered society would be rewarded, but any 'Men & Women […] so thoroughly abandoned in their Wickedness as to have lost every good Principle' would 'inevitably meet with the punishment which they deserved', however much it would 'distress his feelings'. He would encourage regular convict marriages but male prisoners trying to get into the women's tents at night would risk being shot: those convicted of pillaging the colony's precious breeding animals or stealing other produce would be hanged (the first to be made an example of in this way being 17-year-old Thomas Barrett). He hoped that they would be helped by the absence of other tempta-tions – as hopeful escapees to the bush would soon fatally discover – and ended by wishing them all 'reformation, happiness and prosperity, in this new country' and granting the rest of the day as holiday.

For the next four years Phillip's steady resolution in keeping to this agenda was the bedrock of the colony's precarious existence. The beauty of Port Jackson, on which many of the First Fleet's journalists remarked, hid many thorns. The ground at Sydney Cove was rocky and took extensive labour to clear of embedded eucalyptus trees, whose timber proved practically useless except for burning. Until better wood was found, reed-thatched huts and barracks made of cabbage-palm trunks daubed with mud were miserably leaky and a haven for vermin. Phillip's convicts included only one brickmaker, and when he isolated suitable clay, it was a major achievement to build a secure, tiled-roof storehouse and a hospital building, and soon also to get officers' cottages and the permanent, brick-built Government House underway – for long the only dwelling in the colony with glass windows.

Food remained the critical problem in the early 'starvation years'. Animals failed to thrive and fell prey to natural and careless accident: dingoes, over-consumption of personal stock by officers and surreptitious pillage by Aboriginal people and convicts. Breeding rates were also inadequate until new imports came in from 1790 on. Supplementary hunting and fishing had some success but proved too erratic to rely on. Agricultural expertise was seriously lacking; first plantings inevitably put in at the wrong season either died or were sickly, some seed was weevil-infested, and mice proved a problem, as, later, did drought.

Many of the convicts also unsurprisingly proved idle or simply unreformable. They stole private property, produce cultivated by the more diligent, game and fish, food from the government stores and the precious European livestock. Phillip's court backed up his promise of floggings and hangings where necessary, but he also took more constructive measures to promote self-reliance. He devised a system in which reliable individuals and cohesive groups – including the free crews of the *Sirius* and the *Supply* – were made responsible for supporting themselves on allocated plots, or for doing other tasks whose completion left them with time to cultivate crops and other foodstuffs for themselves. Similarly, a dozen trustworthy convicts were formed into an effective though hated night watch to counter theft from gardens and huts after dark. The success of some of the early convict marriages also encouraged family responsibility – and families. Despite often painful rationing, no one died of hunger, while the fine climate and good medical care soon raised general health and the infant survival rate above contemporary English norms. By these means, albeit slowly, the power of example and achievable ambitions started to produce a noticeably reforming effect.

Self-sustaining agriculture really began when Phillip established a farm away from Sydney Cove, on more extensive fertile ground at Parramatta – at the head of Port Jackson – in November 1788. The first year's grain harvest was kept entirely for seed, but some became consumable thereafter. The year 1792 saw the first bumper crop and Parramatta already well established with its own Government House, storehouse and settlement. It was also there that James Ruse – a convict who had been a Cornish farmer – began the first successful personal farm, a project Phillip backed partly as an experiment in what a determined man could do. Ruse started with two government acres in November 1789 and in February

1792 Phillip made over this 'Experiment Farm' to him as the first private land grant in Australia. It had then been expanded to 30 acres to support Ruse, his new convict wife Elizabeth – whose sentence Phillip remitted absolutely in July 1792 – their daughter and two convict labourers. It later rose to 200 acres, though Ruse eventually lost it and ended his life working for another farmer.

While Phillip insisted on good treatment of the local Eora people, the convicts' general attitude to them was poor. They quickly stole essential Aboriginal weapons as 'curiosities' for trade with departing sailors, and began other maltreatment for which the Eora soon exacted lethal repayment on (sometimes innocent) hunters and others in the bush. Phillip refused to countenance revenge and punished those who attempted it, his best intentions inevitably fuelling the vicious cycle. His own early relations with the local people were also fraught and variable, and included the desperate expedient of forcibly detaining three of them long enough to learn their language. The first, Arabanoo, detained in December 1788, ultimately stayed of his own accord but died in May 1789 in a smallpox outbreak, one of several European diseases which soon caused many Aboriginal deaths. Colebee and Bennelong, captured in November 1789, had both escaped six months later. Phillip was himself nearly killed by a spear in the shoulder when leading a party to try and renew contact with them in September 1790, but he again forbade reprisals. Shortly afterwards, the Aboriginal people sought to mend relationships, which

thereafter slowly, if erratically, improved. In the end, Phillip's diplomacy and his willingness to help them with food and medical aid, and to welcome them both into the European community and as guests in his own house, began to normalise their presence in Sydney Cove. Where his enlightened attitude came from other than from Cook's example – itself based on wise advice in London – is hard to say, as is what might have happened thereafter had it continued beyond his time as governor. Regrettably, more familiar attitudes reasserted themselves under his successors, with dire results for Aboriginal society. It was to Phillip's credit that, when he left Australia, Bennelong was one of two Aboriginal men who accompanied him and lived to return home in 1795, though the other, Yemmerrawannie, died in England in 1794.

With nature, inexperience and human folly against him, the new governor had to issue more of the imported dry stores, such as flour, than expected, and then steadily reduce rations as stocks became critically low. The convicts' general good health on the voyage dipped seriously after arrival, affecting their ability to work. Drink and the dislocation of exile also took their toll, with runaways dying or being killed in the bush; others succumbed to depression, madness in one or two cases and general quarrels. In October 1788, with no news of when further supplies – or further convict mouths to feed – would arrive from England, John Hunter left for Cape Town in the *Sirius* for essential replenishments. He took the longer but easier option of sailing round the world via Cape Horn, before returning in May 1789 with 120,000 pounds of flour (four months' supply), new seed stock and much-needed medical supplies. He also brought the first letters from home, which improved morale without giving any news of relief.

A major cause for resentment among Phillip's men – primarily the Marine officers and troops – was his policy of issuing equal rations to all

THE GOVERNOR MAKING THE BEST OF HIS WAY TO THE BOAT AFTER BEING WOUNDED BY A SPEAR STICKING IN HIS SHOULDER (detail), *c.* 1790.

The Port Jackson Painter's record of Philip's wounding while trying to re-establish contact with the Eora people.

and housing both convicts and non-convicts the same way. Like his attitude to the local Aboriginal people, this egalitarianism ran against hierarchical norms. It was impossible to argue with, however, since he applied the same rationing rules to himself and in mid-1790 put all his considerable private supplies into the common stock. There were further particular problems with the Marines. Their officers resented the extension of their role as guards into being working overseers, and the men resented the fact that their own disciplinary code was often harsher than the convicts', and that Phillip also applied justice impartially, hanging six Marines at once for systematic theft from government stores in 1789.

The problem began at the top with the Marine commandant Robert Ross, described by a subordinate as 'without exception the most disagreeable commanding officer I ever knew'. He himself felt slighted by a lack of consultation, although Phillip's commission allowed him to govern without a formal council, and naval captains were neither required nor expected to consult more than they thought fit. Phillip clearly explained his own orders to Ross, and London's expectations, but he continued to be a self-sufficient master of detail in managing the colony and Ross a touchy and bad example of subordinate leadership.

Such 'want of temper' in Ross and other officers added to more material problems until March 1790, when Phillip despatched him along with 280 convict men, women and children in the *Sirius* and the *Supply* to Norfolk Island, 1,000 miles off the coast to the north-west. He had already sent a party of 22 there in February 1789 under King, again to head off possible French occupation. King reported that the soil was rich and cultivable. A further 40 went in October, then Ross's party and many others after the arrival of the Second and Third Fleets. All were sustained by a brutal and eventually exterminating dependence on the mutton bird, a migratory species that spent March to August on the island: it made excellent eating. Despite many difficulties, the establishment of a successful sub-colony seemed possible, but ultimately circumstances were against this outcome. The timber from the tall island pines proved to be too brittle for masts and the local flax too coarse and difficult to work by normal methods for canvas. More critically, while free agriculture could have supported the island under good government, the sadistic incompetence of its regime after 1800 under the New South Wales Corps turned it into a living hell for new convicts and those already emancipated there, and it was abandoned in 1813–14.

By early 1790, poor crop yields and diminished stores meant that starvation loomed at Port Jackson, a principal reason for the departure of Ross's party. No one then knew that Phillip's first reports home had resulted in the storeship *Guardian* sailing from England the previous September. Commanded by Lieutenant Edward Riou – a former midshipman with Cook – she carried two years' stores, agricultural supervisors and two dozen convicts chosen for their farming or building skills.

His Majesty's Brig *Supply* 1790 off Lord Howe Island [and]
His Majesty's Ship *Sirius* in Sydney Cove 1789 (details), by George Roper, 1792.

She also collected many more plants and animals from the Cape but then hit an iceberg in the Indian Ocean on 13 December 1789 and lost her rudder. Riou's brilliant seamanship got her back to Cape Town, where she was wrecked in a storm, although part of her cargo was saved and later sent on. Had Riou arrived at Port Jackson, the *Sirius* would probably not have sailed with Ross to Norfolk Island, from where the *Supply* returned on 5 April 1790 bringing the dreadful news that she too had been wrecked on the surrounding reef, though without casualties.

On 3 June 1790, hungry despondency after loss of the *Sirius* was relieved when Phillip's lookout station on South Head signalled the arrival of the *Lady Juliana*. Nearly 11 months out from Plymouth, the ship brought 225 female convicts and, more importantly, transformed the morale of the colonists. They now learnt of the loss of the *Guardian*, of the outbreak of the French Revolution, and that the *Lady Juliana* was the first of a 'Second Fleet', all of which had arrived by the end of the month – the storeship *Gorgon*, and the transports *Neptune*, *Surprize* and *Scarborough* (again).

The extra mouths to feed, the hundreds who landed sick, the fact that many of the newcomers were too old or infirm to work and the disruptions created by the fresh injection of a criminal element added to immediate problems, which, from July 1790 to October 1791, included drought. Nonetheless, the Second Fleet's arrival proved a watershed. With it came further stores, plants, animals and some of the more skilled convicts and supervisors originally sent in the *Guardian*; all of these helped strengthen the colony and give Phillip means to help those, like Ruse, who were trying to make their own way. He also sent the *Supply* to obtain further supplies from Batavia (Jakarta). It returned in October 1790, followed in December by a hired storeship, these cargoes helping carry them through 1791. The sickly Third Fleet straggled in between August and October of that year, when Phillip sent the *Atlantic* back to Calcutta for further supplies just as the drought broke, ensuring the good harvest of 1792. The *Atlantic* returned in June, two more storeships came in from England by that November, and thereafter Sydney's transformation from harbour to regular port began. By the end of 1792 there were more than 4,000 colonists under Phillip's jurisdiction, some 1,100 of these being on Norfolk Island. By then the principal mainland agriculture took place on a thousand productive government acres and more than 500 in private hands, most on the better land round Parramatta. Phillip had also made land grants to 66 people living there or nearby by that October. Fifty-three of these were emancipated convicts, though one of Phillip's causes for regret was that many of the abler men preferred to work their way home when their sentences expired.

DISTRESSING SITUATION OF THE *GUARDIAN* SLOOP, CAPT. RIOU, AFTER STRIKING ON A FLOATING ISLAND OF ICE; artist unknown, published by Thomas Tegg, 1809.

The rudder and part of the keel were torn off but Riou, one of Cook's third-voyage midshipmen, got the ship and 60 others on board back to Cape Town. The other 259 took to the five boats, of which only the launch holding 15 made it. Most of the stores later salvaged from the *Guardian* eventually reached Australia.

The other great change came in the arrival with the Second Fleet of the first companies of the New South Wales Corps, under Major Francis Grose, to relieve Ross's Marines. Grose had been wounded fighting in America but revived his career by helping raise the corps specifically for Australian service. Unlike with the Marines, the intention was for them to settle there, many bringing wives. The calibre of the corps's men was poor, but its role included the civilian administrative and supervisory tasks to which Ross's officers had objected. Phillip himself foresaw that substantial expansion of agriculture would require a quasi-military organisation but was much disturbed in later years by the immediate direction this took.

Grose was encouraged by what he saw on arrival. As the new lieutenant-governor, he inherited Ross's farm and after Phillip left he and a short-term successor commanded the colony until 1795, when Hunter returned as governor. Grosse militarised the administration, replaced civilian magistrates with his own officers, abolished Phillip's egalitarian methods and accelerated land grants to his own men – most significantly offering his officers 100 acres each with ten convict labourers to work it at government expense. The control of labour was largely vested in his new regimental paymaster, Lieutenant John Macarthur – a central figure in the military 'mafia' which quickly established itself as Australia's first governing and property-owning elite. This shift was commercially launched in 1793 when Macarthur organised the cartel that, using credit accessed against pay, bought 7,500 gallons of rum and the other cargo of an American trader, and sold it on in the colony at a huge profit. The transaction prefigured the corps's ongoing control of trade through Sydney, aided by emancipated convict trader allies, their gains being used to buy up land from the many less successful ex-convict farmers. In this way, arriving transportees effectively became slaves to the 'Rum Corps', as it became known, being used for its private benefit and remaining in its thrall after their sentences expired.

LAST CAMPAIGNS

Phillip was not there to see these developments. Tired and ill by the autumn of 1792, he anticipated formal permission to return home, embarking in the *Atlantic* on 11 December with 'the honors due to his rank and situation in the colony'. With him went his two Aboriginal protégés, live kangaroos, dingoes and other animals, and natural specimens to add to those he had already sent back to Banks and others. He reached England in May 1793 via the Cape and Rio. After reporting to the authorities in London and clarifying legal matters arising from the death (in 1792) of his estranged wife, he resigned his governorship in October and went to Bath to recover his health, though requesting further active service. There he met 43-year-old Isabella Whitehead, a well-provided spinster, and they embarked

FOUNDING OF THE SETTLEMENT OF
PORT-JACKSON AT BOTANY BAY, NEW
SOUTH WALES (detail), by Thomas Gosse,
artist and engraver, 1799.

An idealised image of the foundation of
Sydney, with the town already established in
the background. It emphasises the natural
resources of the land; its amenability to rearing
European stock; the directive role of the naval
and military personnel involved; the presence
of a gentlemanly civilian element among early
arrivals (the man shooting on the left); and
British dominance over both the Aboriginal
population and the convict-colonists, the
latter being reformed by redemptive labour.

Bronze bust (1932) of Arthur Phillip, 'Citizen of London, founder and first Governor of Australia', in the church of St Mary-le-Bow, Cheapside, London, by Charles Hartwell RA (1873–1951). The bust is based on a portrait of 1786 by Francis Wheatley, now in Australia. It was originally in St Mildred's, Bread Street, which was destroyed by wartime bombing in 1941.

in May 1794 on a late and what seems to have been happy marriage.

Well regarded in naval, government and scientific circles, Phillip continued to advise on Australian matters and to support the careers of valued former subordinates there, particularly Philip Gidley King, who succeeded John Hunter as governor in 1800. He himself returned to active service in 1796, commanding in rapid succession the *Alexander* (in which he had been a lieutenant), the *Swiftsure* and the *Blenheim*. In the last two he was in the Earl of St Vincent's Mediterranean Fleet, gaining both his and Nelson's approval, and he pleased St Vincent further in conducting a delicate diplomatic mission at Lisbon for three months in 1797–98. It was thus the worst disappointment of his life when the earl allowed him to be replaced as captain of the *Blenheim* after Rear-Admiral Frederick took her as his flagship in February 1798. Worse, in retrospect, was the fact that Phillip left the *Swiftsure* only at St Vincent's request, which denied him enjoying a captain's glory in her at the Battle of the Nile that August. It was also characteristic of the time that, despite his generous pay and pension as founding governor of New South Wales, that position gained him none of the public honours granted to captains for such fighting service, often only very brief.

Phillip never had another ship and his last naval roles were in command of the Sea Fencibles – volunteer coastal defence forces – in Hampshire, and as general inspector of both the Impress Service (from 1801) and the Sea Fencibles (1803–05). In December 1806 he and his wife moved permanently to Bath, where early in 1808 he had a stroke that left him partly paralysed in his right side, although clear in mind and able to resume a quiet social life. He reached the rank of full admiral by seniority in May 1814 and died with the fading summer on 31 August that year, aged 75.

4

THE 'SPIRIT
OF DISCOVERY'

The Tragic Voyage of Lapérouse

'The former spirit of discovery seemed to have vanished entirely.' —LAPÉROUSE

ON 26 JANUARY 1788, two French ships, the *Astrolabe* and the *Boussole*, sailed into Botany Bay. They were nearing the end of an ambitious voyage of scientific exploration in the Pacific Ocean, begun nearly three years earlier, in 1785, under the command of Jean-François de Galaup, comte de Lapérouse. His ships had originally been under orders to visit New Zealand rather than Australia, but new instructions from Paris had reached him in Kamchatka, on the Russian Pacific coast, that he was to investigate reports that Britain was planning to establish a new settlement in New South Wales. He arrived less than a week after the First Fleet, just as it was on the point of moving up the coast to the more suitable site of Port Jackson.

The two strange ships caused a certain amount of conjecture, if not consternation, in Botany Bay: were they Dutch and coming to dispossess the British? Could they be British ships with stores? If they were French, were the two countries at war again? In fact they were still at peace and the French were welcomed warmly when it was learnt that this was the famous Lapérouse expedition. The benefits of science were considered universal at the time and the great series of eighteenth-century European voyages of exploration, motivated, it was believed, by 'the enlarged and benevolent design of promoting the happiness of the human species', were seen as epitomising these lofty ideals. In consequence, it was not unusual for scientific ships of enemy nations to be helped, even during times of war. 'Europeans are all compatriots at this distance from their countries,' commented Lapérouse on their

OPPOSITE TABLEAU DES DECOUVERTES
DU CAPNE COOK, ET DE LA PÉROUSE
(detail), by Phelipeau (engraver) after Jacques
Grasset St Sauveur, artist and publisher.

The largely fanciful engraving of the lands
and peoples encountered by Cook and Lapérouse
was produced on the posthumous publication
of Lapérouse's voyage narrative around 1797
or 1798, edited by M.L.A. Milet Mureau.

welcome from the British, although in practice he found that their 'offers of assistance were restricted to good wishes for the ultimate success of our voyage' rather than including the stores the French desperately needed. In fairness to Governor Phillip (who had already gone to Port Jackson, and whom he did not meet), the young colony had little enough for itself.

The many savants on board the two French ships made the most of their time in what had become, since Cook's visit nearly 20 years earlier, natural history's most famous bay. The French botanists collected specimens and also planted some of the seeds that they had brought with them, adding to the varieties that Phillip's ships had carried out from Britain. The astronomers set up their instruments ashore in a temporary camp and made their observations. Lapérouse himself sent back copies of his journal and charts to the Ministry of Marine with the returning British convict transports. The French and British officers socialised happily, while on a more sombre note the French chaplain, Father Receveur, who had died as a result of wounds received during an attack on the ships' boats in Samoa, became, as far as is known, the first Frenchman to be buried in Australia. After a month the *Astrolabe* and the *Boussole* left Botany Bay planning, as Lapérouse informed both his minister and Governor Phillip, a sweep north and east into the Pacific before turning west for Île de France (Mauritius) in the Indian Ocean and then home to Brest. They never reached their destination and it would be nearly 40 years before the mystery of their disappearance was solved.

It had been the largest and best-equipped voyage of scientific exploration ever mounted by France to that date. Since Louis-Antoine de Bougainville had crossed the Pacific and landed in Tahiti just before Cook in 1768, France had launched four voyages to the South Seas; none had been particularly distinguished and one had ended tragically. National pride, if nothing else, insisted that Lapérouse's voyage should be of a scale to rival, if not exceed, those of the famous Captain Cook. But there was a problem with this almost immediately, as any new voyage to the Pacific in the wake of Cook could do little more than fill in the few gaps left by the great navigator. The director of the Dépôt de Cartes et Plans, Charles Pierre Claret de Fleurieu, had argued in the original proposal that, while Cook had made Europe

'aware of the existence of vast countries, scattered islands and clusters of islands' in the Pacific, 'it must not be thought that we have a complete knowledge of the Earth; and in particular, of the North-West coasts of America, of those of Asia which face them, and of the islands that must be scattered in the sea that separates the parts of these two continents'. Orders were accordingly drawn up which directed Lapérouse to concentrate on the less well-covered areas of the north and west Pacific. What the expedition would inevitably lack in major new discoveries, however, would be more than compensated for by detailed surveys of those areas only touched on by Cook, and by the range and depth of the scientific research. Louis XVI, himself a keen geographer, took a close personal interest in the voyage, helping to plan its route and discussing its objectives with Lapérouse, while the names of the ships, *Astrolabe* and *Boussole* ('astrolabe' and 'compass'), underlined its navigational aims. This was exploration as high-profile national enterprise. Although France and Britain were at peace, and their scientific communities had cooperated informally on the preparations for the voyage, scientific exploration was by now inescapably part of national rivalry and was effectively being used by France as a way of continuing war by other, more peaceable, means.

Lapérouse was born Jean François de Galaup in 1741, at Albi in south-west France. Although his family had been climbing the social ladder for generations, it was still very much *petit noblesse*, and the name 'de Lapérouse' was acquired for him only when he decided to join the navy, which was a far more class-structured institution than its British counterpart. He was an experienced seaman and navigator who had made his name during the War of American Independence. Significantly, in the context of his Pacific voyage, he had gained a reputation as a humanitarian commander when, during an attack on British trading posts in Hudson Bay in 1782, he had treated his prisoners courteously and left provisions at the destroyed base for those who were away hunting at the time and who would otherwise have been unable to survive the winter. His second-in-command and captain of the *Astrolabe* was Paul Antoine Fleuriot de Langle, an equally experienced officer who had sailed with Lapérouse on the Hudson Bay raid.

PREPARATIONS FOR THE JOURNEY

Lapérouse was to take no fewer than 15 civilian scientists on the voyage, including artists, astronomers, civil engineers, surveyors, botanists, an ornithologist and a clockmaker; even the expedition's chaplain, the unfortunate Father Receveur, was an accomplished botanist. In this the voyage departed from the principle that had eventually been adopted in Britain. After Cook's difficulties with Banks over the structural changes needed to accommodate the large scientific party on the *Resolution*, and his even more uneasy relationship with the naturalist Johann Reinhold Forster on the voyage itself, the number of civilian scientists on the third voyage was cut dramatically. Cook took only an artist and an astronomer, and the rest of the scientific work was carried out by the officers, a practice from which the Admiralty would henceforth only rarely depart. In France in 1785, however, there was real excitement within the scientific community as its members competed for places on this prestigious expedition: the young Napoléon Bonaparte, who was shining in the mathematics class at the *école militaire*, applied unsuccessfully, while Georg Forster, the scientist who had accompanied Cook and his father on the second voyage, was briefly considered but eventually not invited as it was thought that it would ultimately be more interesting to consider the same things in different ways.

The head botanist was to be Joseph de La Martinière. France had long been aware of the commercial possibilities of plants from overseas, and since the 1750s colonial administrators in the French West Indies had been required to send samples of plants back to the Musée National d'Histoire Naturelle in Paris. Georges-Louis de Buffon, the eminent but now ageing author of the influential *Histoire naturelle* and head of the museum, was consulted on the question of appointing a suitable gardener to look after the plants on the voyage, and he referred the matter to Thouin, the King's head gardener, who in turn suggested a young man called Jean Nicolas Collignon and drew up a detailed list of instructions for him on how to collect plants and seeds and store them at sea. While at Brest preparing for the voyage, Collignon fell out with La Martinière, who believed that a botanical scientist should be in charge of a mere gardener, whereas Collignon thought he should be answerable only to Lapérouse. Although Lapérouse appeared to side with Collignon, and tried to keep the two men apart by transferring La Martinière to the *Boussole*, the argument was merely a foretaste of the squabbles that would break out periodically during the voyage.

The botanical objectives were twofold: the King's instructions to Lapérouse specified that on the one hand the botanists were to collect plants and specimens that 'would enrich Europe', and on the other they were to introduce useful European species to 'newly discovered countries', for:

> *Of all the benefits which the King's generosity can bestow on the inhabitants of newly discovered countries, plants that can help feed mankind are without doubt those which will bring them the most lasting benefits, and can best increase their happiness.*

To this end, Collignon carried 59 live fruit trees and shrubs and enormous quantities of vegetable seeds and bulbs. When collecting rather than planting, he was also instructed to ignore as much as possible the distractions of beautiful and exotic flora and concentrate instead on useful plants. Special cases were designed and built and sent to Brest already carefully packed with the live plants, for Thouin considered that they were as vulnerable on the two-week journey from Paris as they would be on the voyage to the Pacific. The plant boxes were an advanced design with three layers of protection. The first was a mesh of fine tin wire that protected the plants from normal shipboard accidents. On top of that was a close-fitting panel of glass designed to be in place virtually all the time. Watering was carried out through two holes in the sides, which would remain open except in the most extreme weather conditions to allow the air to circulate freely in the box.

A glazed cabinet for transporting plants made for the Lapérouse expedition; pen and ink and watercolour, notebook of Gaspard Duché de Vancy (died 1788).

The third level of protection was hinged wooden shuttering, which sealed the box from the elements and prevented undue loss of moisture. Thouin thought that the plants should be able to last two weeks without watering. Forty years later Nathaniel Ward developed the Wardian case in Britain following a similar principle, and this was to revolutionise the notoriously difficult business of transporting plants by sea.

ENTERING THE PACIFIC

The *Astrolabe* and the *Boussole* sailed from Brest in August 1785, heading for Cape Horn and into the Pacific Ocean, which they were to cross before beginning their investigations in the west Pacific. Lapérouse was given considerable freedom to deviate from his orders as circumstances dictated and he took advantage of this immediately. Their first port of call in the Pacific was in Chile, at Concepción, where they stayed for three weeks before setting off for Easter Island, the most easterly of the Polynesian islands. The visit there was as brief as it had been for Cook's *Resolution*, the two ships staying for less than 24 hours. Easter Island was

ISLANDERS AND MONUMENTS OF EASTER ISLAND;
engraving after Gaspard Duché de Vancy.

bleak and its lack of vegetation created a starkly different landscape from the luxuriant greenery found on the many other Polynesian islands. In 1774, Georg and J.R. Forster had described the island as an ecological disaster: 'Its wretched soil, loaded with innumerable stones, furnishes a Flora of only 20 species; among these, ten are cultivated; not one grows to a tree, and almost all are low, shrivelled and dry.'

It was obvious to the French that they had landed among a people who would benefit considerably from the introduction of European plants and vegetables. Accordingly, Collignon set about sowing cabbages, carrots, pumpkins, maize, beet and trees in places he thought them likely to succeed. Thouin's instructions were typically detailed on this and we can assume that Collignon chose his 'favourable aspects' with care and prepared the ground thoroughly. As they left within 24 hours, however, Collignon could not have spent much time establishing the plantation; neither, one imagines, would he have been able to fulfil Thouin's wish to 'inspire the love of gardening in some of the natives', which, if he could also make them understand 'the importance of the vegetables', would 'fill twice the aim of doing good that one hopes from the mission'. In fact, Lapérouse wrote in his journal, the Easter Islanders seemed singularly uninterested in the 'benefits' that Europe was bringing:

> We didn't land on their island to do them anything other than good: we loaded them with presents; we cultivated the weak with caresses, particularly the children. We sowed all sorts of useful grains in their fields. In their houses we left pigs, goats and sheep, which will in all likelihood multiply. Nevertheless, they threw stones at us, and they stole everything that they could manage to lift.

Since Bougainville's voyage had been published 20 years earlier describing Tahiti in terms of classical beauty and simplicity, Polynesians had come to embody the Rousseauesque 'noble savage' living in harmony with Nature. Rousseau's conception had never gained universal acceptance; it was only one of a number of competing theories of human origins, but it was far stronger in France than in Britain, especially among the classically educated classes from whom the scientists on board the *Astrolabe* and the *Boussole* were drawn. The noble savage was a simplified part of what was actually a far more sophisticated theory, but at its heart it was a belief in the essential good of humankind, in a primitive, 'untouched' state once shared by all peoples in which no one knew jealousy, greed, deceit or hate. These vices were supposed to be the by-products of an over-civilised western society; the proper business of enlightened European travellers, therefore, was not to infect 'natural man' with the diseases of civilisation, but simply to help improve their living condition by introducing useful crafts or manufactures, for example, or those useful plants and vegetables cultivated in Europe. While many of the scientists on board the French ships would have seen Collignon's plantings in that philo-sophical light, others, including Lapérouse, did not. The belief in the Polynesian noble savage had already taken a severe battering after the killings of Cook in Hawaii in 1779 and the French navigator Marion du Fresne in New Zealand in 1772, after which even Rousseau professed himself shocked that the 'children of nature' could behave in such a way.

HAWAII, ALASKA AND THE PACIFIC NORTH-WEST COAST

The voyage continued north to the Sandwich Islands (Hawaii) where, mindful of Cook's fate, Lapérouse was careful to protect his landing parties, and then further north to Alaska, where he gave himself three months to explore the North American coastline down to Monterey in California. The northern part of this coast had taken on a new significance to Europe after Cook's discovery of the trade in sea-otter furs and, although the aim of Lapérouse's voyage was scientific explo-ration, as befitted its royal backing, commercial exploitation had always lurked in the background. Lapérouse's ridiculously ambitious survey plan took no account of the intricate nature of the coast; it was to take the British navigator George Vancouver three full seasons to survey the same area. Although it did not help that Lapérouse's ships were held back by the fog, just as Cook's had been ten years earlier, the French survey actually advanced European knowledge of this coastline very little. A few places where the ships anchored for a few days, such as Port des Français about 600 miles north of Nootka Sound, were surveyed and studied to a very high standard. When the size of Port des Français became obvious to Lapérouse he hoped that he had found the entrance to the North-West Passage – 'Imagine a vast basin, whose depth in the centre is impossible to estimate, edged by great, steep, snow-covered mountains,' he wrote; 'this is the channel by which we planned to enter into the heart of America' – but this hope was dashed when they followed the two arms at the head of the bay only to find that both ended almost immediately in huge glaciers.

The botanists were also disappointed: although there was a rich supply of greens, which the seamen ate in soups and salads, as well as large numbers of flowering plants and berries, Lapérouse noted that 'none of this vegetation is unknown in Europe; M. la Martinière found during his various excursions only three plants which he believes to be new, and one knows that a botanist can make a similar find in the environs of Paris'. Neither did the Tlingit people impress Lapérouse: he described them, their customs and their environment at some length, but his underlying attitude is summed up in the dismissive comment that they were 'as rough and barbarous as their soil is stony and untilled'. European reactions to the peoples of the north-west coast of America were complicated and often contradictory. Although Lapérouse, for example, condemned them as barbarous, he also saw their cultures as being more advanced than those of the widely admired Polynesians, who had become the standard by which 'primitives' were judged. The Tlingit could 'forge iron, work copper, spin the hair of various animals and sew with this wool a material similar to our tapestries'. They were also keen and shrewd traders, Lapérouse noticing that the population of the bay quadrupled during his visit as a steady stream of canoes loaded with furs arrived to take advantage of the unexpected commercial opportunity represented by the French ships.

The harbour had been charted accurately by the surveyors de Monneron and Bernizet, but, shortly before the ships were due to leave, Lapérouse gave the order for three boats to complete the survey by sounding the depth of the water around the narrow entrance, through which the tide could rush at up to nine knots. The French ships had entered this dangerous passage only with considerable difficulty, Lapérouse admitting that 'never in the thirty years I have spent at sea have I seen two ships so near destruction'. He placed the boats under the command of his first lieutenant, d'Escures, 'a Knight of St. Louis who [had himself] commanded some of the King's ships'. Ignoring his captain's written and verbal orders to approach the pass only at slack water, and not to approach it at all if there was a swell, d'Escures took the boats in while the tide was still running fast and there was a heavy sea breaking on the reefs; two of the boats, including that of d'Escures, went too close and were sucked into the current and capsized. There were no survivors and no bodies were ever recovered. Lapérouse erected a monument to the sailors on Cenotaph Island, and the physicist de Lamanon composed a short tribute: 'A l'entrée du Port ont péri vingt-un braves marins; qui que vous soyés, mêlés vos larmes aux nôtres' (At the entrance to this port, twenty-one brave sailors perished. Whoever you may be, mingle your tears with ours).

The ships then made their way south, sailing past what would become Vancouver Island without discovering its insularity or spotting the entrance to the huge sound behind it, then down the Oregon and California coasts to the new Spanish colony of Monterey. The Spaniards may have viewed Lapérouse's arrival with as much suspicion as the British would in Botany Bay, for the French ships were one more worrying sign that Spain's traditional monopoly of the Pacific was under threat, but the governor was generous in his welcome and the ships finally left after a ten-day stay loaded down with fresh food. They headed across the Pacific to Macao in China, which they reached on 1 January 1787, unexpectedly discovering and nearly coming to grief on French Frigate Shoal, far to the north-west of the Sandwich Islands.

Macao

Macao had been trading with Europe since Portugal had leased the island from China in the early sixteenth century, so the scientists sensibly decided to take advantage of the comforts of home while they were available and rented a house in the town. They omitted to inform Lapérouse, however, or even let him know where they could be found, and he got his revenge by placing them all under arrest when they finally returned to the ships. Both sides sent strongly worded complaints to Fleurieu, who decided to ignore them, presumably working on the assumption that there was nothing he could do from such a distance and that the problems would have resolved themselves anyway by the time the expedition returned to France. The ships then left Macao, taking six Chinese sailors with them to make up for the losses in Port des Français, and visited Manila in the Philippines before heading north between Korea and Japan, conscious that for the first time they were sailing into waters that few Europeans had navigated and which none had surveyed. Here Lapérouse was able to make a real contribution to cartographic knowledge. As usual, the scientists landed and took samples when they could, with Collignon planting and collecting, often in appalling conditions. At Castries Bay

VIEW AT MACAO NEAR THE ENTRANCE TO THE RIVER OF CANTON, by John Webber, painted in 1784 from sketches taken in late 1779, towards the end of Cook's third voyage. It is presumed to be the picture exhibited under that title at the Royal Academy, London, in 1785. Lapérouse also called at Macao on his outward voyage to the Pacific.

on coast of Tartary he tried to light a fire with gunpowder to thaw out his freezing hands, but his thumb was broken when the powder exploded.

In August 1787 they reached Kamchatka, the most easterly point of Siberia, where Captain Clerke had been buried in 1779 towards the end of Cook's third voyage. It was here that Lapérouse received his orders to investigate Botany Bay as well as the pleasant news that he had been promoted. Before heading south he took the precaution of arranging to send home his up-to-date journal, charts and notes with Barthélemy de Lesseps, a young diplomat who had come on the voyage as Russian interpreter; it took him more than a year to get back to Paris. (Ferdinand, the nephew of de Lesseps, would later build the Suez Canal.)

TRAGEDY IN BOTANY BAY

Lapérouse sailed south in a broad arc through the Pacific Ocean, taking his ships through the Samoan islands. Here tragedy struck again. In a letter sent to Thouin from Botany Bay, Collignon described the incident:

> Since I had the honour of writing you my last letter from Kamchatka, we've disembarked in [a] few more landing places. Amongst others at an island in the Navigators [Samoa], where I was hoping to take some roots of the bread-fruit tree, of which there were many in great quantity. But on the second day of our visit, which I had planned for this task, and for which I had landed the necessary instruments, [there was] a tragic, cruel scene where we lost several men, some of the first rank of officers, and I just escaped becoming a victim myself, having been wounded in several places. But I, as well as several others, had the happiness of escaping from the hands of our assassins, inhabitants and indigenous people of these parts, who behaved in this extreme way despite the fact that our procedures were the most humanitarian imaginable. But unfortunately we have been dupes of our own good nature, and this is what has denied me any possibility up to the present of procuring this most valuable plant.

They had arrived at Tutuila on 10 December 1787 and, after what had appeared to be a friendly reception, the captain of the *Astrolabe*, de Langle, told Lapérouse that he wanted to land and take on board fresh water; in this, Lapérouse acknowledged, de Langle was following 'the system used by Captain Cook [who] believed that fresh water was a hundred times better than the water we had in the hold'. But Lapérouse did not subscribe to this theory and argued in turn that the ships had enough water to get them to Botany Bay and that landing was therefore an unnecessary risk. De Langle insisted and Lapérouse finally agreed, writing later in his journal that 'M. de Langle was a man with such judgment and such qualities that these facts more than anything else caused me to give my consent'. It is interesting to put de Langle's refusal to accept Lapérouse's orders alongside that of d'Escures in Port des Français and to speculate whether they indicate any deeper problems on the expedition. Social rank was a perennial problem in the pre-revolutionary French navy; incidents where subordinate officers refused to take orders from their military superiors because they were their social inferiors were neither unknown nor conducive to the efficient running of ships. D'Escures was the son of an admiral and de Langle a *vicomte*, the social superior of Lapérouse – it was rumoured that de Langle had even been considered for command of the expedition for that reason; while the two men had sailed together for a number of years and clearly liked and respected each other, social rank may have complicated their relationship. Whatever the reason, de Langle had his way at Samoa and led the boats ashore.

Several of the scientists, including Collignon and the physicist Lamanon, joined the watering party of 60 men. Because of the lie of the land, the boats were soon out of sight of the ships, and when they approached the shore they discovered that the tide was out, which meant that the boats grounded, vulnerably, a considerable distance from the beach. A number of Samoans came out to the boats and began trading with the sailors, and the situation appeared fairly peaceful; the seamen started to fill the barrels from the freshwater stream flowing down to the beach, while Collignon began to explore the area around the beach, putting samples of interesting plants into a sack he had slung over his back. According to Lapérouse, who tried to piece together the chain of events later on, the situation deteriorated rapidly when the seamen and islanders began arguing about price. By this time more than a thousand Samoans had gathered on the beach; Collignon began to move back to the boats just as the situation broke into confused and bloody conflict. Both Lamanon and de Langle, as well as ten of their men, were killed.

THE SEARCH FOR LAPÉROUSE

The *Astrolabe* and the *Boussole* sailed on for Botany Bay, whence they were to depart on 10 March 1788 and disappear into the Pacific Ocean. By early 1790 concerns about the expedition's fate were being expressed publicly in France. As the years passed with still no word, the story generated its own literature, with poems, plays, pantomimes and melodramas appearing in Dutch, English, French and Italian. The loss of Lapérouse touched all of Europe, although, admittedly, not to the same degree as the death of Cook. In February 1791 Fleurieu declared the men officially lost. Pressure grew for a search expedition, and later that year the National Assembly gave Bruny d'Entrecasteaux command of two ships, the *Recherche* and the *Espérance* ('search' and 'hope'), which finally sailed in September 1791. It was to be

MASSACRE OF DE LANGLE, LAMANON AND TEN OTHERS OF THE
TWO CREWS; engraving by James Heath after Nicolas Ozanne, from charts
and plates to Lapérouse's *Voyage*, 1798.

both a rescue mission and a voyage of discovery, for d'Entrecasteaux took with him
almost as many scientists as Lapérouse had done.

But where to begin the search? Lapérouse's last letter from Botany Bay said
that he was planning to strike out into the Pacific in order to complete his original
instructions to explore the islands of the western Pacific; this meant that he would
sail to 'the south of New Caledonia, Mendaña's Santa Cruz, the south coast of de
Surville's Arsacides, and Bougainville's Louisiades, to see if they join New Guinea
or not'. He went on:

> By the end of July 1788 I will pass between New Guinea and New Holland by
> another channel than the Endeavour's, if there be one. I will visit, during September
> and part of October, the Gulf of Carpentaria and western New Holland as far as
> Van Diemen's Land, but in a way that will enable me to sail north early enough to
> reach the Île de France.

This was a lot of ocean to cover, and d'Entrecasteaux's search was complicated by a report from Phillip's deputy, Captain Hunter of the *Sirius*, saying that he believed Lapérouse may have been wrecked east of Timor, for he claimed to have seen some Admiralty Islanders wearing French naval uniforms. D'Entrecasteaux would begin the search there, but decided to approach it via the south coast of Australia, where he made the important discovery of the harbour on which the city of Hobart, Tasmania, now stands. The discoveries made by the relief expedition surpassed those made by poor Lapérouse, while the charts of the south coast of Australia produced by d'Entrecasteux's civilian engineer, Beautemps-Beaupré, were models of their type and would be used extensively by Matthew Flinders in his survey of Australia in 1801–03. Beautemps-Beaupré later wrote a textbook on marine surveying which was translated into English in the 1820s and quickly supplanted those by Alexander Dalrymple and Murdoch Mackenzie, published in the 1770s, which had until then remained the only books available on the subject.

OPPOSITE NAUFRAGE DE L'ASTROLABE;
hand-coloured lithograph by Louis LeBreton.
    An imaginative depiction of the wrecks
of the *Astrolabe* and the *Boussole* on the rocks
of Vanikoro. LeBreton sailed as a surgeon on
Dumont d'Urville's Pacific voyage of 1837–40.

RIGHT Medal commemorating the expedition
of the *Boussole* and the *Astrolabe*, by Pierre
Simon Benjamin Duvivier, 1785.

Over two seasons d'Entrecasteaux explored Hunter's theory about the missing ships and retraced as much as possible of Lapérouse's projected route, but he found no trace of them. In May 1793, the search party reached the Santa Cruz group and saw to the north of Santa Cruz itself an island that did not appear on any map; this they named Île de la Recherche, after their ship, but sailed on without further investigation. It was actually the island of Vanikoro, and it was here that Lapérouse's ships had been wrecked – and it is even possible that two of the crew were still alive on the island when the *Recherche* and the *Espérance*

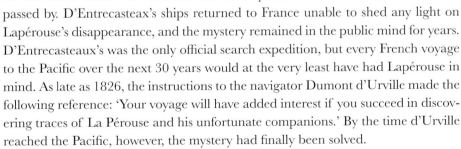

passed by. D'Entrecasteax's ships returned to France unable to shed any light on Lapérouse's disappearance, and the mystery remained in the public mind for years. D'Entrecasteaux's was the only official search expedition, but every French voyage to the Pacific over the next 30 years would at the very least have had Lapérouse in mind. As late as 1826, the instructions to the navigator Dumont d'Urville made the following reference: 'Your voyage will have added interest if you succeed in discovering traces of La Pérouse and his unfortunate companions.' By the time d'Urville reached the Pacific, however, the mystery had finally been solved.

In 1826, an Irish trader called Peter Dillon heard of an islander offering for sale a sword hilt of French design that he had found on Vanikoro. Intrigued and mindful of the reward of 10,000 francs offered way back in 1791 by the French government for news of Lapérouse, Dillon bought the hilt and took it with him to Calcutta, where he managed to persuade the East India Company to let him lead a search expedition to the island. Once on Vanikoro, he was able to buy a number of objects, clearly of European origin, which had come from a reef on the west coast of the island. He also learnt something of the fate of Lapérouse and his companions from questioning the islanders. The two ships, still sailing in company, had struck the reef during a cyclone. One ship had almost immediately broken up and the surviving crew were killed by islanders as they struggled ashore; the other remained relatively intact and the crew were able to stay together as a group and build an encampment on the beach: Dillon was shown a large clearing which was supposed to be the site of the camp. This party managed to construct a boat from the timbers of their wrecked ship and, leaving two men behind on the island, they eventually sailed away to an unknown but imaginable fate. Dillon took the relics and his story to France, where an ageing Barthélemy de Lesseps confirmed that they belonged to the expedition. Dillon was received by the French king, Charles X, who ensured that he received his 10,000 francs as well as a government pension of 4,000 francs per annum, and that he was made a Chevalier of the Légion d'honneur. Dumont

MONUMENT TO MONR DE LA PÉROUSE AND HIS COMPANIONS, ERECTED AT BOTANY BAY; lithograph by William Spreat after R.M. Westmacott, from the latter's *Sketches in Australia* (1848). The monument was erected in 1825 at the instigation of Hyacinthe de Bougainville (son of the explorer Louis-Antoine) and P.-A. de N. du Camper, both of the French navy, during their round-the-world voyage in the *Thétis* and the *Espérance*, 1824–26.

d'Urville arrived on Vanikoro four months after Dillon had left, in response to a message left for him in Hobart, but he was not able to add materially to the story, although he collected a few more artefacts and raised some guns from the wreck site. Over the next 150 years other expeditions and dives on the wrecks would find more objects; the anchors raised in 1883 adorn the statue of Lapérouse in his home town of Albi where, more recently, the Musée Lapérouse has opened.

The journals sent back from Kamchatka and Botany Bay were edited by an army officer, Baron de Milet-Mureau, and published in 1797 as part of an arrangement that would have provided a pension for Lapérouse's widow. But, being incomplete and lacking most of the scientific observations that were the voyage's primary purpose, and with the expedition's fate still unknown, the book did not grasp the public imagination and was not a financial success. Lapérouse's achievements have always been overshadowed by his disappearance in much the same way that Cook's third voyage was by his death on Hawaii. Those achievements were, in fact, considerable, although necessarily diminished by the voyage's abrupt end. Lapérouse consciously adopted many of the practices established by Cook, and with similar success: in just under three years he lost only one man to scurvy, although, like Cook, he was no nearer to understanding the underlying causes of the disease. He used similar navigational and cartographical techniques to Cook and the resulting charts were produced to a high degree of accuracy – the shortcomings in his survey of the American coast were due largely to bad weather and lack of time. While most of the scientific data were lost with the shipwreck, the information that was sent back from Spanish America, Macao and Port Jackson was valuable and the indications are that, although Lapérouse undoubtedly had his problems with the civilian scientists, this did not affect the quality of their work. Perhaps the single most significant achievement was, as the French historian Alain Morgat has observed, that 'Lapérouse ushered in the era of scientific navigation in France and played a role analogous to that represented by Cook in the history of exploration'. While his expedition can be seen as a continuation of an already well-established tradition of French maritime activity in the Pacific, of which Louis Antoine de Bougainville's voyage is the most well-known example, Lapérouse's was the first of a number of large state-sponsored voyages that would make important contributions to Europe's knowledge of the Pacific. These voyages would also eventually usher in colonisation when Aubert Dupetit Thouars annexed the Marquesas and Tahiti in the 1830s, laying the foundations for France's Pacific empire.

Painted from the Life by J.Russell R.A.Crayon Painter to his Majesty
and their Royal Highness's the Prince of Wales & Duke of York.

Engraved by J.Conde.

CAPᵀ BLIGH.

5

THE TRIALS OF CAPTAIN BLIGH

APTAIN COOK'S domination of Pacific exploration makes it easy to overlook the group of younger talents who began their careers under him as midshipmen or master's mates, or in other capacities. George Vancouver is covered elsewhere (see Chapter 7), but, among others less well known, Alexander Hood was the nephew of celebrated admirals and became a captain at 21, dying heroically in a single-ship duel in 1798, and Edward Riou played a small part in the Botany Bay story (see pp.110–12) before being killed under Nelson at Copenhagen in 1801. Richard Grindall (on the second voyage) became a distinguished fighting officer who commanded the 98-gun *Prince* at Trafalgar in 1805. He died as a retired admiral, as did Cook's nephew, Isaac Smith, and James Burney, whose importance as a historian of Pacific exploration augmented the fame of his otherwise artistically talented family. James Trevenen saw much later action and died in Russian service against the Swedes, after war forestalled his attempt to lead a Russian survey voyage to the Bering Strait. Lastly here, the American-born Nathaniel Portlock and George Dixon, the *Discovery*'s armourer on the third voyage, captained the two ships of the King George's Sound Company that pioneered the British fur trade on the American north-west coast in 1785–88. They returned around the world, which Portlock circumnavigated again on a voyage to transport breadfruit from Tahiti to the West Indies in 1791–93. On this occasion it was as commander of the schooner *Assistant* in the second 'breadfruit expedition' led by Cook's third-voyage sailing master in the *Resolution*, William Bligh. Bligh is, of course, best known for his first breadfruit-transplantation attempt in the *Bounty*, which ended in a mid-Pacific mutiny in 1789. Cast adrift, Bligh and 17 companions (an eighteenth was killed early on) were saved only by his own skills as a seaman and navigator after an escape to safety in a voyage of more than 3,600 nautical miles. Had they died – which was a far more likely outcome – we might now know as little of the *Bounty* affair as we do of the disaster that overtook Lapérouse at the same time on the reefs of Vanikoro.

MUTINY ON THE *BOUNTY*, 1787–89

Born on 9 September 1754, William Bligh came from an old Cornish family with naval, military, aristocratic and customs connections, his father being a Plymouth customs officer. He went to sea at the age of 15, rated as an able seaman (AB) until 1774 and as a midshipman thereafter, primarily learning his navigation and seamanship from three years (1771–74) in the 36-gun frigate *Crescent* in the West Indies, and two in the sloop *Ranger*. The latter was involved in anti-smuggling operations in the Irish Sea, based at Douglas on the Isle of Man, where Bligh formed significant connections. It was at that point, when he was 21, that Cook picked him as master of the *Resolution*, undoubtedly over more experienced men.

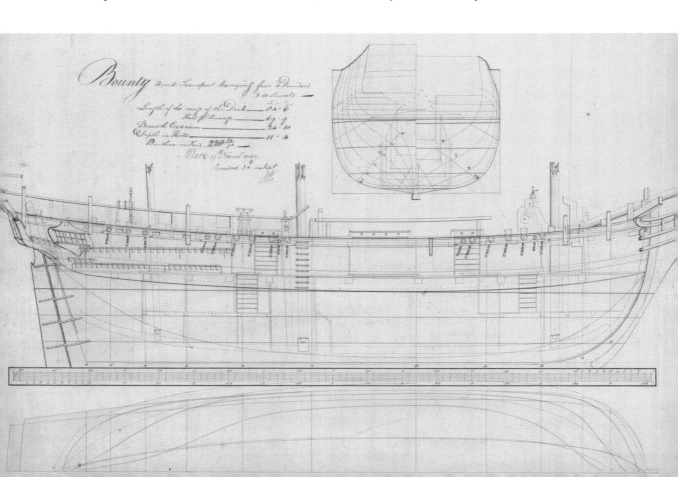

This suggests that someone important recommended him, though Cook must also have been impressed by his journals and charts, which Bligh would have submitted to the Admiralty. None of these from his pre-*Resolution* days survives, and he later stated that he lost all his own early charts from 1774 onward with the *Bounty*.

As master and the expedition's other principal surveyor, Bligh certainly worked closely with Cook. A number of his charts from the latter's last voyage are identifiable, and whatever polish he acquired from Cook as a navigator and surveyor, he closely followed his shipboard regime on both the *Bounty* and the *Providence* voyages. This included insistence on high standards of cleanliness in vessels and men, a good antiscorbutic diet, however much sailors disliked 'greens', and exercise, including compulsory dancing to a seaman fiddler: this was Bligh's innovation in the *Bounty*, even though the man he chose was near-blind and of little other use. He also maintained Cook's then unusual practice of a three-watch system which allowed eight hours' rest in twelve rather than four on, four off. Less admirably, he would have seen Cook's occasional gesticulating outbursts of temper – his own being similar in style – which Cook's crews called his 'heivas', after a vigorous Tahitian dance.

Bligh's failing, though one that only the *Bounty*'s circumstances made critical, was to have a short fuse too much of the time. A cautious and often self-congratulatory perfectionist, he saw others' failures to meet the standards that he required, in both expected ends and the means by which they were to be achieved, as worrying slackness. While 'placid and interesting' in private, on duty he switched from civility to invective with dizzying ease, though he was not physically brutal by the standards of the day. He was not an excessive 'flogger' either of his own men or of light-fingered Tahitians, finding it little deterrent in the latter case. Cook, by contrast, dealt more severely on various occasions with Polynesian pilfering, especially on his last voyage: on Hawaii, his loss of patience with it contributed, in part, to his death.

Bligh's genius – of which he seems to have remained unaware – was for inducing severe stress in subordinates who disappointed him, especially those lacking hardened maturity. The Navy did not recognise this critical weakness either, since it ran by clear rules, with no concept of 'psychological' mitigation to explain disobedience and failure of duty. Bligh's reputation was tarnished by what emerged about his style of command in the court martial of the *Bounty* mutineers – not least since he was by then again in the Pacific and unable to defend himself. However, the worst official reprimand that he ever had was as captain of the *Warrior* in 1805, when one of his lieutenants called him before a court martial for 'tyrannical behaviour'. The charge being partly upheld, he was simply reprimanded and told to moderate his language. It is more notable that while he was one of many captains turned out of their ships during the fleet mutiny at the Nore in 1797, when he was in command of the *Director*, he was not on the mutineers' blacklist of the hundred most unpopular officers, whom the Admiralty agreed to replace.

Rather, he was well respected by his crew and defended them in the affair, blaming agitators who had come aboard from other ships. In short, his fitness to command was well within accepted norms and his competence as a seaman, navigator and guardian of his men's welfare was exceptional. His volatility limited but did not stop his advancement, and it was other exceptional circumstances that combined with it to spark the Royal Navy's most famous mutiny, in the *Bounty*, one that was also very untypical in being neither a fleet 'strike' nor a single-ship revolt against unarguable tyranny.

Signs of Bligh's ability to make himself unpopular appeared on the *Resolution* after Cook's death on Hawaii in 1779. Both in the events surrounding that and on the rest of the voyage, Bligh behaved with resolution and professional skill. However, he did not respect John Gore, to whom command of the *Resolution* eventually devolved, and he appears to have alienated Cook's second lieutenant, James King, who brought the *Discovery* home in 1780. On their return, Gore, King and nearly every other officer were promoted, some less deserving than Bligh. Bligh himself was not, presumably because Gore and King did not recommend him. King was in fact almost Bligh's antithesis in personality, as expert an astronomer as Bligh was a navigator, popular and 'one of the politest, genteelest & best-bred men in the world'. When he completed the official write-up of the voyage proceedings, Bligh was incensed to find that all charts included that were not Cook's were credited to Henry Roberts – another post-voyage 'promotee' who only made fair copies of Cook's and Bligh's surveys. That Bligh received a one-eighth share of the publication profits confirms his creative rights, but King gave him no credit. Personal antipathy aside, the explanation for this probably lies in Bligh's private criticism of those accompanying Cook at his death and the absence of retribution against the Hawaiians. Lieutenant John Williamson's irresolution as the boat commander during that fatal skirmish was notorious but even he was promoted, only to have his cowardice confirmed by court martial after the Battle of Camperdown in 1797, when in command of the *Agincourt*. Bligh, by contrast, showed his courage there and had probably approached the *Bounty* voyage ten years earlier with some bitter memories and a point to prove.

Sitodium altile.

Otaheite.

Sydney Parkinson pinxit 1769.

In February 1781, at Douglas in the Isle of Man, Bligh began a happy 30-year marriage to Elizabeth Betham, intelligent daughter of Richard Betham LL.D, the local Receiver General of Customs there, and two weeks later was appointed master of the frigate *Belle Poule* in the North Sea. That August he fought in the Battle of the Dogger Bank, against the Dutch, after which he was at last promoted to lieutenant, briefly in the *Berwick* and the *Princess Amelia*, and then as sixth lieutenant of the *Cambridge* in March 1782. The *Cambridge* took part in Lord Howe's relief of Gibraltar from Spanish siege later in the year but was paid off at the war's end in January 1783. Bligh returned to his 'Betsy' and daughter Harriet (the first of six) at Douglas, but needed more than his half-pay to support them. Fortunately his wife's uncle was Duncan Campbell, a ship owner and the government contractor for the recently introduced prison-hulk system (see p.91). For the next four years Bligh gained profitable experience as a merchant captain commanding three of Campbell's West Indian traders as well as acting as his agent in Jamaica. It was in Campbell's *Britannia* in 1787 that he was persuaded to take on a well-educated and ambitious volunteer midshipman, of Cumbrian origin and Manx residence. This was Fletcher Christian, who had previously sailed only in the frigate *Eurydice*.

While Bligh and Christian made two voyages together in the *Britannia* and became ill-fated friends, a plan was evolving in London to transplant breadfruit, a staple of the Tahitian diet, to the West Indies as a cheap food for the enslaved African workforce on British plantations there. Cook's voyages had made the plant well known, notably to Joseph Banks, who had sailed on the *Endeavour* voyage and who was now President of the Royal Society. In May 1787 George III instructed Lord Sydney to issue orders for the Admiralty to allocate a ship to the experiment. The small vessel provided and the consequently inadequate command structure and deficient initial planning – none of which was the fault of Bligh – indicated that the Navy was less than enthusiastic. It was, however, a great opportunity for a suitable junior officer, and Bligh's name probably came up early given his Pacific and West Indian experience, with Campbell certainly lobbying Banks on his behalf. On his return in the *Britannia* in August 1787 it was Banks whom he thanked for his 'great goodness' in honouring him with the command, even before the Admiralty confirmed it.

By then the Navy Board had already bought a ship and was fitting her out. It had also been told to choose one no larger than 250 tons and, in the event, the selection fell to Banks and David Nelson, the senior gardener for the voyage, who had also sailed on Cook's last expedition. Their involvement ensured its suitability for plants but not for other factors that might have given pause to an experienced seaman like Bligh. Their choice, a 215-ton West Indiaman called *Bethia* but now renamed *Bounty*, was in fact the smallest vessel considered (90ft 10in x 24ft 4in, or 27.7m x 7.4m, and drawing 11ft 4in, or 3.5m). That was very small considering the nature of her mission

John Adams, alias Alexander Smith; print from a drawing by Midshipman Richard Beechey of HMS *Blossom*, which called at Pitcairn in 1825.

Adams was one of the more violent mutineers, and was their last survivor on Pitcairn Island. He died there aged about 67 in 1829, as the Christian patriarch of the Anglo-Tahitian community the mutineers had created.

and her prescribed passage, which was to be 'west-about' to Tahiti, on the shortest route via Cape Horn. From there, orders also directed her to circumnavigate westward, making up any breadfruit losses with other exotic plants from the East Indies.

By contrast, the solid *Endeavour* was of 368 tons, and after nearly losing her on the Great Barrier Reef, Cook never again sailed with just one ship. Of his other vessels, the *Discovery*, at 299 tons, was the smallest and *Resolution* the largest, at 462 tons. After the *Endeavour* voyage, Cook also never again risked the hazards and delays of beating west round Cape Horn. Instead he took the longer route east before the prevailing winds from the Cape of Good Hope, and used New Zealand harbours as his base for launching out into the Pacific.

The size of 'His Majesty's armed vessel *Bounty*' also defined her administratively as a 'cutter', the smallest of vessels in terms of permitted complement. This ordained only a lieutenant in command, with no other commissioned officers who would have buttressed Bligh's authority and no Marines to defend it or the ship. These were all advantages that Cook had enjoyed even when only a lieutenant commanding the *Endeavour*, which, like all his larger vessels, was rated as a 'sloop'. Bligh himself, together with Banks and others, canvassed for his promotion to rectify this situation; however, Lord Howe at the Admiralty refused.

Bligh had never been round the Horn either way, and the deficiencies deriving from both choice of ship and prescribed route lay not with him but with the Admiralty, which then compounded normal practical delays with an unaccountable one of three weeks to issue sailing orders. This almost guaranteed that they would hit adverse weather at the Horn. Despite heroic efforts, Bligh could not beat into the Pacific and was forced to turn back the long way round via the Indian Ocean, for which he had only contingency permission. Arriving well behind schedule at Tahiti, they then took time to get the plants ready, following which they had to wait to catch seasonal winds for the return voyage. The exhausting struggle with the Horn and incidents that occurred on the long following passage had sapped crew morale in one way, while their overlong dalliance in an aphrodisiacal South Sea paradise undermined discipline in another. Other factors also raised the odds that there would be trouble.

The *Bounty*'s crew was made up of the usual mixture of the reliable, the indifferent, the immature and some confirmed troublemakers. The good men included the armourer John Coleman, the gunner William Peckover and the sailmaker, Lawrence Lebogue. Peckover spoke Tahitian, having sailed on all three of Cook's voyages, while Lebogue – at 40, one of the oldest men in the ship – had been under Bligh in the *Britannia* and would sail with him again in the *Providence*. Some of the hard cases were Charles Churchill, the violent and unpopular ship's corporal, James Morrison, bosun's mate, and able seamen Matthew Quintal, John Williams and 'Alexander Smith' – whose real name was John Adams. Williams was the first of the mutineers to die on Pitcairn Island; Adams survived easily the longest, dying in 1829. William Purcell, the carpenter, proved corrosively insubordinate from an early stage but drew the line between that and mutiny. John Fryer, the master, was competent but soon became anxious and resentful as Bligh's greater competence and censorious style undermined his role, while the surgeon, Thomas Huggan, was a slovenly alcoholic. The meticulous Bligh tried unsuccessfully to shed him before the voyage, during which his growing incapacity proved both dangerous and a standing affront to good discipline.

Of a complement of 44 under Bligh, 25 would be implicated in the mutiny. Two of these, Churchill and Matthew Thompson, were later killed on Tahiti and four died as captives in the wreck of the pursuing *Pandora*, whose captain, Edward Edwards, carried off both the guilty and the innocent, treating them with equal severity, when he found them there in 1791. Nine were eventually tried in 1792. Three, including the loyal Coleman, were acquitted as uninvolved and six were sentenced to hang, though only three 'foot-soldiers' were in fact executed. Those pardoned included the plausible Morrison and the gentlemanly Manxman Peter Heywood, whom Bligh had been pressed to take as a 15-year-old midshipman by his wife's father. Heywood, who later rose to be a naval captain, would have been hanged less for active mutiny – his role remaining somewhat equivocal – than for failure to distance himself clearly from it, and he owed his salvation to being both well defended and well connected. The remaining 14, including another gentleman able seaman, Edward Young, would vanish with *Bounty* herself to a mostly violent fate on remote Pitcairn under their leader, Fletcher Christian. Christian was only 24 when he finally cracked after a trivial row over missing coconuts (Bligh claimed they had been stolen) that involved several of the officers. With the accumulated effects of his captain's temper, their prolonged stay on Tahiti and the suicidal loss of self-esteem that failing to meet his own and Bligh's expectations seems to have induced, this was the last straw for Christian.

Bligh finally sailed from Portsmouth, into bad weather, on 23 December 1787 and on 5 January put into Tenerife. Shortly afterwards he began his three-watch system, but needed a third watch-keeping officer in addition to Fryer and Peckover. For this he picked his protégé Christian, then a master's mate, and early in March rapidly advanced him to acting lieutenant – a rank the Admiralty would customarily have confirmed on return. Compared with the 33-year-old Bligh – and with Fryer, who probably resented the favouritism – he was very inexperienced and, though he knew Bligh to be 'passionate', flattered himself he could deal with this side of his personality. In the event both men had unrealistic expectations: Bligh's disillusionment with Christian and the gradual psychological disintegration that his expression of it induced in him had a devastating finale. 'I am in hell' was the sole, hopelessly inarticulate explanation that the latter could give his astonished mentor when he cast him adrift.

Bounty reached Cape Horn in the last week of March, at the start of the southern autumn, and for a month Bligh tried to fight his way round against huge seas and westerly gales before turning for the Cape of Good Hope. That his crew sustained the struggle for so long was remarkable, since only 13 of those rated as 'able-bodied' (of which his complement was nominally 25) were in fact mature seamen. They were greatly helped by Bligh's well-organised regime in which hot food was regularly provided and clothes systematically dried in the galley. He in turn was proud to reach Cape Town still with a crew free of 'scurvy, flux or fever' and no deaths or serious injuries. The *Bounty* sailed again on 1 July 1788, east for Tahiti, though Bligh also took aboard seeds and fruit plants for Governor Phillip's nascent colony at Botany Bay, in case he accidentally landed up there. Instead, they had a tedious but rough passage straight to Adventure Bay, Tasmania, where the first unusual disciplinary incident of the voyage occurred, when William Purcell twice refused to comply with Bligh's orders concerning wooding and watering ashore. Exactly why this happened is unknown. Purcell claimed that the work was not proper to his carpenter's rating, but Bligh could neither keep so vital a craftsman confined until later court martial nor flog him, warrant officers being exempt from such punishment. Purcell returned to his senses when Bligh told him that no work meant no food, but effectively unpunished defiance of orders was a serious challenge to Bligh's authority.

The breach was widened shortly afterwards by Fryer, who refused to countersign Bligh's audit of Purcell's and Cole's regular accounts without Bligh certifying Fryer's

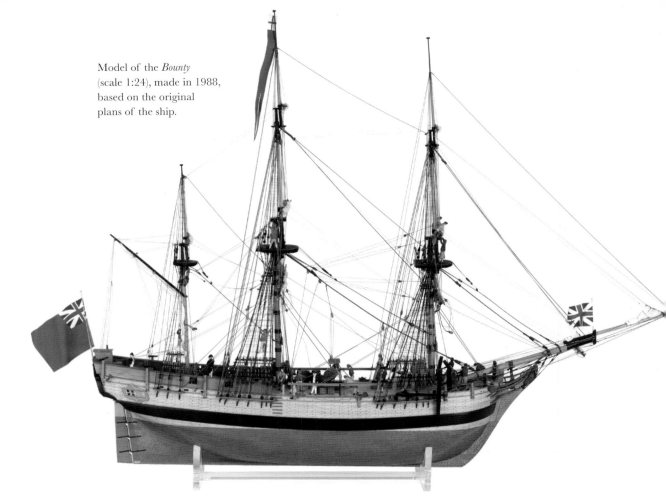

Model of the *Bounty* (scale 1:24), made in 1988, based on the original plans of the ship.

own satisfactory performance. Bligh forced his retreat by reading out the Articles of War and the master's standing instructions before the ship's company. However, it was another extraordinary incident, probably indirectly connected with the death of James Valentine, a seaman, from septicaemia caused by the incompetence of the drunken surgeon, Huggan. Bligh was not satisfied with Fryer, and as master, he should also have been aware of Valentine's condition, Bligh having been made to understand he was recovering. Huggan compounded his ineptitude before they reached Tahiti, first by misdiagnosing scurvy in several men – which incensed Bligh as much as scurvy itself would have after all his precautions – and then by wrongly certifying the crew clear of venereal disease. After a final attempt at reasoning with him failed, Bligh had the surgeon's filthy berth cleaned and his liquor supplies confiscated, though not permanently enough to prevent his death from alcoholism in December 1788 at Matavai Bay.

They had arrived here on 26 October and renewed friendly contact with the local chief, Tinah, well known to Cook by his earlier name of Tu or Otoo.

PACIFIC EXPLORATION

Following Cook's example, Bligh issued strict orders to prevent theft by islanders and to maintain the value of trade exchange through the appointment of a single official 'trader', a task given to the Tahitian-speaking Peckover. He also forbade theft or the violent recovery of stolen items from the Tahitians, as well as any maltreatment of them especially with firearms: these were to be used only where life was threatened. The arrival of the *Bounty* was an opportunity for Tinah to reassert himself following ill fortune in recent local conflict. Bligh had brought many gifts and rapidly secured as many breadfruit plants as he wished for 'King George' in return. When he later said he might move on to other islands, Tinah offered to supply all his needs rather than see him go elsewhere. This suited Bligh well and his only move, at Christmas, was along the coast to the more sheltered anchorage of Oparre. In both places Christian took charge of the shore camp and Fryer of the ship, with Bligh coming and going between the two in close and inevitably critical supervision. Many of the crew, including Fryer – but not Bligh any more than Cook had done – formed liaisons with local women for the duration. Christian's seem to have been unspecific until after the mutiny, when his Tahitian 'Isabella' (the mother of his son, Thursday) accompanied him to Pitcairn. Fryer later caused trouble by misappropriating property of his lover, one of several incidents of casual attitudes to local sensibilities that Bligh had to deal with.

Local theft was a more immediate problem, Bligh's most effective counter-measure being to punish his own men for their carelessness that was usually the cause of the losses. For seamen (such as Adams, alias Smith, on 4 November) this meant flogging; for the officers, a lashing with his tongue. Before long, Purcell again stood on the strict letter of his duty, defied a reasonable request from Bligh and was only briefly confined, while Thompson, a seaman, received 12 lashes for equal 'insolence and disobedience'. By contrast, Coleman earned Bligh's praise for his readiness to help Tahitians by forging useful items from pieces of iron brought to him. For Fryer and Christian, the move to Oparre coincided with a decline in Bligh's opinion of both. Fryer, having surveyed the channel, managed to run the ship aground in it by keeping a poor lookout, while Christian, ahead in the ship's launch, also failed to stay on correct station to prevent this. Bligh was probably incandescent at such bungling of a simple manoeuvre. Fryer and Cole were later also to incur his wrath when sails were taken out of store and found to be mouldy through lack of proper care, a matter well within Fryer's supervisory remit. Bligh recorded that he would have replaced both men had the option existed. Fryer later also let the ship's indispensable timekeeper run down because he forgot to wind it. (This was Kendall's second official copy of Harrison's great prototype; the first, used by Cook, was by then with Arthur Phillip in Australia.)

On 5 January 1789, a week after their arrival at Oparre, desertions finally started to occur – a potentially capital offence, but one already known in the Pacific.

The absconders in the *Bounty*'s small cutter were Churchill, William Muspratt – recently flogged for 'neglect of duty' – and John Milward. A paper found among Churchill's possessions also named three of the shore party, including Christian, though Bligh accepted their denials of being aware of what this implied. Fryer then blundered by not detaining a Tahitian who came on board and admitted to helping the deserters, but on 23 January all three were recaptured. They were put in irons and flogged. All expressed contrition and gratitude for the leniency, being aware that a court martial later would have delivered worse. At the end of their stay a particularly bad case of Tahitian theft earned the perpetrator one hundred lashes. Although this was by far the heaviest beating Bligh ordered, its severity was partly to counter the urgings of local chiefs that the man be killed when they delivered him up, which Bligh of course rejected. The man bore his punishment with apparent indifference.

The *Bounty* at last sailed for the East Indies on 4 March 1789 with over 1,000 plants on board, including more than 700 breadfruit potted up in racks in her great cabin. The ship was also stuffed with supplies of local produce, pigs and goats, as well as private stores and curiosities of all kinds. The farewells were ceremonious and affectionate, but also distressing to many couples about to be separated. Christian's party, especially, now irksomely found themselves back in the confinement of the ship under Bligh's immediate management, after 23 easier weeks ashore.

Things finally came to a head on 24–26 April at Annamooka in Tonga, where Christian, master's mate William Elphinstone and Fryer went ashore with parties to collect wood and water. The result was a spate of thefts arising from the fact that local chiefs were not immediately on hand, the shore parties' inexperience at dealing with islanders less accustomed than Tahitians to European intrusion than the Tahitians were, and Bligh's orders against the use of firearms. Bligh appears to have damned Christian publicly as a 'cowardly rascal' in the matter, and Morrison later recalled that at their departure he berated the assembled crew as a 'parcel of lubberly rascals', pointing a pistol at William McCoy and threatening to shoot him for inattention. The last flare-up was at sea on 27 April, with the coconut incident, when Bligh exploded at several of the officers for at least turning a blind eye to the apparent theft of these supplies, although Christian was cast in the role of principal victim only in accounts written by his subsequent apologists.

By now Bligh clearly considered all his officers lax and again told them so in no uncertain terms. The tempest over, he then characteristically and rapidly forgot the matter, and asked Christian to dine with him. Christian declined and, as night fell, finally succumbed to the private 'hell' boiling in his head since the Annamooka incident. He first contemplated suicide, then the idea of swimming to Tofua, 30 miles away. This developed into an equally wild plan to escape on a makeshift raft, about which he spoke to several people, among them Midshipman George Stewart, who later died in the *Pandora*. Stewart dissuaded him, saying the crew were 'ripe for anything', and this seems to have lit the fuse that led to mutiny.

After a fitful sleep Christian came on watch at 4am, rapidly recruited Quintal, and he in turn persuaded the violent duo of Churchill and Thompson to join them. Smith (Adams), McCoy and Williams also joined and, thanks to Fryer's lax procedures, Christian easily obtained the key to the arms locker from the unsuspecting armourer, Coleman. At daybreak on 28 April 1789, the sleeping Bligh was seized in his bed by Christian and three others, tied up and lashed to the mizzen mast on deck. Fryer was also detained.

In the ensuing hours of chaos, it soon became clear that, while the core of armed mutineers were united and determined, they could recruit only just over half the remaining crew. No one was prepared to kill Bligh and in the end he and 18 men, including Fryer and Purcell, were cast adrift in the ship's 23-foot launch. Other loyal men remained on the ship, since there was no room for more. The *Bounty* then vanished, eventually to remote and mischarted Pitcairn. By 1808, when Captain Mayhew Folger of the American whaler *Topaz* landed there, only John Adams remained, as benign patriarch over a community of 26 English-speaking children of mutineers and eight of their Tahitian mothers. All the other mutineers and their few Tahitian male companions had long since died, mostly through internecine killings. One such death was that of Christian, the first of the five mutineers killed on 'Massacre Day', 23 September 1793, by the Tahitian men, resentful of their inferior treatment and the women's alliance with the Europeans. *Bounty* herself was stripped and burnt in 1790 to preclude detection, including as a result of further flight.

THE VOYAGE OF THE *BOUNTY*'S LAUNCH

Those left in the boat should also have died, as the mutineers expected them to. However, 150 lb of ship's biscuit, 28 gallons of water, a little pork and some rum, wine, coconuts and breadfruit were put aboard in the mêlée, along with clothes and Purcell's tools, Bligh's papers and basic navigational items, including tables and a sextant. Bligh immediately headed for nearby Tofua, where they foraged with only limited success from 29 April to 2 May. The boat held no firearms, something quickly noted by observant Tofuans who arrived on 1 May and who, with easy pickings in view, attacked the following day. Bligh saw it coming and just managed to get the boat away with the loss of a sturdy loyalist, John Norton, who was killed on the beach. In the shocked aftermath it was clear to all that without guns they were unlikely to be better treated elsewhere. Bligh therefore set sail for Dutch Timor in the East Indies, more than 3,600 nautical miles to the west, having

Coconut cup, horn beaker and bullet weight used during the voyage of the *Bounty*'s launch, 28 April to 14 June 1789, after the mutiny.

The cup bears Bligh's inscription, partly cut and partly in ink: 'W Bligh / April 1789 / the cup I eat my miserable allowance out'. The beaker once bore his note: 'Allowance of water 3 times a day'. The bullet's later mount records its use to measure out the thrice-daily bread allowance to the men in the boat. It weighs 1/25 lb (18 g), which is about the weight of a modern digestive biscuit.

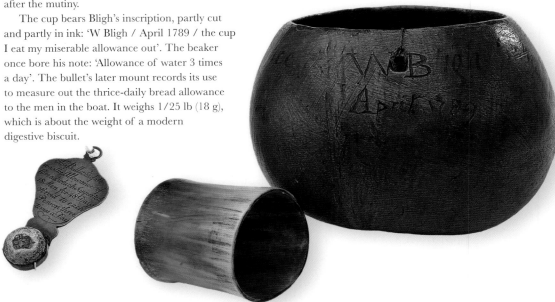

extracted a solemn oath from all to abide by the most stringent rationing of their supplies. This was initially an ounce of bread a day (later reduced), supplemented until they reached Australia only by a couple of birds eaten raw.

The voyage that followed was Bligh's finest. The launch's gunwale was down to inches above the water, and in stormy and often torrentially rainy weather staying afloat required skill and endlessly exhausting bailing. Everyone was perpetually cold and wet and often terrified, and they were able to sleep only fitfully in the exposed and cramped conditions. Bligh had no charts and only his memory of the south-west Pacific to go on, but nonetheless managed to plot an accurate course in a small notebook, using an improvised log line, latitude observations and Peckover's watch. The watch kept going until 2 June, albeit not as accurately as the *Bounty*'s chronometer (which went to Pitcairn). Early on they were pursued by two canoes, but escaped and did not attempt to land again until Bligh predicted that they were approaching the northern Barrier Reef. On 29 May they landed within it on what Bligh called Restoration Island. Here stress-induced disagreements again broke out, followed by a blazing row further up the coast when some men – admittedly weakened – refused to help forage on Sunday Island. Purcell was again insolent and Fryer, attempting to defuse the situation, appeared to side with him when Bligh threatened Purcell with a cutlass. At this point Bligh noted only ten men he felt he could rely on, Fryer and Purcell being among those he could not.

By 4 June they were again at sea north of Cape York but, despite the brief respite, Lebogue and Thomas Ledward, the acting surgeon, were seen to be sinking fast. It was therefore with 'an excess of joy' that early on 12 June they sighted Timor, though another dispute rapidly ensued between Bligh and Fryer about the former's decision to seek a European harbour rather than first get ashore for more food. Nonetheless, on 14 June the launch made port at Coupang (Kupang), Dutch capital of the colonial island of Timor, where they were well received and cared for by the authorities. It was the 48th day since the mutiny; the party had suffered no deaths from exposure or starvation, though Nelson, the gardener, and another man died shortly afterwards from local fevers, as did three others before they reached home.

Their safe arrival did not, however, close the factional breach, which came to its last crisis at Sourabaya that September. Bligh and his men arrived there en route to Batavia, in a schooner that he bought on credit at Coupang and named the *Resource*. On the point of leaving, he found several men incapable of work and asked Fryer if they were ill (they were in fact drunk). On receiving an insolent reply followed by general complaints about ill-treatment from others, including Purcell, Bligh this time reached for a bayonet before calling in the Dutch authorities to support him. In the ensuing local inquiry no one laid a serious complaint against Bligh, although Fryer renewed charges of financial impropriety. He subsequently withdrew these when Bligh produced his accounts.

Bligh later had Purcell tried for insubordination, for which the carpenter was reprimanded, but he laid no formal complaints against Fryer, even though they would have been justified. Likewise, neither Fryer nor Purcell ever complained officially against Bligh. Unlike Christian, all three were tough and understood the unwritten rules. One mutiny was bad enough: more could ruin all concerned, whichever side they had taken.

'K2', the *Bounty* watch.

This is Larcum Kendall's second copy (1771) of Harrison's epoch-making 'H4' chronometer. Taken on the *Bounty*, it went with the mutineers to Pitcairn and, by a tortuous route, came back to Britain only in the 1840s.

At Batavia the fractious company parted, Bligh reaching home on a Dutch ship with his clerk, John Samuel, and another loyal man in March 1790. On his return he rapidly published a preliminary account of the *Bounty*'s loss and his open-boat voyage as part of a campaign to secure his position. Lacking any awareness of his own contribution to the mutiny, he blamed the corrupting effect of Tahiti on evil men. As no contrary view was presented, the subsequent court martial for loss of the *Bounty*, which Bligh and the men he saved faced that October, also absolved them all from blame.

THE SECOND BREADFRUIT VOYAGE, 1791–93

With his published account making him a celebrity, Bligh was rapidly promoted to commander, and then to captain in December 1790. Four months later, on 16 April 1791, he was formally appointed to the new, 420-ton *Providence* to repeat the *Bounty*

LIEUT. BLIGH AND HIS CREW OF THE SHIP *BOUNTY* HOSPITABLY RECEIVED BY THE GOVERNOR OF TIMOR, at the end of the launch voyage; engraving by William Bromley after Charles Benazech, who made the survivors look better than they were in reality. Bligh wrote:

'Our bodies were nothing but skin and bones, our limbs were full of sores, and we were clothed in rags ... the people of Timor beheld us with a mixture of horror, surprise, and pity.'

project of transplanting breadfruit to the West Indies, with a 500-guinea gratuity from the Jamaica Assembly to speed him. This time he selected the ship, launched only on 23 April, and had the 100-ton *Assistant* as consort. She was commanded by Lieutenant Portlock, promoted from master's mate in 1780 after bringing home the *Resolution*'s advance despatches from Cape Town.

The *Providence* voyage had similarities with its predecessor as well as differences from it. Events in the *Bounty* obscure the fact that, for all his troubles, Bligh was an important observer of the geography, society and natural history of everywhere he visited – Tahiti, the East Indies and the Cape of Good Hope. As he explained to Banks, speaking of the *Bounty*'s launch, 'I have endeavoured to make the remaining part of my voyage of some avail even in my distress'd situation,' and he kept a running survey through the Fiji islands (of which he was European discoverer) and up the coast of Australia, through the Prince of Wales Islands off Cape York, avoiding New Guinea only for lack of firearms. This observation continued in the *Providence*. It included discoveries round Adventure Bay, Tasmania, and a swift but competent further recording of the Fiji group on the westward passage from Tahiti. Perhaps the most remarkable achievement was a hazardous 19-day survey through the Clarence Islands of the Torres Strait, punctuated by two attacks from islanders there in which one man died.

However, the essential difference between the two breadfruit voyages was that Bligh's advice underlay all preparations for the second and that they reflected his customary foresight and the example set by Cook: he required two ships and a sound command structure, with a full complement of subordinate commissioned officers and a party of 24 Marines, four of whom were in the *Assistant*. Once at sea, he also reinstituted the three-watch system and the same tight regime as in the *Bounty* for welfare and good order, both afloat and ashore. His irascibility when subordinates failed to meet his exacting standards was otherwise the same, not least since his own health was bad throughout the voyage as a result of the hardships he had already suffered. Young Matthew Flinders, who sailed with him, came to admire but never to like him and the old difficulties soon showed themselves again in Bligh's relationship with Francis Godolphin Bond, the *Providence*'s first lieutenant.

Frank Bond was Bligh's nephew and already a lieutenant with long sea experience when Bligh invited his participation to help his nephew's career. When Bond agreed, Bligh exerted influence to have him appointed, but it was typical of him that, once they were on board, considerate Uncle William became nagging and imperious Captain Bligh. This made the voyage a bitterly remembered purgatory for Bond, whose more easy-going outlook was bound to infuriate his uncle.

Consequently, and knowing his uncle's prior reputation as a 'tyrant', he soon had experience of his 'ungovernable temper' but was wise enough to conceal his resentment, of which Bligh remained unaware. By contrast, the sensible and artistic

OPPOSITE NATHANIEL PORTLOCK (1747–1817); artist unknown.

Born in Virginia, Portlock served as a master's mate on Cook's last voyage and commanded the *Assistant* on Bligh's second breadfruit voyage. This portrait shows him as a merchant captain on his fur-trading voyage to north-west America (1785–88). His ship, the *King George*, and her consort, the *Queen Charlotte*, are in the background. The figure to the left is a man of Nootka Sound, based on an image by John Webber from Cook's last voyage. Portlock is buried at Greenwich, where he died as an officer in the Royal Hospital for Seamen.

George Tobin, making his first commissioned voyage as the third lieutenant, recognised in Bligh 'the quickest sailor's eye, guided by a thorough knowledge of every branch of the profession necessary on such a voyage'. While Tobin's inexperience occasionally brought out 'the Unbridled licence of [Bligh's] power of speech, yet [it was] never without soon receiving something like an emollient plaister to heal the wound', and he rapidly learnt how diligence avoided what he called 'passing squalls'. At the top end of the scale, the experienced Portlock, in the *Assistant*, had a highly successful partnership with his leader. At Tahiti, Bligh noted that his 'alertness and attention to duty makes me at all times think of him with regard and esteem', an encomium not bestowed on any other of his subordinates.

The ships sailed on 3 August 1791, east via Cape Town to Tasmania and thence direct to Tahiti, where they arrived on 9 April 1792. Here Bligh discovered that *Bounty* had twice returned before vanishing, leaving the party that Edwards had already swept up and carried off in the *Pandora*. On 20 July, with 2,126 breadfruit and about 500 other plants on board, Bligh left Tahiti again for the Torres Strait and Coupang, where he learnt a little of the fate of *Pandora* on the Barrier Reef. Mangoes were among the plants that he also collected in the Indies and that he was thereby responsible for successfully introducing to the Caribbean, whither he sailed on the long westward passage via St Helena. He reached St Vincent on 23 January 1793 and went on to Jamaica, breadfruit and other plants from the Pacific and East Indies being landed in both places. After all the trouble, however, breadfruit proved unpopular with the enslaved Africans it was meant to feed, but Bligh and Portlock received a warm welcome from the authorities of both islands, as well as generous immediate rewards for their efforts.

They arrived home in August 1793 with additional plants for the Royal Botanic Gardens at Kew, including (from the Caribbean) the originally West African ackee, today the national fruit of Jamaica, which was classified as *Blighia sapida* in Bligh's honour. The homecoming was otherwise muted: Britain was already eight months into war with revolutionary France and Bligh found his earlier fame soured by notoriety from the trial, in his absence, of the *Bounty* men whom Edwards had brought home. Although the *Providence* expedition ended with complete success and, taken overall, considerable good feeling towards Bligh from his men, the Admiralty granted none of his officers their hoped-for promotions. Bligh himself was much later (in 1801) elected a Fellow of the Royal Society for his 'distinguished services to navigation' but in 1793–94 found himself writing a defensive pamphlet to rebut allegations made against him in connection with the mutineers' defence at trial. The popular myth of 'wicked Captain Bligh' was well planted there while his back was turned and, ever since, it has often needed cutting back to see Bligh the man in true proportion.

Rebellion, Resistance and Retirement

Bligh's last mutiny – more a *coup d'état* – which deposed him as governor of New South Wales owed something to his personality, but little in the way of blame. In this case his assertive rectitude lacked subtlety but helped end a situation too long out of control under his immediate naval predecessors, John Hunter from 1795 and Philip Gidley King from 1800.

Bligh was appointed governor in April 1805 though he did not sail for Australia, accompanied by his second daughter, Mary, until February 1806. By this time his reputation for having a bad temper was augmented by one for being a brave fighting commander. He distinguished himself as captain of the *Director* in Admiral Duncan's victory over the Dutch at Camperdown in 1797 and commanded the *Glatton* at the Battle of Copenhagen in 1801, fighting next in line astern to Nelson's *Elephant* and winning warm praise from him. His later command of the *Warrior* followed a brief spell of survey work in 1803–04, which included being temporarily in charge of the Hydrographic Office, and he gave up the *Warrior*'s captaincy only when Banks – and a generous salary – persuaded him to go to Australia.

The colony at Sydney Cove was by then firmly in the grip of the New South Wales Corps, which included, notably, the able but unscrupulous figure of the 'Perturbator' (now Captain) John Macarthur, a complex, depressive man of 'restless, ambitious and litigious disposition', in Hunter's phrase. This was complicated by conflicts between the officers of the corps; between the corps and the emancipated convicts and free settlers whom it exploited commercially; and between the corps's private-property interests and its official role of supporting the authority of the naval governors who followed Arthur Phillip – a case of 'who will guard the guards', with inter-service discord thrown in. In the three-year interregnum between Phillip's departure and the return of Hunter, the corps had subverted civil government, control of landholding, convict labour and trade through Sydney for its own profit – with Macarthur at the centre of the web as Regimental Paymaster from 1792 and Inspector of Public Works the following year. Both Hunter and

King were well aware of the problem but were unable to deal with it and were duly recalled as this became apparent. London also failed to help in other ways. In 1801 Macarthur was sent home to face court martial for duelling with his commanding officer, Lieutenant-Colonel Paterson. However, the charge was dismissed in England, with Macarthur also using the occasion to win substantial official support for an Australian wool-farming experiment, despite falling foul of Joseph Banks, and he sailed for Sydney again in 1804, taking merino sheep with him. When the government shortly afterwards looked to replace King with someone who was incorrupt, resourcefully independent, firm and 'not subject to whimper and whine when severity in discipline is wanted', Banks had just the man in mind, and Bligh was appointed.

He reached Australia in late 1806, by which time Macarthur had evaded a new ban on corps officers being involved in trade by resigning, and purported instead to represent the 'free inhabitants' – though Bligh quickly found this was not the case. Being well experienced in mercantile finance, and with no reason to favour Macarthur, he had soon acquired a clear picture of his self-interested ways and baleful influence. He also found that, prohibitions or not, the corps was thoroughly corrupt. His conclusion was that the whole corps should be sent home and replaced, a view which threatened the military interest on which his own practical authority rested.

The complex outcome was that by January 1808 Macarthur had manipulated a commercial court case brought against him by another of his enemies, the colony's Judge Advocate, Richard Atkins, to make it a means of undermining Bligh. The aim was to provoke Bligh to take Atkins's side, and Bligh duly fell into the trap, thereby demonstrating an improper bias to which the other six court officers formally objected, as Macarthur had intended. Bligh then ordered them to surrender their papers in the case and explain themselves before him. Macarthur easily presented this as an illegal ultimatum and, with other allies, petitioned Major George Johnston, commander of the corps – who was well aware of what was going on – to rescue the colony from Bligh's usurpation by arresting and supplanting him. This was ostentatiously done on 27 January 1808, leaving both Macarthur and Johnston in control until July, when Lieutenant-Colonel Joseph Foveaux – another appalling and self-interested corps officer – returned from London as Bligh's lieutenant-governor but also refused to reinstate him.

Those involved in the 'rum rebellion' quickly fragmented into factions, and for the next year Bligh remained under arrest at Government House, refusing to return home until London ordered him to do so. In January 1809, when Paterson returned to Sydney as senior officer, Bligh obtained permission to transfer to HMS *Porpoise*, which had come out with him three years earlier. As a ruse, he gave his word that he would sail immediately for London, breaking it once aboard, where his naval authority was unchallenged. Although Johnston and Macarthur left for London in March to prepare their cases, Bligh stayed at sea between Tasmania and the Sydney coast for another year, intercepting ships from home for intelligence and to revictual. His daughter Mary, married and widowed since their arrival in 1806, also remained with him ashore and afloat from the time of his arrest.

In 1809 London at last took decisive action by sending out the 73rd Regiment under Lieutenant-Colonel Lachlan Macquarie. He was also ordered to succeed Bligh as governor after formally reinstating him in order to reaffirm London's sole right to appoint and dismiss. This was not practical as Bligh was off Tasmania when Macquarie arrived on 28 December 1809, but he was nonetheless greeted with proper honours when he landed at Sydney again on 17 January 1810. Macquarie later wrote privately of him as 'most disagreeable [and] ... a very improper Person to be employed in any situation of Trust or Command and ... generally detested...' This harsh opinion clearly has some truth. However, it probably does not take sufficient account of the stress Bligh had then been under for two years, nor of the fact that he certainly still had respectable support in Sydney.

Bligh finally left in the *Hindostan* on 12 May 1810, in a small convoy that carried away the whole 'Rum Corps', which subsequently became the British 102nd Regiment of Foot. This time, however, he left without his daughter. She had what can only have been a whirlwind romance with Macquarie's deputy, Lieutenant Colonel O'Donnell, and assured her bewildered father that she wished to marry him and stay in Australia. Although Bligh was soon brought round, it must have been with mixed feelings that he gave her away in marriage for the second time just before he sailed, at a ceremony in Government House.

He returned to England and the rest of his family in October 1810. In May 1811, George Johnston, now lieutenant-colonel of the 102nd Foot, faced a court martial at Chelsea for 'the act of Mutiny' in deposing Bligh as Governor of New South Wales. A month later an unqualified verdict of guilty saw Johnston cashiered, though the only consequence of his dismissal was his retirement to his substantial farm in Australia. As a civilian, Macarthur faced no charges in London but remained at legal risk in the colony until family lobbying persuaded the government to grant him indemnity from trial there eight years later. In the meantime he was, in effect, trapped in England while his able wife Elizabeth managed his Australian affairs with great success. This included pursuing his wool experiment using cross-bred merino sheep, though it came to full fruition only after Macarthur's return in 1817. As a result, he is still credited as one of the founders of the Australian wool industry; he eventually died insane.

Bligh's promotion to rear-admiral, delayed until after the Johnston verdict, was confirmed in July 1811 and backdated a year. He did not serve again, except in advisory capacities, nor did he long enjoy the company of his much-loved wife

The tomb of William Bligh and his wife at the former church of St Mary's, Lambeth, London (now the Garden Museum), overlooking the Thames beside Lambeth Palace. This photograph shows it before the 2017 completion of the new building extension around it.

Betsy. She died in 1812 and was buried in the graveyard of their London parish church of St Mary-at-Lambeth, leaving him with four unmarried daughters, one of whom was epileptic. Harriet, his eldest daughter, had married the wealthy panorama showman Henry Aston Barker in 1802 and the third – Elizabeth – married Richard Bligh KC, a barrister and her second cousin, ten days before her father's death. Failing health seems to have precluded his attendance, since she went up the aisle with her brother-in-law, Henry Barker. Bligh had spent his last years at Farningham in Kent, rising by seniority to Vice-Admiral of the Blue before he died, aged 63, while under medical care in London. He was buried with his wife at St Mary's, where their imposing monument still bears witness to him as 'the celebrated navigator who first transplanted the Bread fruit tree from Otaheite to the West Indies, bravely fought the battles of his country and died beloved, respected and lamented on the 7th day of December 1817'. The church, however, now has a very different use, and an appropriate one as the final harbour for a navigator whose fame – or notoriety – is for ever linked to a botanical experiment. In 1977 it opened as the Museum of Garden History, now the Garden Museum. Bligh's tomb is today a highlight in the courtyard garden of the striking modern extension that was completed in 2017, just ahead of the 200th anniversary of his death.

6

THE LOST VOYAGE OF ALEJANDRO MALASPINA

For the past twenty years two nations, the English and the French, in noble competition, have undertaken voyages of this sort in which navigation, geography and humanity itself have made very rapid progress… But a voyage undertaken by Spanish navigators must necessarily involve two other objectives. One is the making of hydrographic charts covering the most remote regions of America… The other is the investigation of the political status of America in relation both to Spain and to other European nations.

—ALEJANDRO MALASPINA, 'PLAN FOR A SCIENTIFIC AND POLITICAL VOYAGE AROUND THE WORLD', 10 SEPTEMBER 1788

THE well-equipped expedition commanded by Alejandro Malaspina that left Spain for the Pacific in 1789 represented at one level the philosophical and scientific interests of European Enlightenment, at another a determination to survey the Pacific rim of Spain's sprawling overseas empire. It was intended to reassert the tradition of Spanish voyaging in the Mar del Sur which had faded from view in the glare of publicity that had accompanied the voyages of Cook, Bougainville and Lapérouse. It would not be a voyage of discovery in the traditional sense, Malaspina explained, for 'The safest and shortest routes between the most distant corners of the earth had been pieced together. Any further voyage of discovery would have invited scorn.'

No cost was spared in making the preparations. The corvettes *Descubierta* ('Discovery') and *Atrevida* ('Audacious') were specially built for the voyage, and carried the latest navigational and hydrographic instruments. The officers, scientists

and artists on board were carefully chosen by Malaspina, who had already
completed one circumnavigation while on secondment to the Royal Philippines
Company. Italian born, he had joined the Spanish navy in 1774. He was an experienced hydrographic surveyor, having taken part, as had several of his officers, in
Don Vicente Tofiño's comprehensive charting of the coasts of Spain. In addition,
he was a man of wide reading and radical thinking, whose political and economic
opinions were much influenced by Enlightenment scholars.

Unusually, the initiative for the voyage came from Malaspina and his fellow
commander, José Bustamante, rather than from the Spanish government, and the
expedition as a whole was seen by Malaspina as part of a global project of imperial
regeneration. In the 'Plan for a Scientific and Political Voyage Around the World'
which the two officers presented to the Spanish navy minister in September 1788,

they emphasised that the scientific part of the voyage would follow the model of the expeditions of Cook and Lapérouse as its members collected specimens and made hydrographic and astronomical observations. However, its political tasks would be directed towards strengthening Spain's national interests; for the expedition's duties would include making detailed charts of the coasts of Spanish overseas possessions, investigating the commercial and defensive capabilities of those territories and making political recommendations on their future. Furthermore, it would report on the Russian trading settlements rumoured to exist on the north-west coast of America and on the new British settlement just established at Botany Bay – 'places of interest whether from a commercial point of view or in the event of war'.

The voyage, Malaspina rather optimistically calculated, would take about three and a half years. The expedition would enter the Pacific by way of Cape Horn and sail along the coast from Chile to Mexico, across the North Pacific to the Sandwich Islands (Hawaii), then back to the American mainland to trace the coast north from California before visiting Canton. The second part of the voyage would take the corvettes to the Spanish possessions in Guam and the Philippines, south through the Indian Ocean to New Holland (Australia), and back into the Pacific to Tonga, the Society Islands and New Zealand, before returning home by the Cape of Good Hope to complete the circumnavigation. It was a hugely ambitious project and one whose political objectives of report, recommendation and reform marked it out from its British and French predecessors.

Surveys and Investigations

The expedition sailed from Cádiz in July 1789, calling first at Montevideo, where the corvettes were overhauled after their maiden crossing of the Atlantic. The first year of the voyage along the Atlantic coast of Patagonia to the Falkland Islands (the Malvinas to the Spaniards), round Cape Horn and along the Pacific coasts of Chile and Peru as far north as Callao, the port of the capital Lima, set the pattern for much of what was to follow. Along the coast running surveys were carried out and charts drawn. On land the officers busied themselves with triangulation surveys, the ships' chronometers were rated and a portable observatory was set up in order to make astronomical observations. Later on the voyage, when a specially designed pendulum arrived from Europe, observations related to gravity were carried out in an attempt to determine the true shape of the Earth and, in particular, whether or not the northern hemisphere was flatter than the southern hemisphere. Meanwhile, at the various landing places the naturalists scoured the surrounding region for specimens, while the expedition's artists sketched people and places. This activity would have been familiar to Cook's men, but Malaspina's officers additionally spent much time questioning local officials and collecting information from the archives in pursuit of Malaspina's wider objective of reform of the overseas empire.

Because of the dual nature of Malaspina's mission and the fact that the expedition was in Spanish waters for much of the voyage, it followed a rather

Sketch by Felipe Bauzá of Malaspina's ships *Descubierta* and *Atrevida* at anchor off Mount Saint Elias, Alaska, in July 1791.

different cycle of activity from that of its British and French predecessors in the Pacific. The corvettes spent about 50 per cent of their time in harbour and another 10 per cent at anchor on coasts without harbour facilities. They were therefore at sea for only about 40 per cent of the time, in contrast, for example, to Cook's ships, which, on his second voyage, spent 70 per cent of the time at sea. Although the stays in port allowed for plenty of fresh provisions, and scurvy was comparatively rare, time ashore was not an unmixed blessing, and Malaspina's journal is full of complaints about the problems presented by his crews once in port, relating to lack of discipline, venereal disease and desertion. During the very first stay, at Montevideo, 24 men deserted, and the problem grew worse as the voyage proceeded. A table which Malaspina drew up at Acapulco in April 1791, 20 months or so into the voyage, showed that crew losses from one cause or another, but mostly from desertion, totalled 143 men. Given that the original complement of each corvette was 102 men, this was an extraordinarily high proportion.

THE SEARCH FOR THE STRAIT OF ANIÁN

Until its arrival at Acapulco, near the northern limits of Spanish settlement on America's west coast, the expedition had followed a predictable course, although the original timetable had slipped and Malaspina had decided that he would abandon the projected circumnavigation. Instead he aimed to return to Spain by the same route as his outward voyage, which would allow him to carry out more survey work in Chile and Patagonia. He now estimated that he would be away for five years. It was during the stay at Acapulco, as Malaspina prepared to sail across the Pacific to the Hawaiian Islands, that surprising fresh instructions arrived from Spain. Malaspina was to head north to the Alaskan coast and search there for the passage to the Atlantic reportedly discovered by Lorenzo Ferrer Maldonado in 1588. For centuries the search for the North-West Passage had been encouraged by accounts of voyages that were supposed to have been made through the long sought-after strait, but Ferrer Maldonado's story was the most extraordinary of them all. In 1609 he presented the Spanish court with a memorial in which he claimed that in 1588 he had made a voyage from Lisbon north through Davis Strait and well beyond the Arctic Circle before sailing south-west for more than 2,000 miles to latitude 60° north, where he reached the Pacific through the fabled Strait of Anián. This was the name given to the waterway thought to separate Asia and America, and that provided a navigable route between the Pacific and Atlantic oceans. According to Ferrer, the strait, whose zigzags he showed in several sketches, was 15 leagues long, with high, mountainous sides. Near its opening into the Pacific was a harbour capable of holding 500 ships, and while anchored there the Spanish ship encountered a large vessel bound for the Baltic with a rich cargo of pearls, gold, silks and porcelain. On the return voyage, the narrative continued, the Spaniards found temperatures in the Arctic warmer than those in the hottest parts of Spain.

The lack of interest in early-seventeenth-century Spain concerning this farrago of nonsense is entirely understandable. What is more difficult to explain is why the 'discovery' should be have been taken seriously two hundred years later, in a climate of opinion generally regarded as altogether more critical and less credulous, and after the failure of repeated attempts to find the North-West Passage. The French geographer Jean-Nicolas Buache de La Neuville, who in 1790 presented the prestigious Paris Academy of Sciences with a memoir supporting Ferrer Maldonado's account, must take much of the responsibility. Although the urgency of his new instructions must have startled Malaspina, he was familiar with the account, a copy of which had been found by one of his officers shortly before the expedition sailed. On several occasions in the first two years of the voyage Malaspina had referred to the account as being worth investigating, but by the time the expedition reached Acapulco he had decided to abandon the Alaskan stage of the voyage. However, the matter was then taken out of Malaspina's hands and he prepared to sail north. In an official response to Madrid he referred to some of the 'difficulties' in Ferrer's account, which in private letters he described it as 'apocryphal' and 'false', while on the *Atrevida* Bustamante dismissed the account as fictitious and Buache's memoir as intended 'to delude Europe'. Bustamante pointed out that there was no resemblance between Ferrer Maldonado's description of the Alaskan coast and the recent surveys of it by Spanish and British vessels. In 1774 Juan Pérez had reached the Queen Charlotte Islands on the first Spanish expedition to the north-west coast, and the following year Juan Francisco de la Bodega y Quadra became the first Spaniard to land in Alaska, while in 1778 James Cook had sailed the length of the coast, although without making a close examination. These forays were followed by further Spanish voyages, by Ignacio de Arteaga in 1779 in a belated response to news of Cook's arrival on the coast, and then by Esteban José Martínez in 1788 and Salvador Fidalgo in 1790. Both Martínez and Fidalgo encountered Russian fur traders in Alaska, but neither they nor their predecessors on the coast came across what Ferrer Maldonado had described – a strait 15 leagues long, a harbour large enough to hold 500 ships and vessels carrying Asian trade goods. It was in a mood of resignation rather than optimism, then, that Malaspina and Bustamante sailed north in May 1791, while a dozen seamen attempted to desert when they heard that their destination was Alaska, not Hawaii.

Malaspina took his ships on a long curving track well out to sea before heading in towards the Alaskan coast at latitude 56° north near Cook's Cape Edgcumbe. The snow-covered mountains awed the journal keepers, and the cold was so intense that the artist Tomás de Suria was unable to sketch on deck and was forced to retreat

PIRA, Y SEPULCROS DE LA FAMILIA
DEL ACTUAL AN-KAU, EN EL PUERTO
MULGRAVE; engraving by José Cardero,
1791, showing a member of the Malaspina
expedition at the burial ground of a ruling
Tlingit family at Port Mulgrave, Alaska.

below to complete his drawings. From this landfall the vessels sailed north towards the location of Ferrer Maldonado's supposed strait at latitude 60° north, and on 27 June were off Yakutat Bay. Despite earlier reservations, excitement grew on board as the *Descubierta* and *Atrevida* steered for a great cleft in the coastal range at latitude 59°15' north. Malaspina wrote that the inlet (Yakutat Bay) resembled that described by Ferrer Maldonado, and he added that 'imagination soon supplied a thousand reasons in support of hope'. Five years earlier the expedition of Lapérouse had approached Lituya Bay about a hundred miles to the south with similar hopes. Suria commented on the reaction of Malaspina's officers: 'They believed, and with some foundation, that this might be the so much desired and sought-for strait... Transported with joy our commander sailed towards the opening.' Even the sceptical Bustamante was caught up in the enthusiasm of the moment, and entered in his journal that 'there was hardly anyone among us who was not ready to believe

PLANO DEL PUERTO DESENGAÑO, by Alejandro Malaspina. This chart, printed in *Relación del Viaje hecho por las Goletas Sutil y Mexicana* (1802), shows Malaspina's survey by boat inside Yakutat Bay, Alaska, in July 1791. With his way blocked by the glacial ice shown here, Malaspina turned back and named the inlet 'Puerto del Desengaño' (Disenchantment Bay).

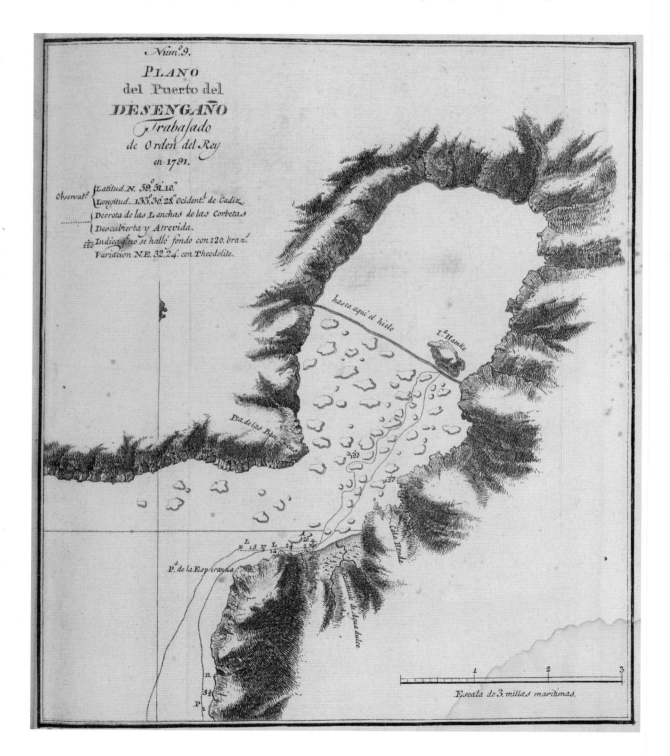

in the probable existence of the longed-for passage'. By nightfall the corvettes had anchored inside the bay, close to a beach and a Tlingit village. Here the portable observatory was set up, the artists began sketching, wood and water were taken on board and a trade for sea-otter pelts took place.

By 2 July Malaspina was ready to explore in person the inner reaches of the inlet in search of the Strait of Anián. He took two launches and 15 days' provisions and left Bustamante in charge of the ships. It took only a few hours to dispel all hopes, for soon the water shoaled and the thunderous sound of large chunks of ice calving from a glacier could be heard. Then the end of the inlet came in sight, its low shore blocked by a glacier behind which rose the steep walls of the coastal range. A frustrated Malaspina named the inlet Puerto del Desengaño (Disenchantment Bay), and after taking possession of the area headed out to sea. Much had been accomplished during the week's stay. The scientists on board had gathered a rich harvest of ethnographic and natural-history material, and the artists had made some superb sketches and paintings, but the overriding disappointment was that there was no strait leading deep into the interior. Later, Malaspina reflected in his journal that a reader in the twenty-first century would be amazed to see how seriously the fictitious accounts of Ferrer Maldonado and other navigators had been taken 'in an age which we call scientific and enlightened'.

From Alaska the ships sailed south to Nootka Sound, flashpoint of the diplomatic crisis of the previous year that had almost led to war between Spain and Britain, and then on to Monterey and Acapulco. On his arrival in Acapulco, Malaspina detached two of his officers, Dionisio Alcalá Galiano and Cayetano Valdés, to carry out a third and final season of Spanish explorations in the Strait of Juan de Fuca. They were instructed by Malaspina to give priority to inlets leading eastward 'to decide once and for all the excessively confused and complicated question of the communication or proximity of the Pacific Ocean and the Atlantic in this latitude'. In two small, locally built vessels, the *Sutil* and the *Mexicana*, Galiano and Valdés spent the summer of 1792 investigating the innermost recesses of the strait. While carrying out their survey, the Spaniards encountered George Vancouver's Royal Navy ships, recently arrived on the coast and engaged in the same task. There was an exchange of information and mutual courtesies, but both sides continued with their independent surveys: the existence, or otherwise, of the North-West Passage was too politically sensitive an issue to be determined by the charts of foreign nationals. Painstaking work by Galiano and Valdés failed to reveal any way through to the east, although of openings, inlets and bays there were more than enough. By late August the Spanish vessels had sailed along the entire east or inner coast of Vancouver Island, and rounded its northern tip to gain the open ocean. On 31 August they arrived back at Nootka, having completed the first continuous circumnavigation by Europeans of Vancouver Island.

THE PHILIPPINES, PORT JACKSON AND VAVA'U

By the end of 1791, as he prepared to set sail once more from Acapulco, Malaspina had finished the main part of his mission. His expedition had produced detailed charts of long stretches of the coasts of Spanish America, established the exact location of the main ports, carried out scientific experiments, collected vast numbers of natural-history specimens (before the voyage ended, just one of the naturalists had collected more than 15,000 plant specimens) and made observations and drawings of the indigenous peoples from Patagonia to Alaska. Less openly, Malaspina had investigated the political and economic state of the colonies, with a view to drawing up recommendations for change. But in terms of distance and time the voyage was only half completed. There was the long run across the Pacific to the Philippines by way of Guam to be made before the ships turned south.

Malaspina spent almost nine months in the Philippines, while Bustamante in the *Atrevida* visited Macao on the coast of China to carry out gravitational observations. Malaspina spent his time in the Philippines making coastal surveys, while his naturalists headed off on inland excursions to collect specimens. During one of these trips the expedition's chief naturalist, the army officer Colonel Antonio Pineda, died – a heavy blow to Malaspina, who wrote in his journal of the 'sudden and irreparable loss'. Malaspina's tribute to Pineda tells us much about his own views on the significance of the expedition's work:

> *His ideas, as ambitious as they were viable, about the land and inhabitants of almost the entire continent of the Americas subject to the monarchy, the comparative exploitation of its minerals, the analysis of its languages, the administration, situation and customs of our colonies, although partially described in his notebooks, have largely perished with him.*

After calling at Mindanao, south of the Philippines, the corvettes followed a semi-circular track into the Pacific. They passed north of New Guinea and then east of the Solomon Islands, the New Hebrides (Vanuatu) and New Caledonia before sailing south to New Zealand. At the end of February 1793 Malaspina reached Cook's Doubtful Sound on the south-west coast of New Zealand's South Island, where he sent his cartographer Felipe Bauzá inshore in the pinnace to examine the area. Neither Cook nor any other European navigator had entered the Sound, and Bauzá's chart for long remained the only survey of this stretch of water. On Bauzá's return, Malaspina set an overnight course to Cook's Dusky Bay (today's Dusky Sound), but when bad weather made it too dangerous to enter he abandoned the attempt and sailed north-west to New South Wales and the newly established British convict settlement at Port Jackson.

Even before leaving Spain, Malaspina had suggested that New South Wales should be viewed for its political significance rather than as a region of interest to his naturalists. His month's stay at Port Jackson reflected this attitude. The courtesies exchanged by the Spanish officers and their British hosts no doubt reflected a genuine warmth between the two sides, but Malaspina's journal also revealed that the ceremonies enabled him to cast 'a veil over our national curiosity'. In effect, Malaspina was engaged in some discreet espionage in a colony which, he reported, had made astonishing progress in the five years since its founding. In a 'Political Examination of the English Colonies in the Pacific', Malaspina described the threat that the new colony posed to Spanish interests in the Pacific, including the possibility that it could even serve as a base for an invasion of Chile and Peru in wartime. His answer to this danger was to suggest trading links between Spanish America and the colony by which cattle and provisions from South America would find a profitable market in New South Wales and so turn a potential enemy into a satisfied trading partner. There was no realistic prospect that the Spanish government would adopt such a policy, but the recommendations reflected the unconstrained nature of Malaspina's thinking on economic and political matters.

On leaving Port Jackson Malaspina decided to sail directly to Vava'u, the north-ernmost group of islands in the Tongan archipelago. This group had not been visited by Cook during his calls in Tonga during his second and third voyages, and Malaspina's stay there had an even clearer political purpose than his stay at Port

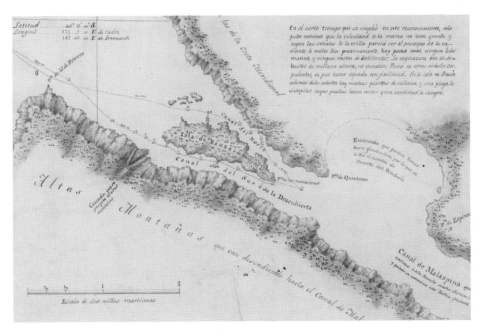

CROQUIS [SKETCH] DEL PUERTO DUDOSO.
Cook's Doubtful Sound was hurriedly surveyed by Bauzá in February 1793.

Jackson. It was a follow-up to the visit made by the Spanish navigator Francisco Mourelle in 1781, and towards the end of his ten days at Vava'u, Malaspina carried out only his second act of possession on the voyage. As at Yakutat Bay, site of the first act of possession, Vava'u had seen few European visitors, so the observations, descriptions and vocabularies compiled by Malaspina and his officers are of particular value. The sketches by the expedition's artists – in this instance, Fernando Brambila and Juan Ravenet – vividly supplement the written word. Relations with the islanders and their chief, Vuna, were friendly apart from the inevitable incidence of petty thieving, and were characterised by the exchanges, commercial and sexual, that had become standard for European callers at the Pacific islands. All in all, the brief interlude at Vava'u had more in common with the previous voyages of the Cook era than any other part of the voyage, and Bustamante's remarks could have been taken from the pages of Hawkesworth or Bougainville:

> *Nothing can compare to the beautiful variety of scenery that met our gaze on this little excursion. The regularity of the plantations, the graceful harmony of the landscape, and the confusion of evergreen trees scattered with flowers all spread before us the marvels of nature in her brightest colours. In these delightful places the dullest imagination could not resist the sweet and peaceful sensations that they inspire. Here our minds were gently drawn to philosophical reflections on the life and happiness of these peoples ... their tranquil existence in the midst of abundance and pleasure.*

El Fondeadero de las Corbetas *Descubierta* y *Atrevida* en las Yslas de Vavao (detail), by Fernando Brambila.

A view of the anchorage at Vava'u in the Tonga islands, May 1793. The observatory set up by the Spaniards is on the right.

PROBLEMS OF DISCIPLINE AND HEALTH

The stay at Vava'u was marred by the unruly behaviour of the crew, many of whom, Malaspina wrote, resented 'the restraint of discipline, however mild'. This was now to be a recurrent theme. By this stage there were problems in working the ships, for the crews were divided between worn-out sailors who had been on board for the whole voyage and inexperienced youths from the Philippines and elsewhere. Some indication of the strain Malaspina was now under can be seen in an angry outburst in his journal little more than two weeks into the voyage from Vava'u across the Pacific to the South American mainland. The trust that he had tried to build up with his crews during the first part of the voyage had 'vanished like smoke'. More worryingly, there was a breakdown in relations between Malaspina and his officers, who were demanding 'more rest and fewer obligations'. The situation was, he said, an odious one in which 'discipline was seen as tyranny, caution as fear, and a normal desire for calm taken as a sign of weakness'. He even hinted at the possibility of mutiny. The rift was also an indication of Malaspina's own deterioration, certainly physically and perhaps mentally and emotionally too. Not only had he been in command for almost four years, but before sailing he had taken only a few months of rest after his circumnavigation in the service of the Royal Philippines Company.

When the corvettes reached Callao in Peru, Malaspina took his instruments and books to the rural retreat of La Magdalena, away from his squabbling officers. There, he wrote, he could 'shake off the hateful guise of commanding officer and attend quietly to the restoration of my own much weakened health'. His state of mind would not have been helped by the fact that, unaccountably, he had not received any official letters or instructions from Madrid since his second visit to Acapulco in October 1791, more than two years earlier. He must have felt betrayed by his closest associates and abandoned by his superiors.

Life ashore was disrupted by the news of the outbreak of war with revolutionary France, for this might have serious consequences for the lightly armed corvettes. The conflict accounts for Malaspina's decision that the *Descubierta* and *Atrevida* should henceforth undertake separate passages to Montevideo, both to increase the amount of surveying they could undertake on the final part of the voyage and to reduce the risk of the expedition and all its work being wiped out by a chance encounter with enemy ships. So severe were the combined losses due to sickness and desertion among the crews that Malaspina and Bustamante were able to sail only after receiving fresh crew members from royal frigates already at Callao. Of all Malaspina's problems, the most intractable was the high turnover of crew members. The records show that during the voyage about 215 served on board the *Descubierta* at different times, and about 240 on the *Atrevida*, making the total number of those who served on the two corvettes (each normally crewed by about a hundred men) in the region of 450. Fatalities among the 250 or so 'losses' suffered by the expedition seem to have been comparatively low, at 20 named individuals, although undoubtedly there would have been further deaths among those crew members left behind in port hospitals whose fate is not known. What is certain is that Malaspina and his officers were faced with continual problems of training and discipline because of changes of crew, and his journal reflects his growing irritation with this situation.

With weakened crews, and worried by the prospect of meeting hostile ships, Malaspina dropped some of the more ambitious parts of the survey of the coasts of South America that he had originally had in mind. He visited Port Egmont in West Falkland to carry out gravity observations and surveyed Puerto San Elena on the east coast of Patagonia before making for Montevideo and his rendezvous with Bustamante. Off Cape Horn he set his own work, not for the first time, in the context of Cook's surveys:

> *Once again we marvelled at the accuracy of Captain Cook's descriptions in this new scene of his navigational success and ability. Thus guided as if by his own hand, we put aside any ideas of discovery and assumed the equally useful role of correcting and at times improving, for public benefit and with a certain scientific curiosity, the original work, which will always be somewhat unfinished, however valuable and impressive...*

For his part, Bustamante surveyed the Spanish settlement in Puerto Soledad in East Falkland, and carried out a search for the Auroras Islands, reported to lie east of the Falklands, before rejoining Malaspina. The last stages of the voyage from Montevideo to Cádiz were an anticlimax as the *Descubierta* and the *Atrevida*, together with a royal frigate, escorted a convoy of slow-moving merchant ships across the potentially hostile waters of the Atlantic. Despite the frustrations of the crossing, Malaspina and his officers continued to make observations and to check their instruments, and it was wholly in character that the final sentence in Malaspina's last entry in his journal for 21 September 1794 concerned the rating of the chronometers. The expedition had been away for five years and two months.

RETURN AND DISGRACE

On his return Malaspina busied himself preparing the account of his voyage for publication. This would be an account on a grand scale that would dwarf the narratives of his predecessors in the Pacific, even the lavish three-volume account of Cook's last voyage. It would answer the accusation that Spain kept its discoveries secret, for, as Malaspina insisted, the publication of the results of his expedition would 'draw aside at last the thick curtain of mystery' which had concealed Spain's overseas possessions. In the first instance there would be seven volumes and an atlas of 70 charts, together with harbour plans and coastal views, and a folio of

VISTA DE LA COLONIA INGLESA DE SYDNEY, by Fernando Brambila, one of several views by him showing the extent to which the colony at Port Jackson had developed since its establishment only five years before the visit of the Malaspina expedition in 1793.

70 drawings. Later, Malaspina hoped that there might be additional volumes of observations based on the work of the expedition's naturalists, Tadeo Haenke and Luis Neé. For Malaspina this monumental work would be more than a matter of factual record, for it would include, in his words, 'An assessment of the political state of the overseas empire, with detailed recommendations for change and reform'. In December 1794 he was received at court together with some of his officers, but felt that he had been fobbed off with mere ceremony. His words in a letter to his friend Paolo Greppi show that deference and tact were not his strong points:

> *One single day would have been sufficient to explain my system. I have seen everything, I have been everywhere. I had hoped that no matter the chaos of the present system it would be realised that there is but a small step from the wrong route to the right one, from absurdity to sane philosophy.*

Nor did Malaspina confine himself to the state of the overseas empire, for at this time he presented the navy minister with a memoir setting out his views on the terms of a peace treaty with France. In commenting on so delicate a matter he enraged the powerful chief minister, Manuel Godoy, who referred to the memoir's 'lack of principles and moderation', and advised that Malaspina should burn it and be told to mend his ways. Malaspina was now treading on dangerous ground,

EXPERIENCIA DEL PENDULO SIMPLE, by Juan Ravenet.

Gravity experiments by Malaspina (right-hand figure in the tent) and others at Port Egmont, West Falkland, in January 1794. This version has the artist, Ravenet, standing just outside the tent drawing the scene.

although he was again received at court by the King and Queen of Spain in March 1795 and was promoted to *brigadier* (admiral).

However, despite this sign of official favour, he became involved in clandestine political activities aimed at replacing Godoy and other ministers. In November, Malaspina was arrested, and after a hurried hearing of his case before the Council of State, he was stripped of his rank and sentenced to ten years' imprisonment in the grim fortress prison of San Antón at La Coruña, while the officers who had been helping him prepare his account of the voyage were ordered to stop work and to surrender all papers relating to the expedition.

Of the proposed seven-volume edition, only one volume was published, in 1802, and this dealt only with a subsidiary part of the expedition (the surveys carried out by Malaspina's officers, Galiano and Valdés, on detachment in the Strait of Juan de Fuca in 1792). The volume was an attempt to offset the publication of George Vancouver's account of his voyage, which included his rival survey of the strait, but although the Spanish account included a handsome atlas, its appearance ten years after the event, and four years after the publication of Vancouver's narrative, was too little and too late. The volume contained no mention of Malaspina other than an occasional reference to the (unnamed) 'commander of the corvettes'. He had been removed from the historical record and so, for the most part, had his expedition, although its astronomical observations were published by one of his officers, José Espinosa y Tello, in 1809. Oddly, the first appearance of Malaspina's own journal came in the form of a Russian translation, issued in parts in a naval periodical in St Petersburg in the 1820s after a Russian diplomat in Madrid obtained a copy of the Spanish original (which, less than ideally, was translated first into French and then into Russian). Finally, almost a hundred years after the expedition set sail, an edited version of Malaspina's journal was published in Madrid in 1885, a belated attempt, as its editor said, at 'reparation'; but the original journal in Malaspina's own hand had to wait until 1990 for publication in Spain as part of a multi-volume series devoted to the voyage. Only in the 1990s were the records of the expedition published on the scale envisaged by Malaspina in 1794.

Malaspina was released from prison in 1803, but spent the remaining seven years of his life in exile in Italy. Although he seems to have had reasonable means during his retirement at Pontremoli (near his birthplace of Mulazzo), among the sad details of his last years is a document dated September 1806 recording that he had sold his sextant, one of a sea officer's most personal and treasured possessions. There was no rehabilitation, no restoration of his naval rank and no resumption of work on the ambitious volumes about the voyage that he had planned so carefully. An expedition that had set new standards in terms of hydrographic, astronomical and natural-history observations slipped from sight, and for a long time Alejandro Malaspina was the forgotten man among the Pacific navigators of the late eighteenth century.

7

'ACQUIRING A MORE COMPLETE KNOWLEDGE'

George Vancouver in the North Pacific

JAMES COOK's chart of north-west America, made in the early summer of 1778 while he was hurrying north to begin his search for the North-West Passage in Alaska, was sketchy and inadequate. Pressed for time in foggy conditions, he had largely kept well offshore and his chart could do little more than indicate the general trends of the coast. While Cook showed that a navigable passage could not exist over the top of the American continent, it was theoretically possible after his voyage that one could still be found along the British Columbian coast. Thirteen years later, in 1791, the Admiralty ordered his old midshipman, George Vancouver, to finish the job and acquire for Britain 'a more complete knowledge' of this extraordinarily convoluted coastline which, with Cook's discovery of the rich trade in sea-otter furs, now had great commercial potential. Vancouver's finished chart reveals the size of the task that faced him: it took him three full seasons to chart an area that Cook had sailed along in four weeks, with most of the surveying having to be done from small open boats, often in appalling weather and with the political responsibility of resolving the Nootka Sound crisis with the Spanish authorities (described in this book's introduction) hanging over him. His survey stretched from California to Anchorage in Alaska; and while it may have lacked the visionary sweep of Cook's great voyages, it was carried out with a determination, with skill and with an obsessive attention to detail that proved conclusively that no passage existed through the continent. It resulted in a set of charts so accurate that many were still being used a hundred years later.

GEORGE VANCOUVER

George Vancouver was born in King's Lynn, Norfolk, in 1757, the son of the deputy collector of customs, and at the age of 14 he was entered on the *Resolution*'s books as an able seaman for Cook's second voyage. He was really one of the ship's 'young gentlemen', trainee officers destined for commissions once they had served the required period at sea and passed the relevant exams. He did his job well, if unspectacularly, a fellow young gentleman describing him as 'a Quiet inoffensive Young man'. In later life Vancouver claimed to have sailed nearer the South Pole than anyone else on this voyage, for when Cook decided that at 71°10' south he had pushed as far south as was humanly possible Vancouver scrambled out on to the bowsprit, waved his hat over his head and shouted '*ne plus ultra*' – no further (has any man ever been). The only source of this story is Vancouver himself and if true it has a certain irony, for, as one of his officers later remarked, he 'was never known to put a favourable construction on the follies of youth'. However, he was a capable officer and for Cook's third voyage he was appointed midshipman in Captain Clerke's *Discovery*.

Two weeks after Cook's ships returned to Britain in 1780, Vancouver passed his lieutenant's examination and was appointed to a sloop under orders for the West Indies. With the exception of a 16-month period on half-pay, he spent the next seven years in the Caribbean, rising to be first lieutenant of the 50-gun *Europa* and recommending himself to the commander-in-chief of the West Indies Station, Commodore Sir Alan Gardner, by surveying Jamaica's Kingston Harbour. The survey was completed with the assistance of the *Europa*'s master, Joseph Whidbey, and the charts themselves were drawn by Joseph Baker, one of the midshipmen, beginning a professional association between the three men that would flower on the north-west coast of America.

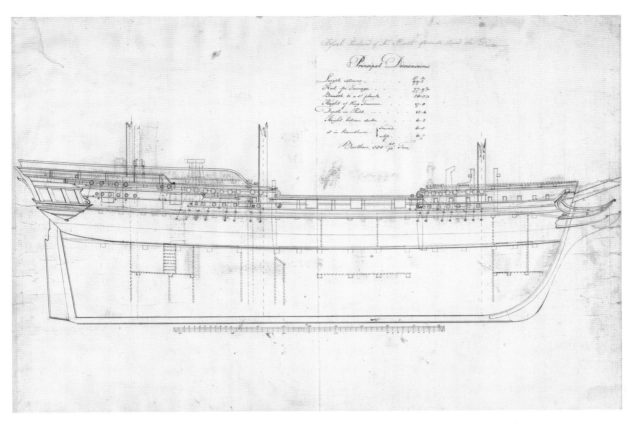

THE *DISCOVERY*

The ship selected for Vancouver's expedition was named after Cook's *Discovery*, the smaller vessel of his last voyage (1776–80). She was a merchantman converted for exploration and had been lying for more than a year in the river Thames under the command of another of Cook's old officers, Henry Roberts, waiting for orders to survey the Southern Whale Fisheries, a large area encompassing the southern Pacific and Atlantic oceans. Vancouver received an appointment as the *Discovery*'s first lieutenant in 1789, almost certainly through the influence of Gardner, who had just become one of the Lords of the Admiralty. During the Spanish Armament of 1790 – Britain's military response to the Nootka Sound Crisis – the fleet was put on a war footing. The *Discovery*'s crew was redistributed and the planned survey voyage suspended. Once a political solution was agreed with Spain, however, the ship was given new orders which combined taking formal possession of the disputed land at Nootka Sound with conducting a survey of the north-west coast on which, under the terms of the new agreement, Britain now had the right to trade. For reasons that are no longer clear, Roberts was relieved of his command and Vancouver appointed in his place.

BANKS AND VANCOUVER

Sir Joseph Banks had been closely involved in planning Roberts's voyage but there was immediate friction between Banks and Vancouver. Banks had persuaded the Admiralty to build a 12ft x 8ft 'plant cabbin' on the quarterdeck to house the collection of live plants he hoped would be brought back, and he personally supervised its installation at Deptford; but Vancouver loathed the large, heavy structure that intruded on the limited deck space and made the ship difficult to handle. Banks had also appointed a Scottish naval surgeon named Archibald Menzies to make 'an investigation of the whole of Natural History of the Countries you are to visit; as well as an enquiry into the present state and comparative degree of civilization of the inhabitants you meet with'. Menzies was an excellent choice for he was a talented naturalist who already knew the area, having just returned from James Colnett's fur-trading voyage to the North Pacific; but he was unambiguously Banks's man. He was appointed to Vancouver's ship as a supernumerary botanist, not as a naval surgeon, and this position placed him outside the ship's formal chain of command, giving him a privileged and protected status that Vancouver was clearly uneasy about – as well as a salary of £150 a year which, an irritated Vancouver later pointed out to the Admiralty, was double his own pay. For his own part, Banks was used to being treated with deference by naval officers and was annoyed by Vancouver's 'arrogance':

How Captain Vancouver will behave to you [Menzies] is more than I can guess, unless
I was to judge by his conduct toward me — which was such as I am not used to receive
from one in his station… As it would be highly imprudent in him to throw any obstacle
in the way of your duty, I trust he will have too much good sense to obstruct it.

Banks advised Menzies to make a note when he felt Vancouver was being obstructive, which he dutifully did. Vancouver had a much freer hand in selecting his officers, however. Joseph Whidbey was appointed the *Discovery*'s sailing master, another shipmate from the *Europa*, Peter Puget, became his second lieutenant, while his third was Joseph Baker. The first lieutenant, Zachary Mudge, had also served briefly on the *Europa*, although he almost certainly got the job through his connections to the powerful Pitt family. The *Discovery* was to be accompanied by the brig *Chatham*, commanded by Lieutenant William Broughton. A storeship, the *Daedalus*, commanded by Richard Hergest, another of Cook's old officers and one of Vancouver's ex-messmates on the old *Discovery*, was to sail to the Pacific separately and rendezvous with them at either Hawaii or Nootka Sound.

There were a number of well-born young men among Vancouver's midshipmen. Thomas Pitt was the 16-year-old son of Lord Camelford and first cousin to both the prime minister, William Pitt, and his elder brother, the First Lord of the Admiralty, John Pitt, Earl of Chatham; Charles Stuart, also 16, was the son of the Marquis of Bute; Thomas Manby, who left a delightful record of the voyage written as a series of letters, was related to the Norfolk family of Lord Townshend, while Spelman Swaine was connected to the Earl of Hardwicke. In addition, Robert Barrie, Henry Humphreys and John Stewart were nephews of admirals. The proportion of well-connected midshipmen on this humble exploration ship was unusually high. This may say something about the growing status of exploration after the Cook voyages, but it was certainly a reflection of the lack of opportunities for young naval officers in peacetime: a long voyage would give them the sea time necessary to gain promotion and with it increased pay and potential prize money.

DISCOVERY'S DEPARTURE

The *Discovery* and the *Chatham* left Plymouth on the unpropitious date of 1 April 1791, entering the Pacific via Cape Town, southern Australia and New Zealand. On the way south there was an incident at Tenerife in which Vancouver was accidentally pushed into the harbour while trying to stop a brawl between drunken members of his crew and a Spanish shore patrol. Menzies described it in detail to Banks and was of the opinion that 'the quarrel originated with our people'. It was probably started by Midshipman Pitt who, in a rare moment of good sense,

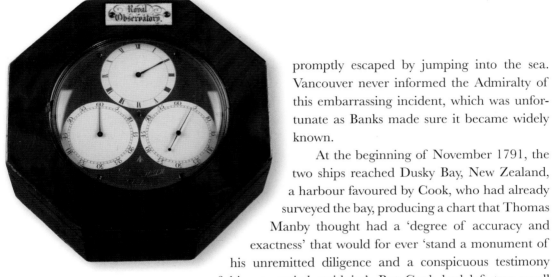

promptly escaped by jumping into the sea. Vancouver never informed the Admiralty of this embarrassing incident, which was unfortunate as Banks made sure it became widely known.

At the beginning of November 1791, the two ships reached Dusky Bay, New Zealand, a harbour favoured by Cook, who had already surveyed the bay, producing a chart that Thomas Manby thought had a 'degree of accuracy and exactness' that would for ever 'stand a monument of his unremitted diligence and a conspicuous testimony of his unwearied assiduity'. But Cook had left two small branches at the head of Dusky Bay unexplored, noting on the chart 'No Body Knows What'; Vancouver surveyed them and in great good humour changed the name to 'Some Body Knows What'. The two ships then set off across the Pacific for Tahiti where, wrote Manby in a mood of eager anticipation, 'the men are benevolent and friendly; the women generous and beautiful'. They arrived on 29 December 1791. In fact, the *Chatham* had arrived a few days earlier; it was already becoming a bit of a joke – an irritating one to the crew of the *Discovery* – that when the two ships sailed together the *Chatham*'s slow sailing held them up, but as soon as they sailed separately the *Chatham* would always beat the senior ship.

After the mutiny on the *Bounty* in 1789, it would be many years before Royal Navy captains would enter Polynesia without being at least aware of the potentially destabilising charms of the islanders. Vancouver, therefore, issued strict orders to manage trade with the Tahitians and keep the crew and the young gentlemen on board unless they were required to go ashore on duty. His orders tried to control contact rather than stop it, but they were nonetheless deeply resented: George Hewitt, the surgeon's mate, suggested acidly that when Vancouver had last been in Tahiti in 1777 he had been 'a Young Man, but that not being now the case the Ladies were not so attractive' to him. Midshipman Pitt was beaten for trying to exchange a piece of iron barrel hoop for sex, guilty in Vancouver's eyes of disobedience, illegal trade and the misuse of ship's equipment. Beating such a well-connected young man was not a good career move for Vancouver and neither did it receive universal approbation on the ship, since warrant officers were normally exempt from it. Pitt had a dangerously unstable personality, but he was also a powerful character who would have considerable influence once he inherited his father's title (which he did in 1793, during the voyage, though he found out only later) and he clearly had a following on the *Discovery*, particularly among the midshipmen. Shortly after they had left Tahiti, a drunken Midshipman Stuart pulled a razor from his pocket, brandished it in front of his captain and proclaimed, 'If, Sir, you ever flog me, I will not survive the disgrace: I have this ready to cut my throat with.' The issue, to these well-born young men, was one of 'honour' and it was destined to become a recurrent theme on Vancouver's quarterdeck.

Vancouver's relations with the rulers of Tahiti and the Hawaiian Islands were, by contrast, generally assured and astute. In Hawaii, where his ships would return to winter in 1792–93 and 1793–94, he took pains to be friendly and diplomatic, even though as a witness of Cook's death he was understandably cautious. Over the course of his three visits to the islands it became clear that Vancouver saw their strategic importance to the development of trade in the North Pacific more clearly than most. Hawaii had gained a deserved reputation as a dangerous place for lightly armed and lightly manned merchant ships and, although it was nowhere in his orders, Vancouver understood part of his mission as being to make the islands safer for European shipping. Establishing a good working relationship with Kamehameha and Kahekili, the two pre-eminent and warring rulers of the island group, was the starting point for this strategy, which, it later emerged, formed part of Vancouver's larger ambition to annex Hawaii. Later in the voyage he took formal possession of a part of the North American coast, in what is now Oregon, also without orders, which suggests that from the first he saw his voyage as a counterpart to the settlement of New South Wales and as part of an active British development of the whole Pacific region.

Vancouver's behaviour could be unpredictable, however. Furious about the theft of some linen in Tahiti, he put a noose round the neck of a Tahitian he knew was merely an accomplice and, according to the ever-critical George Hewitt, 'in a Passion snatched hold of the Halter himself and drew it so tight as nearly to deprive the Man of Life...' In Maui (one of the Hawaiian Islands) the following winter a few ribbons were stolen and Vancouver 'threatened the chiefs with such menacing threats' that the chief of the island leapt out of a window and into his canoe. Vancouver was intolerant of theft, a trait later interpreted by his detractors as an obsession with property which supposedly revealed that, while he may have been an officer, he was certainly no 'gentleman'.

Four Remarkable Supported Poles in Port Townsend, Gulph of Georgia, by Midshipman John Sykes but 'improved' by the artist, William Alexander, for the posthumous publication of Vancouver's *A Voyage of Discovery* (1798). Some 65 drawings survived from the voyage, mainly by midshipmen Sykes and Humphreys, some of which were later engraved for Vancouver's book. This engraving shows the high poles found in several Native American villages, and which puzzled Vancouver's men. The poles were actually used to suspend nets to trap birds.

Surveys and Observations

Vancouver was to start his survey in the Strait of Juan de Fuca, named after a Greek pilot in the service of Spain who was supposed to have sailed up the Californian coast in the 1590s and into a large inlet, the entrance to which was marked by 'a great Hedland or Island, with an exceedingly high Pinnacle or spired Rocke, like a pillar thereupon'. De Fuca claimed to have followed its course for some 20 days before reaching the Atlantic and 'discovering' the North-West Passage. Cook passed by in 1778: 'It is in the very latitude we were now in where geographers have placed the pretended *Strait of Juan de Fuca*, but we saw nothing like it, nor is there the least probability that iver any such thing exhisted.'

But a strait there was, and one that was indeed marked by a pinnacle of rock, today called Fuca Pillar. Vancouver's ships entered cautiously in 'very thick rainy weather' in April 1792, sailing along the south coast of the strait, which he called the 'Continental Shore'. His plan was simplicity itself: he would keep this shore on his right hand knowing that whatever its twists, turns and blind alleys, he would either feel his way into the North-West Passage or find himself back in the open ocean. The next morning dawned with 'clear and pleasant weather', wrote Vancouver, although Manby's prose was more poetic:

Never was contrast greater, in this days sailing than with that we had long been accustomed too. It had more the aspect of enchantment than reality, with silent admiration each discerned the beauties of Nature, and nought was heard on board but expressions of delight murmured from every tongue. Imperceptibly our Bark skimmed over the glassy surface of the deep, about three Miles an hour, a gentle breeze swelled the lofty Canvass whilst all was calm below.

The idyll was cruelly dashed for Manby when he joined his captain in a search for an anchorage, landed and 'killed a remarkable animal about the size of a cat, of a brown color, with a large, white, bushy tail that spread over his back. After firing I approached him and was saluted by a discharge from him the most nauseous and fetid my sense of smelling ever experienced.' Archibald Menzies was keen to take it on board for examination and tied the body to the bow of the cutter, but the smell 'was so intolerable' that it was thrown in the water. The skunk's revenge could never be entirely eradicated from Manby's clothes despite numerous soakings in boiling water, and a chastened midshipman vowed never to disturb another 'on any consideration'.

The two ships anchored in a large bay, which Vancouver named Port Discovery, where three of the ships' boats were victualled for a week and where the survey began. As they started, the weather changed and the gentle breeze that had so enraptured Manby gave way to gales and fog. Obedient to Vancouver's plan to follow the continental shore, over the next few weeks the boats began to trace the coast south into Puget Sound, following every waterway until it either returned them to their starting point or ceased to be navigable. They employed an enhanced version of the 'running survey' that had been used to such good effect by Cook, landing frequently to establish their positions by astronomical observation and measuring base lines on the beach to ensure that their triangulations were accurate. Vancouver soon 'became thoroughly convinced that our boats alone could enable us to acquire correct or satisfactory information regarding this broken country', although he admitted with masterly understatement that 'the execution of such a service in open boats would necessarily be extremely laborious'. Menzies's description of one night during the first survey was typical of many: his boat was battling against a strong ebb tide 'and the night was so very dark & foggy with excessive rain' that they gave up the hope of finding the prearranged rendezvous and pulled ashore to pitch their tents and kindle a fire, but 'the latter was found a very difficult task it being so dark & every thing so wet, it was midnight before we could get under any kind of shelter & then every thing about us was completely drenched & in this situation the greatest part of the Boats Crews passed the night without any covering to shelter them from the inclemency of the weather'. The survey would henceforth be carried out almost exclusively in the boats, rowed mile after aching mile, with the surveyors completing their observations in sections that were then, on their return to the ships, added to the master chart being drawn up by Joseph Baker. The *Discovery* and the *Chatham* would then weigh anchor, move further up the coast, anchor again, and the boats would set out once more.

As the survey progressed over the next three seasons, Vancouver would sight, plot and name hundreds of headlands, bays, mountains and islands. Some names complimented old shipmates such as the astronomer William Wales, who taught Vancouver the principles of navigation and surveying on Cook's second voyage and who was remembered in Wales Point. Others honoured royalty or Admiralty officials – King George Sound and Cape Chatham, for example – or influential people – Port Townshend, named, as Thomas Manby put it, 'in honor of the noble marquis, my sincere and long known friend'. Countless names were descriptive: Desolation Sound is now considered a beauty spot but Vancouver thought it 'a gloomy place' and one that 'afforded not a single prospect that was pleasing to the eye'. A crewman died after eating bad mussels at Poison Cove, and New Dungeness was so called because Vancouver thought it bore a strong resemblance to Dungeness in Kent. He finished his survey three long years later at Port Conclusion.

ENCOUNTERS WITH LOCAL PEOPLES

Vancouver's charts inscribed a specifically British nomenclature on the landscape, reflecting and reinforcing Britain's emerging ambitions in the area, but obscuring a story of contact with Native Americans. The constant, if brief, encounters with the many different peoples living along the coast were a significant side-effect of Vancouver's decision to survey from small boats. In the first survey from Port Discovery alone they passed through the territories of five different clans, and would eventually come into contact with all of the six major language groups on the north-west coast: Wakashan, Haida, Tsimshian, Tlingit, Eyak-Athapaskan and, far to the north, a dialect of the Alutiiq language spoken by the Chugach people. The study of people was hampered by the lack of a professional artist like Hodges or Webber, and although Vancouver's officers made competent sketches of places and incidents, they were surveyors and their drawings were primarily topographical, with human figures almost entirely absent. Some of the published engravings did include people, but they were the later additions of the home artist, William Alexander, who had been hired to improve the sketches for publi-

cation, and they have no ethnographic value. Menzies had official responsibility for ethnography and he steadily accumulated a representative range of artefacts, while the descriptions of peoples left by him, Vancouver and some other officers remain valuable source material for scholars to this day. But although not an unsympathetic observer, and admittedly hampered by the briefness of the meetings, Menzies was never really as curious about human beings, their origins and cultures as J.R. Forster had been on Cook's second voyage, and his ethnography does not compare to that of his predecessor.

MENZIES'S BOTANICAL COLLECTIONS

Menzies began his botanical collections in Port Discovery with the first specimens of the oriental strawberry tree, the arbutus, which bears his name, *Arbutus menziesii*. This, he wrote, 'grows to a small tree & was at this time a peculiar ornament to the Forest by its large clusters of whitish flowers & ever green leaves, but its peculiar smooth bark of a reddish brown colour will at all times attract the Notice of the most superficial observer'. Here, too, he collected the *Rhododendron macrophyllum*, later adopted as the state of Washington's flower. Menzies's most famous introduction to the gardens of Europe was the monkey-puzzle tree, *Araucaria araucana*, which he obtained not in North America but from nuts collected in Chile on the way home. They were planted at Kew and one of the resulting trees, which was known as 'Sir Joseph Banks's Pine', was sketched in the 1830s and is thought to have survived until the end of the nineteenth century.

Menzies put his live specimens in Vancouver's hated 'plant cabbin', but keeping them alive was a constant struggle. As he complained to Banks, 'I have not yet been able to get plants to succeed … in the Frame on the Quarter Deck – for if it is uncovered in rainy weather to admit air, the dripping from the rigging impregnated with Tar & Turpentine hurts the foliage & soil – and if the Side lights are opened Goats – Dogs – Cats – Pigeons – Poultry &c. &c. are ever creeping in & destroying the plants.' He lost an entire collection almost overnight in the cold Alaskan spring, and many more in a sudden squall when homeward bound in the Atlantic.

The survey seemed an endless task at times and tempers became frayed. Menzies and Vancouver clashed over the plant frame and were soon communicating only in writing on the subject. The capable Manby got a brutal dressing down from Vancouver for losing touch with the lead boat one night: 'His salutation I can never forget,' wrote the deeply offended midshipman, 'and his language I will

OPPOSITE A chart showing the area around Vancouver Island surveyed in 1792, with the tracks of the *Discovery* and the *Chatham*.

never forgive unless he withdraws his words by a satisfactory apology.' Vancouver may have been quick-tempered and abusive but he still recognised talent and steadily promoted Manby during the voyage, appointing him sailing master of the *Chatham* – 'a situation I should have refused in England,' Manby said, but one that he welcomed in America 'as it cleared me from a man I had just reason to be displeased with'. Despite his promotions, Manby was true to his word and never did forgive Vancouver. Neither did Midshipman Pitt, who was punished twice more in the first surveying season, being beaten for breaking the glass of the binnacle in a piece of horseplay and put in irons for falling asleep on watch. Vancouver was equally hard with his crew, on one occasion making them tack the ship all day – an exhausting procedure – when he felt that they had been too slow on the first tack.

ENCOUNTERS WITH SPANISH SURVEYORS

And so the first summer progressed, the two ships painstakingly charting the continental shore between the future sites of Seattle and Vancouver. It was near the latter that they met two small Spanish survey vessels, the *Sutil* and the *Mexicana*, offshoots of the Malaspina expedition. They were able to tell Vancouver that Juan

EXPLORING AN ISLAND; engraving by B.T. Pouncey after William Alexander
(from a sketch by John Sykes) from Vancouver's *A Voyage of Discovery*.

Francisco de la Bodega y Quadra was already waiting in Nootka Sound, as agreed by the Spanish and British governments, for the final resolution of the 'incident'. Meanwhile, Vancouver and the commanders of the *Sutil* and the *Mexicana* agreed to pool the results of their surveys, Vancouver honourably recording Spanish names on his charts where they had been the first to survey a coast. Most of the Spanish names, however, were excised and Vancouver's names restored when the charts were prepared for publication back in Britain.

The four ships eventually separated and the *Discovery* and the *Chatham* wriggled through a long and narrow passage which, after a hundred miles, opened out into the broad waters of Queen Charlotte Sound to the north of Vancouver Island. The maze of shoals they found here was far more dangerous than the narrows, and the *Discovery* soon ran aground on a falling tide. Vancouver quickly lightened the ship and ordered the topmasts and yards to be brought down so their weight would not drag the ship over. However, despite these precautions, Manby recorded that 'after lying upright for half an hour a terrible crash ensued which brought the ship on her broadside'. In bad conditions the *Discovery* could have been lost, but fortunately it was calm and the ship floated off with the rising tide some hours later. They had no sooner got off and rerigged than the *Chatham* ran aground and an exasperated Vancouver eventually had to send the boats ahead to find a safe passage.

It was now getting towards the end of August and Vancouver turned his ships towards Nootka Sound to begin negotiations with Bodega y Quadra and rendezvous with the storeship, *Daedalus*, which was waiting for them, but with sad news: Vancouver's old friend Richard Hergest and the young astronomer William Gooch, whose appointment had arrived too late for him to sail on the *Discovery*, had been killed in a brief and confused affray on one of the Hawaiian Islands.

Vancouver's negotiations with Bodega y Quadra were amicable – a mark of their mutual respect was their naming of Quadra and Vancouver Island, which only later became Vancouver Island – but they could not reach agreement on the restitution of British property in the Sound and a frustrated Vancouver wrote to the Admiralty for further instructions (which were never given to him). He then headed south to Monterey, where official reports, charts and specimens were sent back to Britain, while others took the opportunity to send letters home. Manby was one such, writing:

> We are my good fellow spinning about the Globe like a Worligig, seldom in a place, and as seldom like true Seamen contented with our situation. Good health continues in our little squadron, though I am sorry to add not that good fellowship which ought to subsist with adventurers traversing these distant seas, owing to the conduct of our Commander in Chief who is grown Haughty Proud Mean and Insolent, which has kept himself and his Officers in a continual state of wrangling…

THE *DISCOVERY* ON THE ROCKS IN QUEEN CHARLOTTE'S SOUND (detail);
engraving by B.T. Pouncey after William Alexander (from a sketch by Zachary Mudge)
from Vancouver's *A Voyage of Discovery*.

Leaving Monterey, they sailed for the Hawaiian Islands to overwinter. While there Vancouver made strenuous efforts to bring the killers of Hergest and Gooch to justice and, with the help of the Hawaiian rulers, tried and executed three men off Oahu's Waikiki beach. Hewitt, inevitably, criticised the procedure, suggesting that there was no evidence that any of the men had been involved in the killing, but his sentiments do not appear to have been shared by the rest of the crew; even Manby approved. The Hawaiian chiefs, vying for political control among themselves, cooperated because their powerful visitor was a useful ally.

RETURN TO NOOTKA SOUND

Vancouver returned to Nootka Sound in the spring, beginning the survey where they had finished the previous autumn, and the ships gradually worked their way north along an even more intricate coastline. Vancouver had been a sick man before the voyage even started, probably having contracted some form of glandular disease during his time in the West Indies, and by the second surveying season his health was worsening and he was unable to take personal command of as many of the survey trips as before. However, he had made sure during the winter that the boats' crews now had covers to protect them from the incessant rain, bags for dry clothes, and lockers in which to store provisions. The weather was appalling and the local people, the Nuu-chah-nulth, he wrote, seemed 'more daring and insolent' than those in the area around Vancouver Island. They were now in the territory of the Tlingit, and that August Vancouver recorded 'an unprovoked assault on our boats' during which several of the attackers were killed. His boat had landed to fix the outline of the shore, and although four or five Tlingit canoes also landed close by, Vancouver was unconcerned as they appeared 'peaceably inclined' and eager to trade at first. Then the Tlingit began stealing objects and seemed increasingly 'inclined to be turbulent'. 'Our situation,' Vancouver wrote, 'was now become very critical and alarming'; one of the crew was stabbed in the thigh and he abandoned his policy of avoiding bloodshed and opened fire, killing between six and twelve people – the British estimates varied widely – before being able to pull away to the safety of his accompanying boats.

Vancouver was unsure whether in landing he had unwittingly committed an offence, or whether the attack had been in revenge for 'injuries they have sustained from other civilized visitors', by which he meant fur traders, or whether the situation had escalated when 'they conceived the valuable articles we possessed'. Any of these theories could have been valid. Encounters between First Nations people and British, neither of whom understood the other's taboos, cultures or languages, were always complex and potentially fraught affairs, especially as Vancouver's boats were conducting their surveys close inshore and landing often. The British frequently complained of theft but helped themselves freely to wood, water, game and green-stuff, little comprehending that these things had owners and needed to be paid for; and Menzies's interest in burial sites and bones involved trespassing on sacred ground. The violence in what Vancouver referred to as 'Traitor's Cove' was one of the very few occasions on which blood was spilt, which, bearing in mind the tensions inherent in the meetings, shows remarkable forbearance on both sides. The majority of meetings were peaceful and trading often brisk – too brisk, according to Thomas Manby, who, in a letter to a friend, accused his captain of using government trade goods to buy sea-otter furs on his own account, so 'pursuing business and a Trade … unbecoming the Character of an officer in his Honorable and exalted station'.

At some point during this season Midshipman Pitt transgressed for the last time and an unknown member of the crew left a fragmentary record of his illegal trade and punishment:

> the Capt. missing some sheets of copper c[oul]d not learn who had taken them he therefore tied up the Boatswain … during the flogging the Boatswain feeling the pain said Oh Mr. Pitt how can you see me thus used. Capt. V. perceiving that Mr. Pitt had taken the copper ordered the boatswain to be released and Mr. P. to take as many lashes as the boatswain had recd.

Vancouver had had enough of Pitt and when the ship returned to Hawaii the following winter he sent him and a couple of other troublemakers back home on the *Daedalus*. During the winter of 1793–94 Vancouver had a diplomatic victory on Hawaii when 'the principal chiefs of the island ... unanimously ceded the said island of Owyhee to His Britannic Majesty, and acknowledged themselves to be subjects of Great Britain'. Vancouver overstated his case as Kamehameha was putting only Hawaii under the protection of Britain, and had his own purposes for doing so, but it was a skilful piece of diplomacy nonetheless, and one that would have secured an important strategic base for Britain had the fur trade developed. Curiously, Vancouver never informed the Admiralty and the first the British government appears to have heard of the cession of Hawaii was when Vancouver's journal was published in 1798, by which time he was dead.

The following spring the ships returned to North America and this time Vancouver sailed straight to Cook's River, the northern extremity of the survey. Sixteen years earlier, it had seemed to Cook's officers to hold promise of being the North-West Passage they sought, but Cook cut short the survey, writing tetchily in his journal that they had all wasted enough time on a 'trifling point of geography'. Vancouver briskly established that no navigable 'river' existed and changed the name to Cook('s) Inlet, noting in his journal that 'had the great and first discoverer of it, whose name it bears, dedicated one more day to its further examination, he would have spared the theoretical navigators, who have followed him in their closets, the task of ingeniously ascribing to this arm of the ocean a channel, through which a north-west passage ... might ultimately be discovered'. It would have saved Vancouver much trouble as well, but this remains unsaid in a rare criticism of the captain he normally revered.

The two ships steadily worked south, finishing at the end of August 1794 at 56° north, Port Conclusion, where the north-going survey had ended the previous year. When the boats finally returned to the *Discovery* and the *Chatham* after their last extended survey, Vancouver proudly wrote:

> *the hearty congratulations that were mutually exchanged by three cheers, proclaimed not only the pleasure that was felt in the accomplishment of this laborious service, but the zeal with which it had been carried into execution, and ... laudable pride ... in having been instrumental to the attainment of so grand an object.*

There was also a strong sense of relief: Midshipman Barrie probably spoke for many when he said that he would never go through another such voyage 'if a Post Captain's commission was to be my reward'. It had been a hard, troubled but successful expedition. The boats had charted more than 5,000 miles of heavily indented and dangerous coastline 'with,' Vancouver said, 'a degree of minuteness far exceeding the letter of [his] commission'. He had lost but six men and only one of them to disease. Although himself a very sick man and with nagging concerns that he had never managed to resolve the Nootka Sound problem, he was clearly looking forward to a happy return and the recognition he felt he deserved. It was not to be, however, for the waters in London were to prove far more treacherous than those of America.

VANCOUVER'S DECLINE

In the intervening years Sir Joseph Banks had been busy maliciously planting the shipboard gossip sent back by Menzies along with his regular packages of seeds. Banks got more useable information when he heard that the simmering feud over the plant frame had erupted one last and violent time on the way home and that Vancouver had placed the naturalist under arrest and had demanded a court martial as soon as they landed. The affair was smoothed over when Menzies apologised to Vancouver, who then dropped the charges. Banks, however, continued his campaign, encouraging Menzies to publish an account of the voyage before Vancouver's official narrative came out, but, Menzies being 'but a slow hand with the pen', the book never materialised.

More damaging to Vancouver was the return of Midshipman Pitt, now Lord Camelford. His hatred of Vancouver had festered during his journey home in the *Daedalus*, and when both men returned to Britain Pitt pursued his victim remorselessly, challenging him to a duel and once actually trying to thrash him in public. The political caricaturist James Gillray published a print of *The Caneing in Conduit Street* which shows a heroic Pitt raising his stick to a fat and cowardly Vancouver hiding behind his brother and standing in front of 'The South Sea Fur Warehouse' advertising 'Fine Black Otter Skins' – a reference to his trading activities. On Vancouver's back is a feather cloak bearing a label reading 'The Present from the King of Owyhee to George III forgot to be delivered', referring to another scurrilous story. The savage cartoon showed the extent to which many of the less savoury events on the voyage had become common currency in London, where the stories of a hard, vindictive and bullying captain in the Pacific seemed all too familiar after the trial of the *Bounty* mutineers.

It is hard to say what effect the 'Camelford Affair' and Banks's lobbying actually had on Vancouver professionally, but while the Admiralty accorded him the honour of promoting all those he recommended – and he was generous in his recommendations – he was certainly beset with a number of official irritations, obstructions and delays. These were to an extent the normal workings of a bureaucracy, experienced before and since by many returning commanders, but in a letter to Lord Chatham Vancouver complained that since his return he felt 'as it were

insulated, from all connections with persons of consequence' who would normally have been willing to help resolve the issues. Vancouver was up against the Establishment, but it must have been particularly distressing to him when his oldest and most trusted colleague, Joseph Whidbey, was recruited by Banks to support the criticism of his style of command. Conspiracy theorists will note that Banks later proposed Whidbey as a Fellow of the Royal Society.

In the few years left to him Vancouver worked on writing his account of the voyage. That he was able to do so at all bearing in mind his failing health and other problems bears testimony in no small way to the powers of determination and concentration that made him such a good, if demanding, surveyor. Vancouver died in May 1798. For the last few months he did not have the strength to write, so his brother John completed the last pages of *A Voyage of Discovery*, which was published posthumously later that year. It was reviewed favourably in the *Naval Chronicle* as a 'naval classic', although Midshipman Barrie probably reflected the response of more general readers when he complained to his mother that 'I think it is one of the most tedious books I ever read'. In the Hakluyt edition of *A Voyage of Discovery* (1986), the editor, W. Kaye Lamb, wisely left the last word of his comprehensive introduction to one of Vancouver's harshest critics, Archibald Menzies, who said in his eightieth year: 'those books that Vancouver wrote – strange that he could put so much of himself into the printed page. He was a great Captain.'

OPPOSITE THE CANEING IN CONDUIT STREET; coloured etching by James Gillray, 1796.

This satirical cartoon shows the infamous incident when Vancouver's erratic ex-midshipman, Thomas Pitt (by then 2nd Baron Camelford), tried to give his old captain a public thrashing. In 1804 Pitt insulted another naval officer and former friend, leading to a pistol duel in which he was mortally wounded, aged just 29.

BELOW Vancouver's old ship, the *Discovery* (detail), as a prison hulk on the Thames at Woolwich; watercolour by Thomas Hosmer Shepherd, *c.*1830.

The ship had been converted into a bomb vessel after Vancouver's voyage and became a prison hulk in 1808. It was finally broken up in 1834.

CAPTAIN FLINDERS. R.N.
Autograph Copy of Parole on his release from six years Captivity
in the Isle of Mauritius.

I undersigned, captain in His Britannic Majesty's navy,
having obtained leave of His Excellency the captain-general to return in.
my country by the way of Bengal, Promise on my word of honour not to
act in any service which might be considered as directly, or indirectly hostile
to France or its Allies, during the course of the present war.

Port Napoleon, Isle de France, 7th June 1810

(Signed) Matth. Flinders

8

'AN HERCULEAN LABOUR'

Matthew Flinders's Circumnavigation of Australia

'I have ten-thousand difficulties and dangers to encounter. I have undertaken an Herculean labour.'

—MATTHEW FLINDERS

IN THE AUTUMN OF 1800 a young naval lieutenant, having recently returned to Britain, wrote an excited letter to his future wife. In it he described what he saw as a turning point in his life:

> You see that I make everything subservient to business. Indeed my dearest friend, this time seems to be a very critical period of my life. I have been long absent, – have done services abroad that were not expected, but which seem to be thought a good deal of. I have more and greater friends than before, and this seems to be the moment that their exertions may be most serviceable to me. I may now perhaps make a bold dash forward, or may remain a poor lieutenant all my life.

MATTHEW FLINDERS

The young lieutenant's name was Matthew Flinders, his future wife was his childhood friend Ann Chappelle and the 'services abroad' were a series of charts he had made of Australia with his colleague, the naval surgeon George Bass. In a succession of boats – the smallest an eight-foot dinghy called *Tom Thumb* – the two men had started to survey the coast on either side of Port Jackson, but the feat that

PREVIOUS PAGES Matthew Flinders (1774–1814); with a facsimile of his autograph parole after six years in captivity on Île de France (Mauritius).

OPPOSITE Admiralty plan of the *Investigator*'s quarterdeck showing the 'plant cabbin' that Sir Joseph Banks had ordered to be taken out to Australia and erected in Port Jackson.

It was designed to hold the live plants he hoped his naturalists would collect. A number of ships converted for voyages of discovery would be equipped with a plant cabin. They were universally unpopular with the seamen as they adversely affected the handling of the ships.

got them really noticed was the circumnavigation of Van Diemen's Land (Tasmania), which proved its insularity and established, in Bass Strait, a much shorter passage for ships sailing the southern route from the Cape of Good Hope to Port Jackson.

Flinders had sailed as a midshipman on William Bligh's second breadfruit voyage to Tahiti and the West Indies (1791–93). Although he and Bligh fell out, Flinders managed to pick up three things on the *Providence*, all of which were to affect him in later life: the basics of marine surveying; venereal disease; and an appreciation of the influence that Sir Joseph Banks had in all matters to do with exploration. On his return in 1800 from Australia, where his ship the *Reliance* had been stationed for nearly four years, Flinders shrewdly dedicated his charts to Banks – surely the most important of the new and great friends he mentions – and sent him an ambitious plan for a complete survey of the coast of Australia.

Very little more had been learnt about Australia's shores since Cook's running survey of the east coast, while, as Flinders himself put it, 'the vast interior of this new continent was wrapped in total obscurity' to Europeans. Flinders proposed a full scientific expedition to survey the entire coast for possible harbours and rivers, while an on-board party of scientists and artists would explore the land's natural resources. This was to be scientific exploration in the style of Cook, although with a more openly colonial purpose.

Two years earlier, Banks had had a similar project turned down by an Admiralty understandably preoccupied with the war at sea; but, undaunted, he endorsed Flinders's plan and sent it off, and this time it was accepted. What caused the change of heart was that the French government had just requested a passport guaranteeing safe passage for a scientific voyage to Australia under the command of Nicolas Baudin. Although the subsequent history of Flinders's voyage would show only too clearly that the gentlemanly scientific ideals of the Enlightenment were under pressure after years of war, the Admiralty had little choice but to grant Baudin a passport. But neither was it blind to the potential embarrassment of France exploring and naming what was, arguably at least, a British possession. In reality, the Admiralty had very little strategic interest in Australia at that time, but it had no intention of being beaten by the French in any aspect of maritime activity.

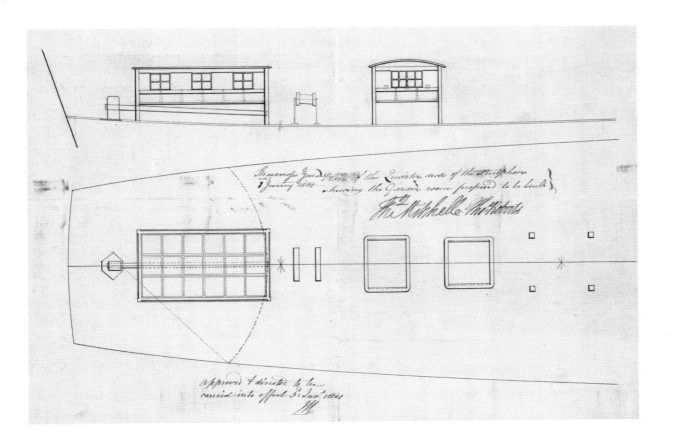

THE *INVESTIGATOR*'S PREPARATIONS

The ship selected was a northern collier, originally built as the *Fram*, then bought by the Navy, converted into a sloop-of-war and renamed the *Xenophon*. The choice followed Cook's famous championing of roomy, sturdy and round-bottomed colliers for long voyages of exploration. However, the *Xenophon*'s structure had been strained by the original conversion and the ship leaked badly from the first – a weakness that would eventually have disastrous effects on the voyage. It was, wrote Flinders, choosing his words carefully some years later, 'the best vessel which could, at that time, be spared for the projected voyage'. Neither he nor Banks felt inclined to risk its abandonment by pushing for a better ship and so *Xenophon* was renamed once again, this time as the *Investigator*. Flinders was appointed its captain and, in February 1801, promoted to the rank of commander. The hope that he had expressed in his letter to Ann Chappelle had been realised: he would now no longer stay a 'poor lieutenant' for the rest of his days.

The Admiralty gave Banks virtually a free hand in planning the voyage and selecting the scientific personnel, telling him that 'any proposal you may make will be approved, the whole is left entirely to your decision'. For the all-important post of naturalist, Banks turned once again to Scotland, appointing a graduate of Edinburgh University named Robert Brown, who was to be assisted by a gardener, Peter Good. There were to be two artists: Ferdinand Bauer, responsible for the 'natural history' – the plants, animals and fish collected on the voyage – and a young man named William Westall as the landscape painter. In addition, there was to be a mineralogist and an astronomer, although the latter, John Crossley, left the ship at Cape Town because of illness and his role would be filled for the rest of the voyage by Flinders and his brother Samuel, who had been appointed as one of the *Investigator*'s lieutenants.

Banks made sure that the ship was supplied with the finest scientific equipment. He personally sent a set of the *Encyclopaedia Britannica* on board and arranged for the East India Company, which had some interest in the outcomes of the voyage, to give Flinders and his officers 'table money'. The Board of Longitude equipped

the *Investigator* with astronomical instruments and chronometers; 'K3' (Larcum Kendall's third chronometer which had accompanied Vancouver) was later sent to join Flinders in Australia. For Banks as well as Flinders this was undoubtedly conceived of as a voyage of scientific exploration in the manner and spirit of Cook; its scale suggests that in some ways Banks saw it as the one he had planned but finally withdrawn from on Cook's *Resolution* in 1772.

Flinders busied himself preparing his ship for its long voyage. When he had a problem he went first to Banks, who generally managed to fix it. Flinders, conscious and proud that he was the second generation of Cook's lieutenants, followed the great navigator's advice on scurvy by loading anti-scorbutics such as sauerkraut and malt extract, insisting that each man drank a pint of this 'wort' every day. The Navy had adopted lemon juice as the most effective countermeasure for the disease in 1796, and while Flinders's use of ineffective ones may have shown admirable loyalty to the memory of Cook, his reliance on them was destined to cost him dear during the voyage.

The Admiralty received a passport from the French guaranteeing the *Investigator* safe passage and by June 1801 the ship was ready. *The Times* reported that 'she is admirably fitted out for the intended service, and is manned with picked men, who are distinguished by a glazed hat decorated with a globe, and the name of the ship in letters of gold'. One sees the purse of Banks rather than the hand of Flinders behind this delightful bit of theatre.

WRECK REEF BANK TAKEN AT LOW WATER, AUGUST 1803 (detail), by William Westall.

The uncharted reef where the *Porpoise* – on which Flinders and Westall left Australia in 1803 – was lost. The wreck is included on the left. Westall did the painting from a drawing he made there at the time, and it was one of the few Australian scenes to which he would return repeatedly. He was working on another version of it when he died.

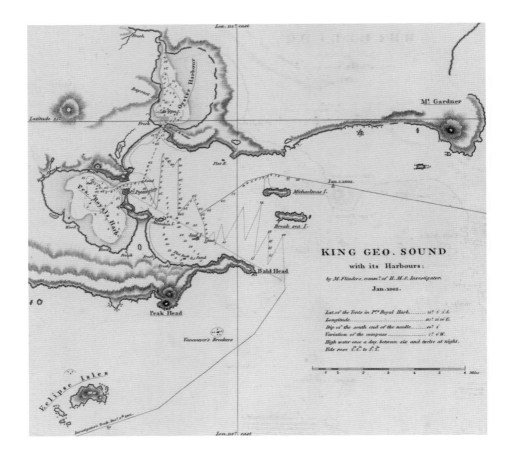

KING GEO. SOUND
with its Harbours;
by M. Flinders, comm.ʳ of H.M.S. Investigator.
Jan. 1802.

Lat. of the Tents in Pᵗ Royal Harb........ 35° 1′ 55″ S.
Longitude.............................. 117° 55′ 10″ E.
Dip of the south end of the needle........ 64° 1′ W.
Variation of the compass............... 7° 0′ W.
High water once a day, between six and twelve at night.
Tide rose 2 ft. 5 in. to 5 ft. 5 in.

MARRIAGE TO ANN CHAPPELLE

Alongside the public preparations for the voyage, which can be traced through Flinders's journal *A Voyage to Terra Australis* (1814) and official documents in British and Australian archives, a personal drama was unfolding. Flinders was a prolific, entertaining and revealing letter writer and his letters to Ann Chappelle offer a rare glimpse of the personal problems that must have hovered behind many such voyages. Ann was clearly very attracted to Flinders and had agreed to marry him, but once she realised that his plans for the immediate future involved him returning to Australia for another three or four years she cooled noticeably. Flinders visited her in Lincolnshire at Christmas 1800 and the visit was not a success: 'Thou didst not just return me answers to questions put', he wrote as soon as he got back to London, 'thou offered nothing for me to consider. Thou asked me no question. Thou seemed to wish no conversation upon the subject that I was so interested about [...] tears are in my eyes – I am torn to pieces.'

At the Christmas meeting Ann gave Matthew 'Pleasures of Memory' (perhaps a souvenir scrapbook of happier times, or the popular poetry collection published by Samuel Rogers in 1795), and both of them seem to have considered the relationship at an end, although they continued to correspond. Flinders's letters between January and April 1801 have not survived. In April 1801, however, he came up with a bright idea:

> *Thou has asked me if there is a* possibility *of our living together. I think I see a* probability *of our living with a moderate share of comfort. Till now I was not certain of being able to fit myself out clear of the world. I have now done it, and have accommodation on board the* Investigator, *in which as my wife a woman may, with love to assist her, make herself happy.*
>
> *It will be much better to keep this matter entirely secret. There are many reasons for it, and I have also a powerful one. I do not know how my great friends might like it.*

Flinders had changed the cabin layout in the *Investigator* to create a small private bedroom off the great cabin, and his plan was that Ann would sail with him to Port Jackson, where she would be able to live relatively cheaply and see her husband whenever the ship returned there to refit. Flinders was right in thinking that this should be kept 'entirely secret'. Sir Joseph Banks was no romantic, thundering some years later when hearing of the marriage of one of his Australian plant collectors, and probably thinking of Flinders that 'this marrying has often been in my way… I did not hire him to beget a family in N.S. Wales.' Flinders and Ann duly married, but Banks heard of it when he, a Lincolnshire man like Flinders, was sent a local paper. By ill chance, the new First Lord of the Admiralty, Earl St Vincent, also paid the *Investigator* an unscheduled visit and was surprised to find the captain's wife on board, and obviously not simply visiting. No official decision had been made on Ann when the *Investigator* left Sheerness at the end of May and began to work its way down the English Channel with her still on board. Bad luck struck again when the *Investigator* ran aground off Dungeness while captain and wife were below and at this point Flinders was in real danger of losing his job. Although Banks was furious

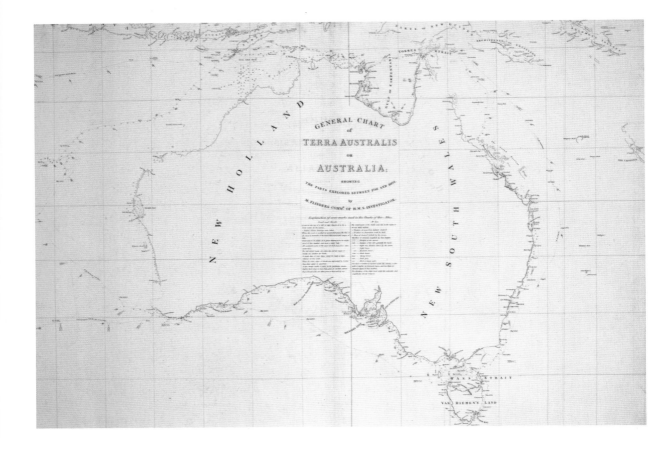

that Flinders had put him in an embarrassing situation, he did not want the voyage compromised before it had even started and so did his best to ease the situation. Flinders kept his command, although he never again really had the full trust of the Admiralty, and Ann was packed off to live with her family. As a memento of her time on the *Investigator*, Ann left a few words pencilled on their cabin wall, which the couple referred to as her 'forget me not'. They were not to see each other again for more than nine years.

The incident throws some aspects of Flinders's character into sharp relief. When faced with a choice between marriage or exploration he chose the latter, which suggests, incorrectly, that he felt a burning desire to be an explorer. He was indeed an intensely ambitious man, but he saw a career in the Navy entirely pragmatically: 'Sea; I am thy servant', he once wrote, 'but thy wages must afford me more than a bare subsistence.' Money was always important to Flinders and while exploration gave him the chance to stand out from the mass of other unconnected and unknown lieutenants, it more importantly allowed him to make his fortune. He calculated that the voyage would earn him the substantial sum of £1,500 from wages and the publication of the official narrative and charts. Flinders was a very intelligent man but one who knew it all too well. His confidence in his own abilities led him to take risks; this made him an effective explorer but occasionally led him into extremely dangerous situations, for his self-confidence could seamlessly blend into an arrogant conviction that he could get away with anything. He probably left Britain feeling elated that he had managed to marry Ann and still keep command of the voyage rather than concerned that he had lost the trust of Banks and the Admiralty and, temporarily at least, embittered his wife.

Ann resented the forced separation deeply and her first letters to him when they were apart again, which he received more than a year later, were clearly cudgelling him for following the 'call of his profession' and showing 'poor proof' of his love for her. Flinders, for his part, simply missed their brief period of intimacy From Cape Town in November 1801 he wrote:

> *Oh, write to me constantly, write me pages and volumes. Tell me the dress thou wearest, and at what time in the morning thou puttest on thy stockings; tell me they dreams, – any thing: so do but talk to me, and of thyself. When thou art sitting at thy kneedle* [sic] *and alone, then think on me, my love; and write me the uppermost of thy thoughts. Fill me half a dozen sheets and send them when thou canst.*

TOWARDS PORT JACKSON

After a stop at Cape Town where the ship was recaulked to try and stop a worrying leak that had first made its appearance in the English Channel, the *Investigator* made landfall at Vancouver's old anchorage in King George III Sound on the south-west tip of Australia, after a passage of just under five months. Flinders's instructions allowed him to stop here briefly for water, but then ordered him to hurry on to Port Jackson for refitting before commencing the survey. The Admiralty had divided the mammoth task of charting Australia's 30,000-kilometre coastline into sections and gave Flinders unambiguous instructions on the order in which he was to complete them, in accordance with navigational, scientific and political priorities. Typically, Flinders promptly ignored the orders and spent some weeks in the Sound (now the site of the city of Albany) refitting the *Investigator* and resurveying the harbour before starting his survey of the south coast of Australia on the way to Port Jackson.

The southern route was the quickest for ships sailing to Port Jackson from Cape Town, but they sailed well south of the coast itself, usually making their landfall at Tasmania. Bruny d'Entrecasteaux had surveyed parts of the coast in his search for Lapérouse in 1791–93, but a full and accurate chart was long overdue. There would be obvious advantages for colonial development if Flinders were able to discover usable rivers and harbours along this stretch; there was also a persuasive but incorrect geographical theory that Terra Australis was not one single continent but two, split in half by a waterway stretching from the Gulf of Carpentaria in the north to the south coast, and Flinders had orders to search for it. In addition, he was acutely aware that Nicolas Baudin's expedition had set off before him, and Flinders was anxious to claim the honour of being the first to survey and name the jewel in the crown of Australian marine surveying.

SURVEYING THE SOUTH COAST

There was nothing fundamentally wrong with Flinders's decision to survey the south coast immediately: the Admiralty had made it his number one task anyway and, as Flinders pointed out in his published account, he was going to have to follow it to get to Port Jackson, so it made sense to survey as he went along. The real problem was that instead of exploring during the cooler months, as originally planned, it was actually done at the height of summer, when the blistering heat created an arid desert where the botanists had hoped to find new and exotic plants. The naturalist Robert Brown always felt bitter about Flinders's decision to survey that area first and complained about it to Banks, noting in addition that Flinders gave the scientists few opportunities to go ashore. Banks, however, backed the captain, telling Brown that he did not know how lucky he was: 'Had Cooke [*sic*] paid the same attention to the naturalists as he [Flinders] seems to have done we should have done much more [on the *Endeavour* voyage].'

By the end of February 1802 Flinders had surveyed most of the Great Australian Bight, that enormous curved coastline stretching from the south-west tip of Australia to the approaches to Bass Strait. It was here, at a place that Flinders named Cape Catastrophe, that tragedy struck. 'It will grieve thee, as it has me,' he wrote to Ann, who of course knew the *Investigator*'s crew personally, 'that poor Thistle was lost upon the south coast.' John Thistle was the ship's sailing master and had sailed with Flinders for some years. 'Thou knowest how I valued him;' Flinders continued, 'he is however gone, as well as Mr Taylor and six seamen, who were all drowned in a boat. No remains of them were found; but the boat, which was stove all to pieces against the rocks, was picked up.'

Flinders described in *A Voyage to Terra Australis* how 'he caused an inscription to be engraven upon a sheet of copper and set up on a stout post' in Memory Cove, the little bay where the boat was found, while the names of the drowned men – Thistle, Taylor, Little, Lewis, Hopkins, Smith, Williams and Grindal – were remembered in nearby islands which still bear their names today.

ENTRANCE TO PORT LINCOLN; Westall's finished watercolour of Port Lincoln, on the south coast of Australia, from which the plate of this title was engraved in Flinders's published voyage account.

Meeting with French Ships

Little more than a month after the tragedy, the expedition met Baudin's ship, the *Géographe* (which had become separated from its consort, the *Naturaliste*), surveying the coast from east to west. Curiously, Flinders makes no mention of the meeting at Encounter Bay in his letters to Ann, but describes it fully in his book. The two ships approached each other cautiously, Flinders recording that 'we veered round as *Le Géographe* was passing, so as to keep our broadside to her, lest the flag of truce should be a deception', before being rowed over to the French ship with Robert Brown who, unlike Flinders, spoke good French. The ships stayed in company for two days and the meeting was courteous, if a little strained. According to Flinders he first asked to see Baudin's passport, and 'when it was found and I had perused it, [I] offered him mine from the French marine minister, but he put it back without inspection'. Unusually, Flinders's passport was made out in the name of the ship, not of its captain, and while this minor detail was either not noticed or not remarked on by Baudin or Brown it was destined to play a significant role in the last part of the voyage.

After exchanging information on their surveys the two ships parted, the *Géographe* to continue west for a while and the *Investigator* to complete the survey of Bass Strait and then head for Port Jackson. It arrived there on 7 May 1802 and Flinders immediately began the process of refitting and reprovisioning his ship, although finding time to write proudly to Ann, in 'a moment snatched from the confusion of performing half a dozen occupations', that they had:

> done much towards the accomplishment of the service for which we came out…
> Had we found an inlet which would admit us into the interior of New Holland,
> I should have been better pleased, but as such did not exist, we could not find it;
> several important discoveries however are made, of islands, bays and inlets; of these,
> when the charts go home thou wilt probably see something said in the newspapers.

He also brought her up to date with the ship's news, telling her of his improving relationship with his first lieutenant, Robert Fowler; of the growing distance between him and his brother Samuel, who 'is satisfied with being as much inferior to other officers as I would have him superior to them'; of the impressive ability of his kinsman, the young midshipman John Franklin (the future governor of Tasmania and Arctic explorer, who would die looking for the North-West Passage), who 'is capable of learning every thing that we can shew him'; and of the robust health of his cat, Trim, named after the faithful servant Corporal Trim, a character in Laurence Sterne's novel *Tristram Shandy*.

A month later, in July 1802, Flinders received two letters from Ann, only six and nine months after they had been written. A further two letters predating them failed to arrive. In them Ann complained about his abandonment of her, and while he made no apologies for his decision to go to Australia, he reassured her eloquently of his love, telling her again that the survey would make their fortunes and urging her 'to submit to what has been decreed for us, and look forward with our best hopes for the good which is in store for us'. He also had to give her the following news:

> *I had desired Elder [his servant] to scrub out the little cabin, and to scour the paintwork; – this was done, and when afterwards I looked for thy forget me not, to indulge myself with fond thoughts of thee, – it was not to be found … I sighed myself to sleep and dreamed of thee; and although it is now sometime since, I am not reconciled. I thought of tracing them again, but it would not be thy writing, and unless it was so, it was nothing; the sentence, however, is so engraven on my memory, that the place where it was written brings every letter of it to my recollection, even to the cross on the T, at the end of not.*

SURVEY OF THE NORTH-EAST COAST

Flinders ended by telling Ann that he would not be able to hear from her again for at least a year as the *Investigator* was about to embark on the second phase of the voyage – the survey of the north-east coast, the Torres Strait, the Gulf of Carpentaria and north Australia. Flinders, typically, interpreted his instructions freely and began with a section of the east coast that he had been expressly ordered to leave to the last. The *Investigator* was to be accompanied by the brig *Lady Nelson*, which boasted an innovative sliding keel designed by Captain John Schank for navigation in shallow waters; unfortunately the design did not work and the *Lady Nelson* became more a liability than a help, Flinders eventually sending her back to Port Jackson. Flinders also took with him an old companion from an early Australian voyage, a man called, in Flinders's spelling, Bongaree, one of the Eora tribe that lived in the Port Jackson area. While his use as an interpreter had been limited, as different tribes spoke very different languages, Flinders had found him very useful in establishing and mediating contact with Aboriginal peoples and had no hesitation in employing this 'worthy and brave fellow' again.

Flinders sailed the *Investigator* up the east coast, following Cook's route between the Great Barrier Reef and the open ocean and missing, as Cook had done before him, the eight rivers that empty into the sea along a 200-mile stretch of New South Wales, today called the Northern Rivers District. The governor of Port Jackson, Philip Gidley King, asked Flinders to survey the section between Cape Tribulation – where the *Endeavour* had nearly been lost – and the Torres Strait in order to find a passage through what Cook had called 'The Labyrinth'. It would have been an important discovery as ships heading up or down the east coast of Australia usually made a wide detour around the coast of New Guinea in order to avoid the dual dangers of the reef and the strait. Although Flinders did find a route through the Great Barrier Reef, later named the Flinders Passage, he had left the coast too far to the south for it to serve King's purpose, and the Labyrinth would eventually be surveyed in 1819 by King's son, Phillip Parker King (who would be accompanied by Flinders's Aboriginal companion, Bongaree), in the *Mermaid*.

Because Flinders had been delayed on the east coast, and was consequently worried about being caught by the approaching monsoon, his survey of the Torres Strait was far from adequate. More worrying for him was the reappearance of the *Investigator*'s leak, which was soon running at the rate of 12 inches an hour. Nevertheless, Flinders continued to follow the north coast of Australia, surveying the Gulf of Carpentaria and Arnhem Land, which were known at that time only through the inaccurate seventeenth-century charts of Dutch navigators. Some of Flinders's surveys of the Gulf were still in use during the Second World War, although this was less because of their quality than because the swampy and remote area had not merited more accurate charting in the intervening years.

By the following June, the *Investigator* was back in Port Jackson. The leak had worsened, and while on the north coast Flinders ordered a survey of it, which, he later wrote to Ann, 'proves her to be so very much decayed as to be totally irrepairable [*sic*]. It was the unanimous opinion of the surveying officers that had we met a severe gale of wind in the passage from Timor, that she must have been crushed like an egg.' Flinders abandoned his cartographic survey and sailed back via Timor and the west coast of Australia, so becoming the first to circumnavigate the continent. The poor state of the ship was matched by that of the crew, who were badly hit by disease caught in Timor as well as by scurvy: 'Douglas – the boatswain, is gone, – the sergeant, two quarter masters and another followed before we got into this port; and since, the gardener and three others are laid in earth.' The cat Trim, he reported, 'like his master is becoming grey', for Flinders had also suffered during the voyage from scurvy and lameness, the latter caused by 'the gravelly', the kidney complaint which made urination painful and which was eventually to kill him at the age of 40. Modern medical opinion is that Flinders's 'gravelly' was a long-term effect of the gonorrhoea he had contracted in Tahiti as a young man, or more probably of the surgeon's treatment of the disease, which consisted of cleansing the urinary passage with a solution of mercury nitrate.

RETURN TO PORT JACKSON

Flinders began that letter to his wife while he was in Port Jackson, but it was finished and finally posted in Île de France (Mauritius). Once the *Investigator* had been condemned as irreparable in Port Jackson, Governor King gave Flinders and the majority of his crew permission to sail back to Britain on HM sloop *Porpoise*; he gave Flinders's first lieutenant, Robert Fowler, the command, so leaving Flinders free to complete his charts during the voyage. They sailed in company with two other ships, the *Bridgewater* and the *Cato*. Seven hundred miles north of Port Jackson, *Porpoise* and *Cato* struck a reef and were lost – and the *Bridgewater* sailed on in full knowledge, leaving the shipwrecked crews to their fate. After transferring as much of the *Porpoise*'s stores ashore as possible on what became known as Wreck Reef Bank, together with his valuable manuscript charts, Flinders and 13 others set off for Port Jackson in the ship's cutter, christened *Hope* for the occasion.

Thirteen days later he brought the small open boat into Port Jackson, where King gave him command of yet another vessel, the 29-ton colonial schooner *Cumberland*, and sent him back to pick up the survivors. They were accompanied by the East Indiaman *Rolla*, which was contracted to take the majority of them back to Britain via Canton, while Flinders was to sail directly home on the schooner with a small crew.

ÎLE DE FRANCE

On 11 October Flinders left the *Rolla* at Wreck Reef and set sail for the Torres Strait and then for Cape Town, in a schooner that was really designed for short coastal voyages. The *Cumberland* was small, wet and cramped – Flinders described filling in his daily journal in her as being like trying to write while riding a horse in a thunderstorm – and it leaked badly. The ship became even more unsafe when one of the two pumps, which together had barely kept ahead of the leaks, broke down in the Indian Ocean. Flinders felt he had no choice but to put into Île de France and rely on his passport from the French government either to

A VIEW OF THE EUROPEAN FACTORIES AT CANTON; painting by William Daniell showing the strictly controlled European area of the Canton waterfront in the 1790s.

Most of those stranded on and rescued from Wreck Reef were taken to this busy Chinese port of Canton in the East Indiaman *Rolla*. From there, they were able to find passages home with no difficulty.

permit him to make repairs to the *Cumberland* or to negotiate a passage home on a larger vessel. Much to his surprise and outrage it soon became clear that he was not to be treated as a distinguished scientific officer and honoured guest but, rather, that the island's governor, General Decaen, suspected him of being a spy. Flinders made the situation worse by deliberately insulting Decaen, not removing his hat in his presence and curtly turning down an invitation to a dinner that was probably being offered as an olive branch.

Flinders was to remain a prisoner on Île de France for six years, despite a number of formal and informal requests for his release. The imprisonment was not altogether unpleasant as he was eventually permitted to stay in the country with the d'Arifat family. He also made a number of close and lasting friends among the island's upper classes, many of whom were royalists and as opposed to the Bonapartist government of Decaen as Flinders. But to a man of Flinders's energy and ambition any imprisonment was torture: "'I can't get out!' cried the starling.

"God help thee," says Yorick, "but I'll let thee out",' he wrote to Ann, quoting again from Laurence Sterne and expressing his sense of helplessness. Flinders probably feared anonymity more than anything and when he did finally return home in 1810, it must have been obvious to him that during the long imprisonment his voyage had faded from both the public's and the Admiralty's minds.

Worse, perhaps, was that the narrative and charts from Baudin's voyage had already been published while Flinders was imprisoned (although Baudin himself had died on Île de France only weeks before Flinders's arrival), and Flinders was furious to see that the names Terre Napoléon, Golfe Bonaparte and Golfe Joséphine appeared on coasts he had originally charted and named: 'not even the smallest island [was] left without some similar stamp of French discovery…'

The long separation was also difficult for Ann, who at one stage appeared to be prepared to join Flinders on Île de France. She also had to cope with his airy and somewhat insensitive descriptions of his friendships with the pretty daughters of Madame d'Arifat – 'I am not one of those suspicious husbands that think their wives are necessarily doing wrong whenever they have anything they desire to keep to themselves,' he said in what was possibly a veiled suggestion that Ann should not be suspicious of him. Some believe that Flinders did have an affair with Delphine d'Arifat, and even that she had his child; but while a flirtation is possible, even probable, there is absolutely no evidence of an affair and his letters to Ann are consistent in their expressions of love:

> *I am as it were shut up in a cask that has been rolled with violence from the top of hope down into the vale of misfortune; I am bruised and well nigh stunned out of my senses; but canst thou imagine the addition it would be to this misery for the cask to have been driven full of spike nails; – such is the increase of misery to my feelings on thinking intensely on thee.*

Ann saw her husband again on 25 October 1810, nine and a half years after they had parted. John Franklin witnessed their meeting but, feeling 'so sensibly the affecting scene of your meeting Mrs Flinders that I could not have remained any longer in the room under any consideration', he tactfully slipped out of the door. The remaining four years of Flinders's life were spent preparing his charts and book for publication; he died on the day the first copies came off the press.

THE *INVESTIGATOR* AND FLINDERS'S LEGACY

The *Investigator*'s had been the best-equipped British voyage of scientific exploration since Cook's. It had some great successes: the voyage's natural-history finds were outstanding, a contemporary botanist writing that 'the specimens, the descriptions

& drawings brought home from New Holland by Brown & Bauer, are by far the most excellent that ever resulted from any expedition'. Flinders's surveys were often of a high order, but the ambitious programme gave him little time to do more than trace the outlines of the coast and he has frequently, if rather unfairly, been criticised for missing important rivers and harbours. Flinders brought many of his problems on himself: altering the order of the surveys had a far greater impact on the voyage than he could have realised, while 'playing free with the land', as he described his determination to ensure accuracy by following the coast as close inshore as possible, led to the repeated groundings that materially weakened the already strained structure of the *Investigator* and contributed to the vessel's eventual abandonment, and so to the premature end of the survey. His arrogant attitude to General Decaen was undoubtedly the cause of his extended imprisonment, and this effectively meant that the narrative and charts of the voyage did not appear until 1814, when the *Investigator* and its commander had long faded from the public memory.

Flinders has remained a little-known name in the history of British maritime exploration since that time, but he has long been acknowledged in Australia as one of the key figures in its early colonial history, and rightly so. He is widely believed to have been the first to use the word 'Australia' in print, although sadly for history that distinction actually belongs to the less well-known George Shaw, who referred to the 'vast Island or rather Continent of Australia, Australasia, or New Holland' in his 1794 book *Zoology of New Holland*. But Flinders did use 'Australia' both in the text and in the general chart of his *Voyage to Terra Australis*, against the strong preference of Sir Joseph Banks, and it was Flinders's use of it that led to the name's general acceptance some years after his death.

WILLIAM WESTALL: ARTISTIC CIRCUMNAVIGATOR OF AUSTRALIA

William Westall (1781–1850) was a watercolourist, oil painter and printmaker, and younger half-brother of the painter Richard Westall RA, who was his early teacher.

He had just joined the Royal Academy Schools in 1799 when he was engaged as landscape draughtsman for Flinders's prospective *Investigator* voyage, replacing William Daniell, who had withdrawn to marry Westall's older half-sister, Mary. When the ship reached western Australia in early December 1801, Westall began a series of sketches, including coastal profiles, landscapes and Aboriginal figure studies, as Flinders began his survey down to and round the south coast, arriving at Sydney in May 1802. Among drawings Westall made there, a commissioned watercolour of Government House was one of the few finished works he did in Australia. In July they sailed north, rounded Cape York and surveyed the Gulf of Carpentaria in a more productive period for Westall, for whom figure subjects and voyage events had overtaken landscapes as his principal personal interest: during this passage he was also the first westerner to record Aboriginal rock art. By the time they called at Timor the poor condition of the *Investigator* prompted a rapid return to Sydney, again via the west and south coasts of Australia, thereby completing its first mainly inshore circumnavigation. When the ship was condemned on arrival

at Sydney, Westall sailed for home with Flinders in the *Porpoise* and managed to save most of his Australian sketches when it was wrecked in the Coral Sea in August 1803. Picked up from Wreck Reef by the *Rolla*, bound for Canton, he worked both there and for a few months in Bombay before reaching England again late in 1804, a diversion that provided the subjects for some of the most admired later work of his career. With Flinders's imprisonment on Mauritius delaying any Australian publication, Westall then made a new voyage to Madeira and Jamaica. On his return home in 1806, work done there and in India and China formed the basis of his engraved *Foreign Scenery* (1811). This was a commercial success and established him as a sought-after landscape illustrator. It was only in 1809 that the Admiralty filled the void of Flinders's continuing absence by commissioning a series of nine Australian paintings – eventually ten – which took him three years to complete. Those shown at the Royal Academy in 1810 and 1812 led to his election as an Associate of that body and eight paintings, along with one other and 28 coastal profiles, were the basis of his engravings for the *Investigator* account when that finally appeared in 1814. Westall's Australian landscapes are historically important but have been criticised for his introduction of picturesque inaccuracies that mar their value as topographical records. He certainly told Sir Joseph Banks that he found the terrain he was engaged to record uninspiring and, while some of his sketches were undoubtedly lost, he was less productive than Ferdinand Bauer, the expert botanical artist on the voyage: some 140 of Westall's Australian drawings are now known, compared with 2,000 by Bauer. Against this, his artistic quality as a coastal draughtsman has been favourably compared to that of both Hodges and Webber. Westall married in 1820 and soon had four sons. It was his prolific ongoing illustrative work that mainly supported his family, but he also remained a successful London exhibitor, especially of watercolours, until 1848. His wife Ann's brother, Adam Sedgwick, Professor of Geology at Cambridge, was one Charles Darwin's teachers.

VIEW OF MALAY ROAD FROM POBASSOO'S ISLAND, February 1803. The place is on the western side of the Gulf of Carpentaria, where Flinders met Pobassoo, a Malay captain in the trade of fishing for sea cucumbers, then sold on to China. The figure is probably Pobassoo (though Flinders said he was short and elderly), with Malay fishing praus offshore. This is thought to be the first meeting between Asians and Europeans in Australian coastal waters. An engraved version appeared in Flinders's voyage account.

HMS *Beagle* off Fort Macquarie,
Sydney Harbour (detail). This watercolour,
the best-known picture of the *Beagle*, is by Owen
Stanley, captain of its sister ship HMS *Britomart*.
The *Beagle* was commanded at the time by John
Lort Stokes, who had risen from midshipman to
captain during his 19 years' service in the ship.
Both vessels were then engaged on the 1837–43
survey of Australia.

9

'A CHEERLESS PROSPECT'

HMS *Beagle* and the South American Surveys, 1826–36

THE FIRST VOYAGE OF THE *BEAGLE* (1826–30)

BRITAIN finally emerged from the endless-seeming cycle of eighteenth-century European wars with an empire that girdled the globe and a navy that no other nation could match, or would attempt to, until the naval arms race nearly a century later. The Royal Navy's power was built on the strength of its battle fleet, which by the end of the Napoleonic War boasted some 99 ships-of-the-line in commission and ready to sail. Peace in Europe meant that these ships, designed to batter equally powerful opponents into submission, soon had a more marginal role in the Navy's strategic thinking. Although there was no shortage of small wars during the nineteenth century, there was little in the way of major naval conflict and the numbers of large warships were relentlessly reduced. By 1817, according to Paul Kennedy's classic study, *The Rise and Fall of British Naval Mastery*, the 99 had dropped to 80; by 1828 to 68; and by 1835 to 58. The Navy of necessity began to rebuild itself as a predominantly small-ship force able to cope with the new demands and responsibilities of a huge maritime empire. The number of positions for commissioned officers began to shrink, while those who did get posts were typically better educated than their forbears, and better connected. The inexorable advent of steam power within a few decades of the French wars also began to demand new mechanical and technological literacy in the officer corps.

Maritime trade grew rapidly during the nineteenth century as British manufacturers sought to exploit and develop new markets around the world. From the 1850s on most of the world's trade was being carried by British ships, and the Royal Navy's role was increasingly focused on protecting that merchant shipping, policing the empire and improving navigation within it. As Admiral Ritchie succinctly put it in his history of the Navy's hydrographic service, trade needs ships and ships need charts. They particularly needed accurate, detailed coastal charts like those of George Vancouver, rather than the magisterial oceanic sweeps of James Cook.

Britain was especially keen to open up South America to its merchant shipping. For centuries Spain and Portugal had firmly controlled, but never entirely managed to prevent, trade between their Southern American colonies and other European interlopers. But their ability to protect and police these colonies had been seriously weakened by the European wars. For Britain, the routes between the Atlantic and Pacific oceans were the key to this trade, particularly the Strait of Magellan, between the mainland of Patagonia to the north and the islands of Tierra del Fuego and Cape Horn to the south. This northern, continental route, found by Ferdinand Magellan, had the advantage of being the shortest, and also had a certain amount of protection

Lines plan of HMS *Cadmus*. Over 100 Cadmus/Cherokee/Rolla-class sloops were built between 1807 and 1830. The *Beagle* was built at Woolwich Dockyard but remained 'in ordinary' (i.e. in reserve) until 1825, when it was commissioned for the survey of South America.

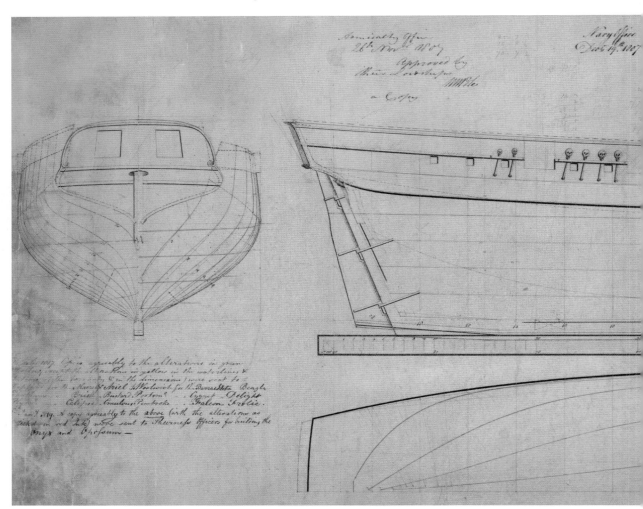

from the elements, but it was navigationally challenging. The longer alternative around Cape Horn was relatively straightforward, but it was exposed to the full fury of westerly gales, as George Anson had discovered in 1741 when he lost three of his six ships as they attempted to beat their way into the Pacific Ocean. Other channels had been glimpsed over the years, some even entered and briefly followed, but none had been mapped in any structured way. The whole area was rightly feared for its constant, strong and freezing winds, hidden rocks and shoals, narrow channels, dead ends, fast-flowing tides and currents and poor visibility. It was not a place to linger and, despite their strategic importance, knowledge of these waters had advanced slowly and none too accurately since 1520, when Magellan first worked his way through the strait that would be named after him. More recently, southern-ocean waters had become valuable in their own right, as increasing numbers of British and American whalers and sealers had begun to exploit their commercial potential that Cook had been the first to describe. The trade came at a terrible price, however, for ship losses in these bleak and largely uncharted seas were common.

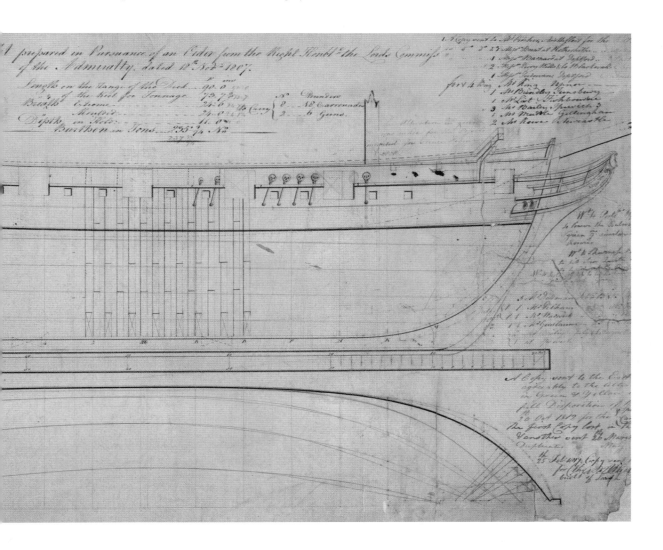

The Admiralty decided upon a survey of the region. Captain Phillip Parker King – an officer who had distinguished himself in four surveys of the Australian coast carried out in the *Mermaid* and the *Bathhurst* (1817–22) – was given command of the senior ship, HMS *Adventure*, and of the expedition. Command of its consort, HMS *Beagle*, went to Commander Pringle Stokes, who had served on the South American station as a midshipman and later as lieutenant in HMS *Owen Glendower*. The *Adventure* was a converted storeship, ideal for carrying the enormous amount of supplies and general goods needed for the voyage but undeniably a poor sailer. The *Beagle* was a 10-gun barque, one of the Cherokee/Cadmus-class, 102 of which had been built between 1807 and 1829 to serve as the Navy's imperial maids of all work. A number had been converted for surveying. The class as a whole had a deserved reputation for being extremely 'wet' boats: one captain described his ship as 'one of his Majesty's bathing machines', and they were popularly known in the service as 'half-tide rocks', for they spent as much time below the surface of the sea as on it. More worryingly, a quarter of the class were lost at sea, which earned them another nickname: 'coffin brigs'. The *Beagle* shared their predilection to roll heavily and sharply in any sort of sea, but was to prove generally a good and reliable sea boat when well handled in the extreme conditions around Cape Horn.

King's orders were for his ships to survey the 'Coasts, Islands, and Straits' of South America from the Rio de Plata (River Plate) to the island of Chiloé on Chile's Pacific coast. They were to 'continue on this service until it should be completed'. The

MONTEVIDEO FROM THE
NORTH-WEST, by Conrad Martens.
During the southern winter the ships
would retreat north to refit and survey
the eastern and western coasts of South
America. Over the *Beagle*'s two South
American surveys, Montevideo became a
familiar port. This is a later watercolour
version of half of a fuller panoramic
drawing that Martens did from the deck
of the *Beagle* in December 1833, while
the ship was anchored in Montevideo
harbour during her second South
America survey. (See also illustration
on pp.164–5.)

primary object of the survey was to 'open up' the Strait of Magellan for commercial
traffic, which generally opted for the longer, more open ocean route around the
Horn rather than risk the dangers of the strait. King took advantage of the leeway
in his orders, ignoring the long stretch south from the River Plate, and instead sailing
directly for the entrance to the Strait of Magellan, which they reached at the end
of November 1826. He justified this decision by arguing that he thought it best to
tackle one of the hardest stretches of the survey first 'while the crews were healthy –
and while the charms of a new and difficult enterprize had full force'.

Merely working their way into the strait took King's ships nearly a week, for
its entrance was guarded by two narrows less than a mile wide in places, through
which the tides raced furiously. Working out how best to use these singular tides to
their advantage, and fighting their way against the strong westerly winds, both ships
anchored in Gregory Bay on the north bank of the strait at the end of November
1826. Here they met their first Patagonians, the Tehuelche, a nomadic, horse-riding
people who inhabited the mainland coast. King distributed some brass medals
commemorating the voyage of the *Adventure* and the *Beagle* that he had had struck in
England – much as Banks had commissioned medals for Cook's second voyage. A
Spanish-speaking Tehuelche woman called Maria agreed to provide fresh guanaco
meat (guanaco being llama-like animals abundant in the area). She was, said King,
a 'rather remarkable woman' of about 40 years of age who, proving reliable and
honest in doing business, would become an important figure in supplying the

survey with fresh provisions. There was a downside, however, for Maria was fond of tobacco and strong drink: King once described her sleeping with her head on the *Adventure*'s windlass and being 'so intoxicated that the noise and concussion produced by veering eighty fathoms of cable around it did not awake her'.

Although there were neither professional naturalists nor artists on either ship, the collection, recording and drawing of 'such objects of Natural History as may be new, rare, or interesting' was a requirement of all officers and enshrined in the official orders. It was, though, the formal responsibility of the surgeon, who on the *Beagle* was E. Bowen, who was invalided out of the ship early on in the voyage, in 1827. His role was then assumed by the assistant surgeon, Benjamin Bynoe, who developed a keen interest in collecting. A rider to the Admiralty's instructions stated firmly that the collections 'must be understood to belong to the Public' rather than the individual. The officers of both ships would assiduously measure and describe the people, plants, birds and animals they saw to the best of their ability, although Charles Darwin would later dismiss the *Beagle*'s early forays into the natural history of the region as being 'of a very trashy nature'.

Leaving Gregory Bay, and still following the continental shore, the ships sailed in company to Port Famine, site of Pedro Sarmiento's disastrous attempt in 1583 to establish a Spanish colony in the strait. Here King divided his forces. Pringle Stokes's *Beagle* would survey the strait through to its westerly exit into the Pacific, returning to Port Famine within three months. John Clements Wickham, first lieutenant of the *Adventure*, would explore some promising channels closer to home in the *Hope*, a small, decked boat brought out in the *Adventure* specifically for close surveying work, while the *Adventure*'s other boats would survey the waters around the port. Avoiding the innumerable rocks and shoals and fighting every inch of the way against fierce westerly winds, the *Beagle* finally reached the strait's Pacific entrance, the Harbour of Mercy, after 30 days' sailing from Port Famine. Although it seemed a long passage to the battered 'Beagles', it was actually a remarkably fast one in comparison with many earlier voyages: Magellan had managed a respectable 38 days, Byron had taken 42 days in 1764, Wallis and Carteret 82 and 84 days respectively in 1766, and Bougainville 40 in 1768. Privately, Pringle Stokes saw little point in surveying some of the dangers, for, as he noted in his journal, they only needed to be seen to be avoided.

The *Beagle* returned to Port Famine, arriving a month late after a 200-mile diversion to rescue the crew of a sealer, the *Prince of Saxe Cobourg*, lying wrecked in Fury Harbour, off the west coast of Tierra del Fuego. Reunited once more, the *Beagle* and the *Adventure* made their way back through the Strait of Magellan and returned to Montevideo, pausing briefly at Gregory Bay to buy more meat from Maria and her people. They arrived in Montevideo on 24 April 1827, soon moving north to Rio de Janeiro to reprovision and refit for the second survey, and report to the commander-in-chief of the Royal Navy's South American squadron, Sir Robert Otway. With Otway's blessing, King wrote to the Lord High Admiral (the Duke of Clarence and future William IV, the 'sailor king') asking for permission to hire a second boat like *Hope*, for the need for small, handy, fore-and-aft-rigged vessels had become abundantly clear after the first survey season. Permission eventually arrived and an appropriate vessel was bought and named *Adelaide* (after William's wife, the Princess of Saxe-Meiningen).

Returning to Tierra del Fuego, Stokes exceeded his orders and surveyed the whole American coast south from Port Desire, about halfway between Montevideo and the strait, arriving late at Port Famine yet again. Once more the expedition was divided, with King taking command of the *Adelaide* to find and explore the St Sebastian Channel, an opening that a number of earlier vessels had reported seeing but had not been able to follow up. The *Beagle* got the unenviable job of fighting its way through the strait once more, picking up the survey where it had finished the year before, and extending it nearly 300 miles north up a complex and unforgiving lee shore as far as Chile's Gulf of Peñas.

It must already have become obvious to everyone on the *Beagle* that Stokes was in no real condition to carry out another such arduous survey. His late arrival at Port Famine may have been, in part at least, due to a dread of what was to come, and with good reason. The crew were still physically and mentally exhausted from the previous year's survey and the prospect of having to repeat it, just to get to the beginning of what promised to be an even more perilous voyage, probably pushed Stokes over the edge. The weather was – if such a thing were possible – even worse, with the constant driving, freezing rain reminding Stokes of John Bulkeley's graphic description of the shipwreck of the *Wager* in the same waters in 1741, where he faced 'showers of rain and hail, which beat with such violence against a man's face, that he can hardly withstand it'. The impenetrable clouds louring over the *Beagle*'s decks 'seemed as immovable as the mountains'. The weather, to Stokes, was not just 'horrid' or 'horrible', but actively malicious in seeking out the *Beagle* and relentlessly attacking him and his men. The destruction of his yawl, battered to pieces in a storm, affected him deeply: it had been 'a beautiful boat … pulled and sailed well, and was roomy, light and buoyant'. He mourned its loss as he would have done the death of a friend. To add to their woes, the ship's company began to be affected by the endlessly cold and wet conditions, which Stokes noted brought on 'pulmonic …, catarrhal and rheumatic complaints'. Unsurprisingly, scurvy had set in as well. On the surgeon's advice Stokes returned to the relatively safe harbour of Port Otway, which they had only just discovered, snugged the ship down and allowed the crew to rest for a fortnight before returning to the rendezvous at Port Famine. Stokes took little interest in the workings of the ship thereafter and spent most of his time in his cabin, where, finally back at Port Famine, but in the grip of a terrible depression, he shot himself in the head. He lived for another 12 days, eventually dying in great pain.

This 'fatal event', as King described it, 'cast an additional gloom over every one' and he quickly prepared his ships for sea. He made *Beagle*'s first lieutenant, William Skyring, its acting commander and they sailed for Rio de Janeiro to reprovision and prepare for a third surveying season. Admiral Otway, however, chose to appoint his 23-year-old flag lieutenant, Robert FitzRoy, to command the *Beagle* in place of Skyring, who reverted to being first lieutenant and assistant surveyor. He had every right to feel bitter, but if he did he kept it to himself and King would later praise him generously for his professionalism in the published voyage narrative. FitzRoy would also acknowledge his debt to Skyring by naming a large sea lake after him.

Setting forth once more, the *Adventure* made its way through stormy waters off Cape Horn to Chile to await the *Adelaide* and the *Beagle*, which were again bound for the Strait of Magellan. The *Beagle* would initially survey part of the strait's southern shore and the Jerome Channel. The little *Adelaide*, under Skyring's command, would survey the Magdalen and Barbara Channels, which it was hoped might provide alternative exits or entrances to the strait, before rendezvousing with the *Adventure*.

As Keith Thomson has neatly put it in *HMS Beagle: The Ship That Changed the Course of History*, FitzRoy's task with the *Beagle* was not an easy one: 'to take on a battered ship and a demoralized set of men and lead them straight back to the same desolate region where their previous captain had been driven to suicide'. Later in life, FitzRoy would himself become no stranger to the depression that killed Pringle Stokes, but through leading by example, caring for his men's well-being, and praising and punishing consistently when necessary, he brought new energy and determination to his physically and mentally exhausted crew.

Entering the Strait of Magellan through the narrows as usual, the two ships made their way to Port Famine, arriving there on 14 April 1829. They set sail together three days later, separating after a few hours for the *Adelaide* to follow the Magdalen Channel, while the *Beagle* continued its way along the strait. Strong contrary winds slowed the *Beagle*'s progress and much of the work had to be done from the ship's boats. On 3 May they anchored in Port Gallant – a 'perfectly secure' but 'dismal harbour in winter', according to FitzRoy. From here he prepared for a boat expedition. Taking provisions for a month, he and John Lort Stokes (the *Beagle*'s young midshipman, a promising surveyor and no relation to Pringle Stokes) took two boats to examine the Jerome Channel. The weather, declared FitzRoy, was so mild that he was able to enjoy a refreshing morning swim, recording the water temperature as 42°F (5°C) and the air temperature as 39°F (4°C). Tough FitzRoy may well have been, but one senses more than a hint of showmanship

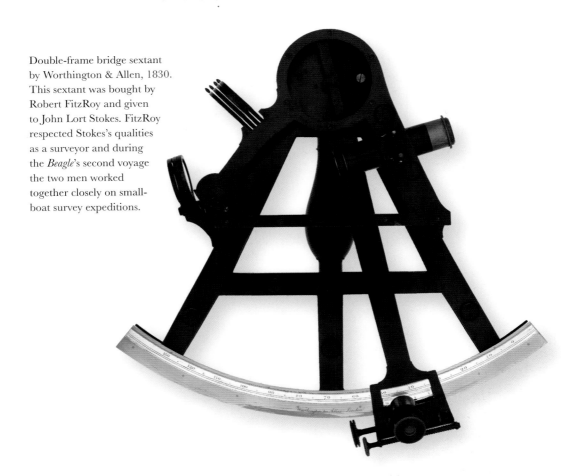

Double-frame bridge sextant by Worthington & Allen, 1830. This sextant was bought by Robert FitzRoy and given to John Lort Stokes. FitzRoy respected Stokes's qualities as a surveyor and during the *Beagle*'s second voyage the two men worked together closely on small-boat survey expeditions.

here. As the boats followed the channel it began to open up into a large saltwater lake, which they would name Otway Water after their commander-in-chief. Here they met a group of Fuegians who were, commented FitzRoy, 'very rich in Fuegian wealth, such as skins, arrows lances &c', but little else. After an initially cautious meeting during which FitzRoy optimistically attempted some understanding of their origins, language and religion, there were some tensions when a tinderbox was stolen, but, said FitzRoy, 'we parted without a quarrel'. They rowed along the shore of the lake, camping in an inlet they named Donkin Cove 'as a mark of respect to the preserver of meat, to whom we had been so often thankful'. Donkin was one of a number of manufacturers supplying tinned, pre-cooked provisions which FitzRoy thought ideal for exploration as they did not need to be cooked. This was an important consideration, as Fuegian weather could be so appalling that lighting a fire ashore was impossible, while lighting one in the ship's galley under local conditions could be downright dangerous. Ironically, given the earlier tinderbox theft, FitzRoy would later come to admire the Fuegians for their ability to light fires without them in situations that defeated the seamen. The boats found a navigable channel that would later be named FitzRoy Channel, which they hoped might lead back to the Strait of Magellan, but it just led to another huge saltwater lake, the one they named Skyring Water. They returned to the *Beagle* a month later, FitzRoy declaring that 'I never was fully aware of the comfort of a bed until this night. Not even a frost-bitten foot could prevent me from sleeping soundly for the first time during many nights.'

Skyring and the *Adelaide* soon joined the *Beagle* having, as FitzRoy wrote approvingly, 'thoroughly completed the work they had to perform without loss, or even an accident. The difficulty of their task was increased by very bad weather; but they succeeded in tracing and surveying the Magdalen Channel to its junction with the sea, and returning by the Barbara Channel … carrying on a regular chain of triangles and connecting their work with points previously fixed in the Strait.' (Triangulation was the fundamental method of the surveyor.) They were then free to follow the Pacific coast and meet up with King's *Adventure*, which was due to be waiting for them in San Carlos. King's original orders instructed him to complete the survey by returning to Britain via Australia, but he later received permission to return by the shorter Atlantic route. FitzRoy was ordered to carry out a survey of the south coast of Tierra del Fuego on the way back before meeting up once more with the senior ship at Port Famine, or at Rio de Janeiro should they miss the first rendezvous.

The *Beagle*'s was a dangerous task, FitzRoy describing the long stretch from the Agnes Islands to Cape Schomberg as 'the worst I have seen, it is so very broken, and has so many rocks and dangerous breakers lying at a long distance from shore'. This last part of the voyage is remembered particularly for the four young Fuegians – Fuegia Basket, York Minster, Jemmy Button and Boat Memory – who over a period of days were taken hostage by FitzRoy against the return of a stolen whaleboat. The bizarre course of events following the theft shows two sides of FitzRoy: on the one hand, he publicly supported the master who had been in charge of the whaleboat, stating firmly that 'had I been with the boat, I should have probably lost her in the same manner'. On the other, his fury at its loss –it was vital for the survey – led to an absurd wild-goose chase around the islands. His overre-action was reminiscent of Cook's vengeful rampage through Moorea in search of a stolen goat on his third voyage. While Cook's scorched-earth policy eventually got his goat back, FitzRoy never saw his whaleboat again. Both men had acted in anger, probably exacerbated by the other tensions of their voyages.

The immediate problem for FitzRoy was that he now held four young Fuegians hostage with no obvious way to return them to their families and a limited amount of time to complete his survey and reach Rio de Janeiro. Precisely when he decided to take them back to England to be 'civilized' and returned to Tierra del Fuego as interpreters is not entirely clear, but once he realised that returning them was already impossible, he really had no other option. The *Beagle* turned north and reached Rio a day after the deadline, on 2 August 1830. With the *Adventure*, they sailed for Plymouth, arriving on 14 October. They had achieved much, and in gruelling conditions, but their most significant discovery must have been that the survey was far more difficult than anyone had anticipated and that, as yet, the work was unfinished.

THE SECOND VOYAGE OF THE *BEAGLE* (1831–36)

On the return of the *Beagle* and the *Adventure*, FitzRoy learnt through King that the Admiralty was receptive to the idea of a second voyage to complete the South American survey and return the Fuegian hostages. Boat Memory had died from smallpox soon after reaching Britain while the remaining three had been enrolled at FitzRoy's expense in a children's school founded by the Reverend William Wilson in 1825. Here, with mixed results, they were taught English and 'the plainer truths of Christianity' alongside more practical skills of husbandry and gardening. FitzRoy hoped that in three or four years, and with suitable guidance, they would be able to rise above their perceived savage state and return to their home able to demonstrate the benefits of civilisation and Christianity to their fellow Fuegians. This strategy was already proving successful in the Pacific, where the London Missionary Society started to be dramatically more effective once it began to use indigenous converts to communicate with other islanders, simply because they understood the islands' cultures and languages. To FitzRoy, the three Fuegians were to be the foundation stones of the first European mission in Tierra del Fuego. At first things seemed to go well: York Minster, Jemmy Button and Fuegia Basket soon became celebrities and were apparently introduced to William IV and Queen Adelaide. A young trainee missionary, Richard Matthews, volunteered to accompany them to Tierra del Fuego. However, it was becoming obvious that the 'civilising' programme was not advancing at anything like the rate FitzRoy had anticipated: if anything he saw them becoming more and more depressed and actively resisting their lessons. At this point he appears to have been leaning towards returning them rather earlier than the originally planned three or four years. Then, in what FitzRoy tactfully described as a 'disappointing' decision, the Admiralty suddenly changed its mind and informed him that it had no intention of commissioning a second South American survey. Quite apart from putting an end to FitzRoy's professional ambition to complete that project, the abrupt volte-face made him feel honour-bound to return the Fuegians at his own cost. The reasons for the Admiralty's change of heart have never been entirely clear, but to FitzRoy's great credit he bit

the bullet, immediately applied for a year's leave and set about hiring and provisioning a suitable ship for the long voyage south. Then the Admiralty changed its mind once more and approved a second voyage, although this time the reasons were obvious: it had been persuaded to reconsider the original plan by one of FitzRoy's influential relatives, most probably his uncle, Lord Londonderry. An additional factor, arguably more persuasive, was that a second survey would also suit the purpose of Francis Beaufort, Hydrographer of the Navy, who was planning to establish a chain of chronometric observations at key points around the world. These 'standard points' would provide accurate locations for future voyages. It was therefore swiftly agreed that once the *Beagle* had safely taken the Fuegians home and completed its hydrographical responsibilities, it would make its way back to London via a west-about circumnavigation of the world.

By the end of June 1831, FitzRoy had assumed command of **HMS** *Beagle* for the second time. He brought with him a number of officers and men from the first voyage. Benjamin Bynoe, the assistant surgeon, returned in the same position, and the impressive young midshipman John Lort Stokes was promoted to lieutenant, serving as Admiralty Mate and assistant surveyor. Philip Gidley King, son of the first expedition's commander, joined the *Beagle* as midshipman; he had been listed as a volunteer on his father's *Adventure*, although he would have been little more than 11 years old – not an unusual age to go to sea at that time. John Wickham, the *Adventure*'s second lieutenant, became the *Beagle*'s first. William Skyring was unavailable, having finally received the promotion he deserved and been given command of the survey vessel HMS *Ætna*, engaged on the West African survey in support of the Navy's anti-slavery squadron. But bad luck still followed him, for in 1833 he was killed in a brief but bloody encounter at Cap Roxo, just to the south of the Gambia River. Cap Skirring, just to the north of the spot, was named after him.

The *Beagle* had been decommissioned on its return from the first survey, and after a five-year voyage in some of the most testing conditions in the world it needed a thorough and thus costly refit: indeed, as the work steadily mounted up it would have been little more expensive to have built a new ship. FitzRoy had his own ideas on what was needed to improve its handling and, for example, insisted on the main deck being raised a foot, an unusual suggestion, but he correctly thought it would reduce its unpleasant roll and make it a drier and more comfortable ship. The *Beagle* was the first vessel consistently to employ Beaufort's method of recording wind speed and sea conditions; the Beaufort Scale is still in use today. FitzRoy was also using the voyage to test the value of barometers to the emerging science of 'weather forecasting' (a term he first introduced when he was appointed 'meteorological statist' in 1854). William Harris's recently invented lightning conductors were fitted to the masts and spars, and John Frazer's newly designed stove was installed in the galley. The stove's performance had been tested for three years in one of the *Beagle*'s sister ships, the *Chanticleer*, where it was claimed that even in the worst of conditions its performance had been such that it received 'the constant admiration of everyone on board'. Twenty-two chronometers were embarked, 11 of which were supplied by the Admiralty and the balance largely by FitzRoy himself. Chronometers were scarcely an innovation by the 1830s, being taken routinely on voyages of exploration, but the large number was exceptional. This reflected not only the importance of completing the survey and the global chain of longitude readings, but also FitzRoy's interests. Prior to going to sea he had been educated at the Royal Naval College, Portsmouth, where he became the first winner of the mathematical prize aged 14, in 1819. He was an intellectual, absorbed by time and mathematics. In many ways he was uniquely qualified for the job, but he also typified the new breed of scientific officer being drawn to work for Beaufort's hydrographic department.

Beaufort's post – that of Hydrographer to the Navy – had been created only in 1795, with the appointment of Alexander Dalrymple. Under him the Hydrographic Office, as it would later become, had remained a small body largely dedicated to printing charts. By the time of Captain Beaufort's appointment in 1829 it was able to commission its own surveys, allocate resources and build a body of officers whose careers depended on their skills as surveyors. Beaufort, it could be said, assumed the role of Sir Joseph Banks (who had died in 1820) as the 'common centre of we discoverers', as Cook's lieutenant, James King, had described Banks many years earlier. Beaufort was a member of the Royal Society, the Royal Geological Society and the Royal Astronomical Society, as well as being a founding member of the Royal Geographical Society. He valued science, moved in scientific circles and understood the close links between science, surveying, empire and discovery. FitzRoy, perhaps mindful of the stresses and loneliness of command that had led to the suicide of Pringle Stokes, approached Beaufort, asking if he might be able to recommend a gentleman interested in science and natural history to sail as his companion on the forthcoming voyage. Through Beaufort and the recommendation of his friend the Reverend George Peacock, Charles Darwin was offered the position and accepted it. This immediately created a tension, for naval custom dictated that the official naturalist was the surgeon, but *Beagle* already had a surgeon, Robert McCormick, as well as an assistant surgeon, Bynoe. Although Darwin claimed in a letter that 'my friend the Doctor is an ass, but we jog on amicably', relations between the two men were, at best, strained during the voyage. McCormick was actually angry at FitzRoy rather than Darwin for giving collecting opportunities to his friend but not himself as ex officio ship's naturalist. He finally left the *Beagle* in high dudgeon at Rio de Janeiro before the survey proper had even really started. He was not missed. In fact his departure allowed Bynoe to be promoted to acting surgeon, and he and Darwin worked together closely and harmoniously for the rest of the voyage.

'Perhaps no vessel ever quitted her own country with a better or more ample supply … of every kind of useful provision', wrote FitzRoy. But quitting the country took a little longer than expected; for although *Beagle* had been ready for sea by the end of November 1831, a series of westerly gales pinned her in Plymouth until the end of December. FitzRoy's determination to sail on 26 December was thwarted by the crew's celebration of Christmas, which left the ship without enough sober men to handle her. She finally sailed on the 27th, and two days later came the reckoning, with four men being flogged for drunkenness, insolence and disobeying orders. The punishments seemed severe to an already seasick Darwin, confined to the cabin he would share with John Lort Stokes and Philip Gidley King for the next five years. Without openly mentioning the floggings, FitzRoy was unrepentant in the published narrative, writing that 'every naval officer knows the absolute necessity of a certain degree of what inexperienced persons might think unnecessary coercion when a ship is recently commissioned'. Flogging would continue in the Royal Navy for a further 30 years before finally being abolished.

The *Beagle* made her way down and across the Atlantic. Frustrated by unfavourable tides, they were unable to land at Madeira so sailed on to Tenerife, where they were refused entrance because of a rumoured outbreak of cholera in England. They instead continued down to the Cape Verde islands, landing on the island of St Jago, where Darwin was first overwhelmed by the rich, breathtaking beauty of the tropics: 'it has been for me a glorious day, like giving to a blind man eyes', he wrote in his diary. Then on to Bahia in Brazil and south to Rio de Janeiro, passing the wreck site at Cabo Frio of FitzRoy's old ship, the *Thetis*, which had been carrying bullion worth $800,000 to England. Two Royal Navy vessels were in the process of salvaging as much of this as possible as the *Beagle* sailed past. FitzRoy was obviously affected by the sight but later, in the voyage narrative, he philosophised: 'Those who never run any risk; who sail only when the wind is fair; who heave to when approaching land, though perhaps a day's sail distant; and who even delay the performance of urgent duties until they can be done easily and quite safely; are, doubtless, extremely prudent persons: but rather unlike those officers

whose names will never be forgotten while England has a navy.'

On their arrival in Rio de Janeiro FitzRoy made his observations but discovered a difference of four miles between his observed longitudes for Bahia and Rio and those of a French expedition led by Admiral Roussin in 1828. This was meat and drink to FitzRoy, who promptly returned to Bahia – a distance of some 1,000 miles – and then sailed back down to Rio once more, double-checking his observations and confirming that his calculations were correct and Roussin's wrong. He was exceeding his orders but 'trusted to the Hydrographer for appreciating his motives'. Beaufort accepted the reasoning but would not always be so accommodating of FitzRoy's spirited independence. Darwin, meanwhile, had remained at Rio, taking advantage of the *Beagle*'s unscheduled absence to conduct his researches further and further inland. This arrangement established a comfortable pattern for Darwin, who thereafter stayed ashore whenever he had opportunity, often for weeks at a time, returning to the *Beagle* when necessary.

The survey pushed steadily south towards Tierra del Fuego, where the Fuegians were to be returned to their respective peoples. En route, FitzRoy nearly created a minor international incident with his robust refusal to stop for the guardship at Buenos Aires, and later got caught up with a military revolution in Montevideo, which saw him leading an armed party from the ship through the streets of the city. Further south, at Punta Alta, Darwin made one of his most important discoveries: the fossilised remains of long extinct mammals, which he had crated up and sent to England. As Keith Thomson has observed, the find made Darwin famous years before he was able to return home. The survey work continued, but it was soon

clear to FitzRoy that the *Beagle* alone would not be able to complete the South American work, at least not to the level of detail required. He needed auxiliary vessels, smaller shallow-draught boats able to sail closer to the wind than the *Beagle* – the type, in fact, that had been used with such success by Pringle Stokes and Phillip Parker King on the first voyage. The impulsive FitzRoy hired and fitted out two small schooners, the *Paz* and the *Liebre*, from an English trader, Mr Harris, giving command of the little squadron to his first lieutenant, John Wickham. The not inconsiderable cost was met by FitzRoy, in the confident expectation that the Admiralty would 'approve of what I have done'. Unfortunately for him, the Admiralty did not approve and he eventually had to meet all the charges himself.

Just before Christmas 1832 the *Beagle* passed through the Strait of Le Maire between Cape Horn and the Fuegian mainland. After celebrating Christmas in Good Success Bay, FitzRoy planned to sail up the coast to the area where he had first taken York Minster and Fuegia Basket hostage. After returning them he would retrace his course back down the coast, through part of the Beagle Channel, surveying it as he went before leaving Jemmy Button, along with Matthews the

THE *BEAGLE* IN THE MURRAY NARROW, BEAGLE CHANNEL; watercolour by Conrad Martens, based on a drawing he made on 3 March 1834. An engraved version appeared in FitzRoy's voyage account and Martens also did a later oil painting of the same view. The Beagle Channel is a separate 150-mile (240-km) land-bound route between the Atlantic and Pacific, south of the Strait of Magellan, but less easily navigated.

missionary, with Jemmy's people, the Tekeenica. The plan was thwarted by two things. First, the weather on this exposed coast was appalling. The *Beagle* almost capsized when struck by three huge waves in a row which left the ship heeled right over with three feet of water on the deck and at the mercy of a fourth wave, which would have certainly sunk her. The ship was saved only by the quick thinking of the carpenter, Jonathan May, and the first lieutenant, Bartholomew Sulivan – both stalwarts of the first voyage – who knocked out the ports in the bulwarks, releasing the *Beagle* from the weight of water and allowing her to roll slowly back, 'like a cask' according to FitzRoy, proud and relieved that his little ship had survived such a test. Darwin had a different take on the same incident, noting sadly that 'I have suffered an irreparable loss from yesterday's disaster, in my drying paper and plants being wetted with salt-water.–Nothing resists the force of an heavy sea; it forces open doors and sky-lights & spreads universal damage.' The weather did not improve and further progress up the coast would clearly be difficult. The second factor in turning back was that York Minster unexpectedly decided that he did not wish to return home but was content to remain with Jemmy, Fuegia and the Reverend Matthews. FitzRoy accordingly retraced his course back to the Beagle Channel.

A favourable spot for the mission was found near the Murray Narrows on 18 January 1832, at a place called Woolya, where the *Beagle's* crew built small dwellings and dug and planted a vegetable garden without opposition. FitzRoy was apprehensive nonetheless, worrying about the implications of endemic theft, suspecting a sudden attack and becoming increasingly doubtful of York Minster's motives for wanting to stay there rather than with his own people much further up the coast. To allay his fears a short trial period was agreed upon and the missionary, Matthews, was left alone in the camp for nine days while FitzRoy, Darwin and a boat's crew left to explore further part of the Beagle Channel, a long and open passage that reminded Darwin of Loch Ness, stretching 120 miles from the south-eastern shore of Tierra del Fuego to the Pacific Ocean. This potentially important sound had been seen towards the end of the first voyage by the *Beagle's* sailing master, John Murray, but lack of time had precluded a survey. After the agreed nine days had passed FitzRoy returned to Woolya to find Jemmy Button and York Minster in good spirits but Matthews terrified: robbed of most of his possessions and fearing for his life, he was desperate to be taken back on board the *Beagle*. The mission was duly abandoned. Darwin's sadness at leaving the three young Fuegians to face an uncertain future among a people he later described as being 'in a more miserable state of barbarism than I had expected ever to see a human being' probably reflected a general concern, for the trio had been popular with the crew. Darwin tried to look on the positive side, writing in his journal that they did not appear to be at all worried, but then contradicting himself to note that Jemmy 'looked rather disconsolate & would certainly have liked to remain with us'.

Beaufort's orders for FitzRoy included conducting a survey of the Falkland Islands, the ownership of which had been disputed regularly between France, England, Spain and Argentina since the 1760s. They had been taken over once more by Britain little more than months before the *Beagle* arrived, her job being in part to maintain a token and temporary naval presence. Hydrographical knowledge of the islands remained sketchy, wrote Beaufort, 'however often they have been visited', justifying the need for the *Beagle* to conduct 'a rigorous survey' while at the same time acknowledging that the cost would probably be 'very disproportionate to its value'. These sentiments were shared by Darwin, who normally welcomed any chance to get ashore but remarked of the islands: 'We have never before stayed so long in a place & and with so little for the Journal... the place bespeaks what it has been, viz. a bone of contention between different nations.' Here FitzRoy bought a third schooner which he named the *Adventure* after Captain Phillip King's old ship, and with more than a nod to the *Adventure* of Cook's second voyage. Once more FitzRoy took pen in hand to write to the Admiralty in the hope that his actions would be acceptable (at this stage he had not received its blunt refusal to sanction the hiring of the *Paz* and the *Liebre*). In the meantime the *Adventure* remained in the Falklands to continue the survey while the *Beagle* sailed north to Maldonado, where Darwin left the ship for a few weeks' botanising, and Montevideo, where he rejoined it.

Between May and November 1833 the *Beagle* was refitted while the small boats were engaged on a number of local surveys on the east coast of South America, with Darwin spending as much time as possible exploring and collecting ashore: during the last four months of the year he reckoned that he had slept ashore every night but one. By the beginning of 1834 the ship was once more working her way south after having celebrated Christmas in Port Desire, a little to the north of the Strait of Magellan. This was a healthy outdoor Christmas with games, competitions and prizes, a very different affair from the one that had delayed the *Beagle*'s departure from Plymouth. FitzRoy ordered the *Adventure* to the Falkland Islands to continue the survey started the year before, while the *Beagle* entered the Strait of Magellan through the two narrows as usual, where the ship's company were able to renew their acquaintance with Maria and the Patagonians. They dropped anchor at Port Famine, staying for some days to rate the chronometers, then doubled back through the narrows and headed south along the eastern shore of Tierra del Fuego. They called at Woolya for a brief visit, arriving on 5 March 1834 and finding hardly a trace of the mission. Then, much to their surprise, they saw Jemmy Button paddling furiously towards the ship and bringing, said Darwin, 'two beautiful otter skins for two of his old friends and some spearheads & arrows of his own making for the Captain'. He told FitzRoy that York Minster had taken Fuegia Basket to their own country, robbing Jemmy of all his possessions before they left. Despite this treatment Jemmy appeared to be very happy to be with his family once more and Darwin was reassured that 'he was clearly now well established'.

After a fast passage from Woolya with the wind behind her for a change, the *Beagle* sailed once more to the Falklands, where it rendezvoused with the *Adventure* before sailing west to the Santa Cruz River in southern Argentina. Pringle Stokes had tried to survey the river on the *Beagle*'s first voyage but his boats had been defeated by its strong currents. FitzRoy's team for his attempt included Darwin, the artist Conrad Martens, Sulivan, Lort Stokes and 20 members of the crew. Martens, new to the *Beagle*, had joined at Montevideo to replace the sick Augustus Earle, who had sailed as FitzRoy's first privately engaged artist but whose poor health forced him to withdraw there. The expedition would have tested the enthusiasm of anyone as it rowed, surveyed and staggered a gruelling 250 miles up the Santa Cruz. Much of the time they had to haul their small boats bodily through its shallow and fast-flowing waters, surrounded by stark countryside that a disappointed Darwin described as having 'the curse of sterility' on it. Eventually, on 29 April, they sighted the snowy summits of the Andes forming a 'lofty & imposing barrier to this flat country' many miles ahead of them. Frustratingly, the mountains never seemed to get much closer, despite their continuing upstream for another four days, so FitzRoy then decided that his exhausted party should return to the coast to wait for the *Adventure*. Unsurprisingly, descent of the river was far quicker than ascent, with the boats shooting downstream at ten knots, and in one day covering a distance that had taken them five and a half to struggle up. They reached the *Beagle* on 8 May, after an overall foray of 21 days. The survey of the Patagonian coast was now as complete as it needed to be, and once the two ships were reunited they made their last traverse through the Strait of Magellan and sailed north for Valparaíso, Chile, arriving on 22 July 1834.

Delighted to be on terra firma once more, Darwin followed his by now familiar routine and began a series of extended rambles that took him up and down the coast and into the foothills of the Andes. There he found more evidence to support his growing conviction that the Pacific coast of South America was gradually rising. He returned to Valparaíso at the end of September with a fever, the first serious illness he had suffered during the voyage. No sooner had his health recovered than he learnt that FitzRoy had received a letter from the Admiralty stating firmly that

PORTRAIT COVE, BEAGLE CHANNEL; watercolour by Conrad Martens.

This view of Fuegians, with the *Beagle* behind, appeared as an engraving in FitzRoy's voyage account. It is a little mysterious since the account and the resulting charts record no 'Portrait Cove' in the Beagle Channel, only a spot so called outside it on the east side.

'Their Lordships do not approve of hiring vessels for the service', a harsh judgement that forced FitzRoy to bear the full and substantial costs both of hiring the *Paz* and the *Liebre* and of buying the *Adventure*. Darwin believed that the Admiralty's decision was politically motivated. FitzRoy was furious, complaining that 'Captain King – with far less extensive orders – had *three* vessels upon this station'. The decision affected FitzRoy considerably and was a major cause of the gloom into which he sank at Valparaíso. Like his predecessor, Stokes, the physically and mentally exhausted FitzRoy had become more and more depressed for months by the amount of work still necessary. Darwin described him as having lost all decision and resolution – two of FitzRoy's outstanding characteristics as a commander. The Admiralty's letter, showing neither tact nor understanding of the physical and mental pressures facing surveyors in this inhospitable region, was enough to tip him over the edge. A furious and now financially stretched FitzRoy had to sell the *Adventure* and pay off the artist, Conrad Martens. He resigned command of the *Beagle* in favour of Wickham and withdrew from the day-to-day running of the ship. Darwin and Wickham agreed that this was a highly undesirable state of affairs and set about trying to talk him round and persuade him to withdraw his letter of resignation, which to everyone's relief he finally did.

THE VILLAGE OF ALMANDRAL IN THE BAY OF VALPARAÍSO WITH A DISTANT VIEW OF THE ANDES, 1798, after John Sykes, midshipman on Vancouver's voyage.

FitzRoy reorganised the expedition at Valparaíso to continue without the *Adventure*. This Chilean port also served as base for the British Pacific squadron in the mid-nineteenth century.

The survey of the Pacific coast continued after the *Beagle* had been given a refit, Darwin as usual spending as much time ashore as he could. FitzRoy, perhaps considering that he might as well be hanged for a sheep as a lamb, acquired another auxiliary vessel, the *Constitución*, a 35-ton schooner, which he immediately despatched under the command of Stokes to conduct a detailed survey further north. While the *Beagle* was in the southern Chilean harbour of Valdivia on 20 February 1835 a powerful earthquake struck, virtually destroying the town, as it did at Talcuhano and Concepción further up the coast. 'It is indeed most wonderful to witness such desolation produced in minutes of time', commented an awed Darwin in a letter home. The *Beagle*'s surveyors confirmed that the earthquake had pushed up the height of the land by 8 feet (2.44 metres), giving Darwin yet more evidence of a steadily rising South American mainland.

By June 1835 the American survey was virtually done and the *Beagle*'s departure to complete the chronometrical chain was imminent, when word reached them that an English ship, the 28-gun frigate *Challenger*, had been wrecked south of Concepción. The senior British naval officer at Valparaíso, Commodore Mason, was reluctant to mount a rescue operation on such a dangerous lee coast. This was the sort of situation for which the energetic and active FitzRoy, no longer depressed but given new life by the emergency, was ideally suited. Showing little tact or respect for the hesitant Mason's rank, FitzRoy bullied him into taking his ship, HMS *Blonde*, to the rescue, with FitzRoy himself offering to act as pilot. The operation was far from straightforward, but eventually all of the *Challenger*'s men but two (who had actually died in the shipwreck itself some weeks earlier) were rescued.

The *Beagle* was then free to set out for the Galápagos Islands, the first step in the voyage across the Pacific and then home. After a fast passage of just over a week they reached the archipelago on 15 September 1835. The importance of the Galápagos and their famous finches to Darwin's evolutionary thinking can hardly be overstated, for they provided a unified framework for the collections, questions, thoughts and observations that had been made over the five-year voyage. It would take time – years in some cases – before the theories all made sense, but the geology and wildlife of the islands were the key. As Alan Moorhead wrote 50 years ago in *Darwin and the Beagle* (1969):

> *Darwin's thesis was simply this: the world as we know it was not just 'created' in a single instant of time; it had evolved from something infinitely primitive and it was changing still... Quite recently [the islands] had been pushed up out of the sea by a volcanic eruption such as they had seen in Chile, and at first there was no life at all upon them. Then birds arrived and they deposited seeds from their droppings, possibly even from mud clinging to their feet... Floating logs may have transported the first lizards across. The tortoises may have come from the sea itself and have developed into land animals.*

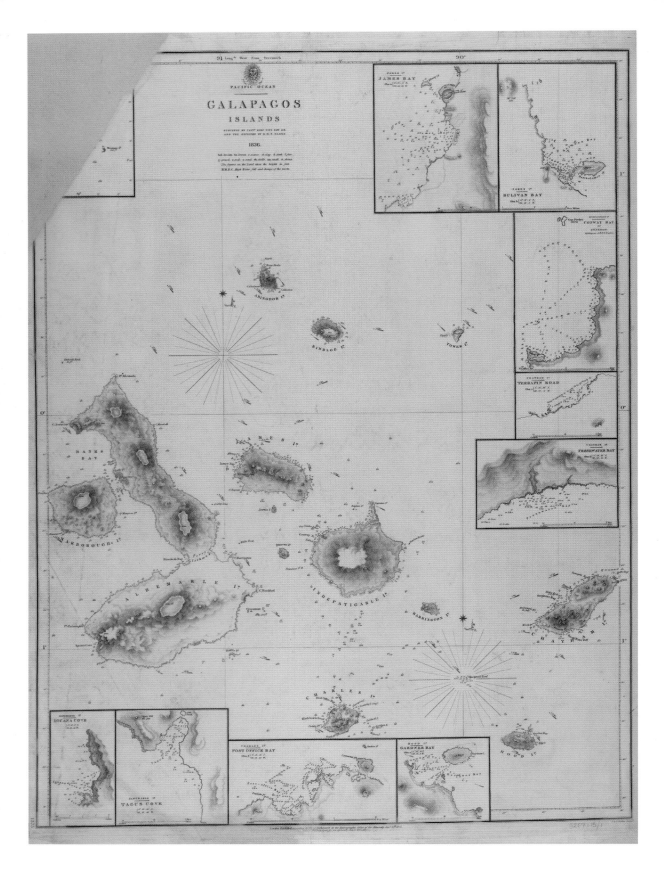

PACIFIC OCEAN

GALAPAGOS
ISLANDS

1836

JAMES BAY

BULIVAN BAY

CONWAY BAY

CHATHAM I.
TERRAPIN ROAD

CHATHAM I.
FRESHWATER BAY

ABINGDON I.

BINDLOE I.

TOWER I.

BANKS
BAY

JAMES I.

NARBOROUGH I.

ALBEMARLE I.

INDEFATIGABLE I.

BARRINGTON I.

CHATHAM I.

CHARLES I.

HOOD I.

IGUANA COVE

TAGUS COVE

CHARLES I.
POST OFFICE BAY

HOOD I.
GARDNER BAY

After just over a month on the islands, during which time the surveyors produced a detailed sea chart of them, the *Beagle* left and headed for Tahiti, dropping anchor at Cook's old anchorage in Matavai Bay on 16 November. FitzRoy made his longitude observations from Point Venus, the very spot first used by Cook to observe the transit of Venus 66 years earlier, before sailing for New Zealand, reaching the Bay of Islands after a three-week voyage. At this point the Reverend Matthews went ashore to live with his brother, as he and FitzRoy had agreed when he left Woolya. The *Beagle* pressed on to the now thriving city of Sydney, where FitzRoy and Darwin caught up with Martens, bought a few drawings from him and arranged for more to be made for the expedition publication. From there the ship crossed the Bass Strait, originally surveyed by Matthew Flinders and George Bass, to Hobart, Tasmania, and then sailed to George Vancouver's old anchorage in King George III Sound (Albany). Darwin, by now homesick, bade a needlessly waspish farewell to Australia, which had been hospitable and generous to the 'Beagles': 'Farewell, Australia! You are a rising child … but you are too great and ambitious for affection, yet not great enough for respect. I leave your shores without sorrow or regret.' The voyage home continued via the Keeling (Cocos) Islands, Mauritius, Simonstown (Cape of Good Hope), St Helena and Ascension, and, in a change of course neither anticipated nor welcomed by some of the officers and crew, it crossed the Atlantic to close the global circle of meridian measurements at Bahia in Brazil, before making for England. The *Beagle* dropped anchor in Falmouth on 2 October 1836, Darwin jumping ship immediately to go home to Shrewsbury, while FitzRoy continued up the English Channel and the River Thames to Greenwich for the final rating of the chronometers: remarkably, after an absence of five years, there was a discrepancy of only three seconds in the readings.

EPILOGUE

The *Beagle* had one more survey voyage in her. In 1837 she was recommissioned under the command of John Wickham, with John Lort Stokes as surveyor and lieutenant and Benjamin Bynoe as surgeon, to build on the Australian surveys of Flinders, Bass, Phillip Parker King and others. In 1841 Wickham, in poor health but obviously seeing things in the young colony that Darwin had not, resigned his commission during the survey to settle in Australia. Stokes was appointed captain in his place, completed the job and took the *Beagle* home in 1843. The latter had spent his entire seagoing career in the ship – just under 19 years at that time – and on his return home was saddened that her prospects held little more than being allowed to rot slowly on her moorings at Sheerness. The Admiralty was not noted for its sentimentality, so it was a rather surprising development that before the publication of Stokes's *Discoveries in Australia* (1845) the *Beagle* had been re-coppered and transferred to the Coast Guard Service, and then sailed across the Thames estuary to a permanent mooring on the River Roach in Essex. Here she joined a number of coastal stations trying to prevent smuggling. In 1870 it was finally sold for breaking up and disappeared from history.

In 2002 a group of academics, local historians and curators met on a windswept marsh near the town of Paglesham, also on the river Roach. The group included Colin Pillinger, Professor of Planetary Science at the Open University, and Dr Robert Prescott, a marine archaeologist from the Scottish Institute for Maritime Studies, University of St Andrews. What had originally brought this unusual pair together was the charismatic Pillinger's '*Beagle 2* Mars Explorer' project, which he had named after HMS *Beagle*. Pillinger's ambitious plan was for his *Beagle 2* to hitch a ride on the larger European Space Agency's *Mars Express* orbiter, which was due to reach the 'red planet' around Christmas 2003. While the ESA's craft would remain in orbit, Pillinger's *Beagle 2* would be released, pass through the atmosphere of Mars, land and begin to send back data to Earth. It was hoped that this might indicate whether or not life had ever existed on Mars. Increasingly struck by parallels between the missions of both *Beagle*s, Pillinger had approached Prescott in 2000, asking him if any remains of the ship had survived. Prescott knew of none but found Pillinger's plan to bring together ship and spacecraft irresistible and, as he said, 'simply too tempting … to ignore'. The result was that by 2002 Pillinger was sure his team had tracked down the ship's last resting place in the Essex marshes. A third party involved was the National Maritime Museum at Greenwich, which, with some gentle persuasion from Pillinger, was soon considering a small exhibition entitled 'The *Beagle* Voyages from Earth to Mars'.

Prescott's archaeologists had found evidence of a structure buried deep in the Essex mud, which ground radar and other geophysical techniques suggested

ADMIRAL JOHN LORT STOKES, by
Stephen Pearce, c.1879. On *Beagle*'s third
voyage (to Australia), Stokes took command
after the resignation of John Clements
Wickham. As captain of HMS *Acheron*,
Stokes would conduct the first consistent
survey of New Zealand since Cook.

was the remains of a vessel of around
90 feet long and 30 feet wide (27.43 x
9.14 metres) – roughly the size of the
Beagle. The next step would have been
a painstaking excavation of the site
and the extraction of core samples
that might reveal enough of the ship's
history to identify it. Theoretically, they
could provide evidence of the oceans
in which the vessel had sailed: a sample
that pointed to the South American
waters of the *Beagle*'s first two commissions, for instance, would be sufficiently
unusual to rule out it being a local craft
and could be 'the killer's fingerprint', as
one of the St Andrews team put it.

However, two of the three linked
projects came to an abrupt halt. On
Christmas Day 2003 *Beagle 2* entered the atmosphere of Mars travelling at 12,000
mph but then, in effect, vanished. It was generally agreed to have been destroyed;
only later was it discovered that it had survived entry and landed, but had been too
damaged to communicate with Earth. Prescott's project foundered on the familiar
reef of funding, the costs of undertaking deep physical excavation on the unstable
marshy Essex site proving prohibitive. However, the display at the National
Maritime Museum did go ahead successfully, opening some months before *Beagle 2*
disappeared and later being despatched on a voyage of its own as a small travelling
exhibition. As its introduction said: 'separated by vast times and distances the
voyages of the two *Beagles* are surprisingly similar... The materials and technol-
ogies that make up *Beagle 2* would be unrecognisable to the 19th-century sailor, but
the skills, ambition, and imagination of the people that made them possible remain
the same.' For both *Beagles* it is an appropriate epitaph.

FITZROY'S *BEAGLE* ARTISTS

Poor Earl[e] has never been well enough since leaving England & now his health is so entirely broken up that he leaves us – & Mr Marten[s], a pupil of C[opley] Fielding & excellent landscape drawer has joined us. He is a pleasant person & like all birds of that class, full up to the mouth with enthusiasm. CHARLES DARWIN, 13 November 1833, at Montevideo

As on Cook's *Endeavour*, both the professional artists on the *Beagle* in 1831–36 were privately engaged, this time by Captain FitzRoy, with the Admiralty just providing victualling. FitzRoy himself, and other artistically competent officers, also helped illustrate the voyage, but he knew they would have little time to do much, so initially recruited Augustus Earle (1793–1838), a widely travelled landscape and history painter. Half-American but London-born, Earle worked first in England and then in the Mediterranean (sailing with his older half-brother, the Royal Navy surveyor, William Henry Smyth). From 1818 he moved on to North and South America, India, Australia and the East Indies. Unfortunately, as one of the oldest on board the *Beagle*, he was becoming rheumatic, and after recovering during two months ashore with Charles Darwin near Rio de Janeiro, he had to end his voyage at Montevideo in 1833 and return to England. He was replaced from Montevideo by the half-German but also London-born Conrad Martens (1801–78), who heard of the vacancy while already at Rio, en route to work in India. Martens was a picturesque landscape watercolourist, and – like William Hodges – well trained in composition deriving from French seventeenth-century landscape classicism. He had so far largely done southern English views, but the scientific purposes of the voyage and the wild terrain he first saw in South America refocused him on factual recording and gave scope to his talent for dramatic and atmospheric set pieces. His watercolours from the voyage, many converted into illustrations for FitzRoy's official *Narrative*, were mainly worked up from detailed pencil sketches and skilfully convey the scale of the vast panoramas he saw round to the west coast of Patagonia. Over 300 *Beagle* voyage sketches and drawings by him, including variants, are still known. He also formed a lasting friendship with Darwin, which continued by correspondence into later life after Martens too left the ship at Valparaíso, Chile, in October 1834. This was because FitzRoy had to cut personal costs and reorganise to continue in the *Beagle* alone, without the assisting schooner *Adventure* (which he regretfully sold at Valparaíso), but it meant that the rest of the voyage, including Darwin's famous stay in the Galápagos Islands, was not so well pictorially recorded. Martens went on alone to work briefly in Tahiti and New Zealand, and in mid-1835 reached Sydney, New South Wales. When the *Beagle* arrived there in 1836, he again met FitzRoy and Darwin to discuss the voyage publication, resulting in his

worked-up drawings – including a few of Tahiti – being sent to England for engraving. Only one or two by Earle were used, though both he and Martens did many coastal profiles still held in Hydrographic Office records. Martens soon found new artistic opportunities in Sydney. He married there in 1837, started a family, and had a successful later career both painting widely in Australia and as a teacher. Sydney remained his permanent home and frequent subject until his death there in 1878.

----

opposite CORDILLERA OF THE ANDES AS SEEN FROM MYSTERY PLAIN, NEAR THE SANTA CRUZ; watercolour by Martens. FitzRoy's survey party, including Martens and Darwin, spent 16 days struggling 250 miles up the Santa Cruz River, in south-eastern Argentina. All they found was arid country populated by guanacos, seen far right (and their bones, left).

below MOUNT SARMIENTO FROM WARP BAY (detail); Martens's watercolour looks east across the Magdalen Channel of the Magellan Strait to the 7,369-foot (2,246-metre) peak that Darwin called 'the most sublime spectacle in Tierra del Fuego'. The ship shown in two positions – and certainly that in the distance – appears to be FitzRoy's auxiliary schooner *Adventure*, originally an English private yacht built on the River Medway.

SOURCES AND FURTHER READING

ALEXANDER, Caroline. *The Bounty: The True Story of the Mutiny on the Bounty* (New York, 2003).

AUSTIN, K.A. *The Voyage of the Investigator* (London, 1964).

BARNETT, James K. and NICANDRI, David (eds). *Arctic Ambitions: Captain Cook and the Northwest Passage* (Seattle and London, 2015).

BEAGLEHOLE, J.C. *The Life of Captain James Cook* (London, 1974).

BEAGLEHOLE, J.C. (ed.). *The Journals of Captain James Cook on His Voyages of Discovery* (6 vols, London, 1955–74).

BROWNE, Janet. *Charles Darwin: Voyaging, Vol.1. A Biography* (London, 1996).

CLAYTON, Daniel W. *Islands of Truth: The Imperial Fashioning of Vancouver Island* (Vancouver, 2000).

COOK, Warren L. *Flood Tide of Empire: Spain and the Pacific Northwest, 1543–1819* (New Haven and London, 1973).

DAVID, Andrew, FERNÁNDEZ-ARMESTO, Felipe, NOVI, Carlos & WILLIAMS, Glyndwr (eds). *The Malaspina Expedition, 1789–1794: Journal of the Voyage by Alejandro Malaspina* (3 vols, London, 2001–04).

DUNMORE, John (ed.). *The Journal of Jean-François de Galaup de la Pérouse* (2 vols, London, 1994).

FISHER, Robin & JOHNSTON, Hugh (eds). *From Maps to Metaphors: The Pacific World of George Vancouver* (Vancouver, 1993).

FLINDERS, Matthew. *A Voyage to Terra Australis undertaken for the purpose of completing the discovery of that vast country and prosecuted in the years 1801, 1802 and 1803* (London, 1814).

FLINDERS, Matthew. *The Flinders Letters Online*, http://flinders.rmg.co.uk/

FROST, Alan. *Arthur Phillip, 1738–1814: His Voyaging* (Melbourne [Oxford University Press], 1987).

FROST, Alan. *The Global Reach of Empire: Britain's Maritime Expansion in the Indian and Pacific Oceans, 1765–1815* (Melbourne, 2003).

GASCOIGNE, John. *Encountering the Pacific in the Age of the Enlightenment* (Cambridge, 2014).

GOUGH, Barry M. *The Northwest Coast: British Navigation, Trade and Discoveries to 1812* (Vancouver, 1992).

GUNSON, Niel. *Messengers of Grace: Evangelical Missionaries in the South Seas, 1797–1860* (Melbourne, 1978).

HAUPTMAN, William. *Captain Cook's Painter: John Webber 1751–93, Pacific Voyager and Landscape Artist* (exhibition catalogue in German and English) (Berne, 1996).

HOARE, Michael E. (ed.). *The Resolution Journal of Johann Reinhold Forster* (London, 1982).

HOWSE, Derek (ed.). *Background to Discovery: Pacific Exploration from Dampuier to Cook* (Oxford, 1990).

HUGHES, Robert *The Fatal Shore* (London, 1987).

INGLETON, Geoffrey. *Matthew Flinders* (2 vols, Guildford, 1986).

JOPPIEN, Ruddiger & Smith, Bernard. *The Art of Captain Cook's Voyages* (3 vols [in 4], London and New Haven, 1985–88).

KENDRICK, John. *Alejandro Malaspina: Portrait of a Visionary* (Montreal, 1999).

KENNEDY, Gavin. *Captain Bligh: The Man and His Mutinies* (London, 1989).

KEYNES, Richard Darwin. *The Beagle Record: Selections from the Original Pictorial Records and Written Accounts of the Voyage of HMS Beagle* (Cambridge, 1979).

KING, Jonathan. *The First Fleet: The Convict Voyage That Founded Australia, 1787–88* (London 1982).

KING, Phillip Parker, FITZROY, Robert & DARWIN, Charles. *Narrative of the Surveying Voyages of His Majesty's Ships Adventure and Beagle Between the Years 1826 and 1836…* (London: 1839).

MABBERLEY, David. *Ferdinand Bauer: The Nature of Discovery* (London, 1999).

MACKAY, David. *In the Wake of Cook: Exploration, Science and Empire, 1780–1801* (Beckenham, 1985).

MORGAN, Kenneth. *Matthew Flinders, Maritime Explorer of Australia* (London, 2016).

NAISH, John M. *The Interwoven Lives of George Vancouver, Archibald Menzies, Joseph Whidbey and Peter Puget: The Vancouver Voyage of 1791–1795* (Lampeter, 1996).

NOKES, Richard *Almost a Hero: The Voyages of John Meares, R.N., to China, Hawaii and the Northwest Coast* (Pullman, WA, 1998).

PEMBROKE, Michael. *Arthur Phillip: Sailor, Mercenary, Governor, Spy* (Melbourne and London, 2013).

PHILLIP, Arthur. *The Voyage of Governor Phillip to Botany Bay: with an account of the establishment of the colonies of Port Jackson and Norfolk Island* (London, 1789 [reprinted 1982]).

QUILLEY, Geoff & Bonehill, John (eds). *William Hodges, 1744–97: The Art of Exploration* (London and New Haven, 2004).

RABAN, Jonathan. *Passage to Juneau: A Sea and Its Meanings* (London, 1999).

THOMPSON, Keith S. *HMS Beagle: The Ship that Changed the Course of History* (London, 2003).

TOLSTOY, Nikolai. *The Half-Mad Lord: Thomas Pitt, 2nd Baron Camelford* (London, 1978).

VANCOUVER, George. *A Voyage of Discovery to the North Pacific Ocean and Round the World, 1791–1795*, ed. W. Kaye Lamb, 4 vols (London, 1984 [1798]).

WILLIAMS, Glyn. *Naturalists at Sea: Scientific Travellers from Dampier to Darwin* (London, 2013).

WILLIAMS, Glyn. *Voyages of Delusion: The Search for the Northwest Passage in the Age of Reason* (London, 2002).

For other general background works, see the present authors' *Captain Cook in the Pacific* (London, 2002).

PICTURE CREDITS

INDEX